THE UNIVERSAL
HUNGER FOR LIBERTY

OTHER BOOKS BY MICHAEL NOVAK

The Spirit of Democratic Capitalism

Choosing Presidents

The Experience of Nothingness

Free Persons and the Common Good

This Hemisphere of Liberty

Ascent of the Mountain, Flight of the Dove

The Catholic Ethic and the Spirit of Capitalism

Business as a Calling

The New Consensus on Family and Welfare (Editor)

On Two Wings

The Guns of Lattimer

Belief and Unbelief

The Open Church

The Joy of Sports

Unmeltable Ethnics

FICTION

The Tiber Was Silver

Naked I Leave

THE UNIVERSAL HUNGER FOR LIBERTY

*Why the Clash of Civilizations
Is Not Inevitable*

MICHAEL NOVAK

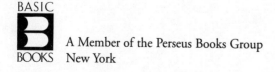

A Member of the Perseus Books Group
New York

Published by Basic Books
A Member of the Perseus Books Group

Books published by Basic Books are available at special discounts for bulk purchases in the
United States by corporations, institutions, and other organizations. For more information,
please contact the Special Markets Department at the Perseus Books Group, 11 Cambridge
Center, Cambridge, MA 02142, or call (617) 252–5298 or (800) 255–1514, or e-mail
special.markets@perseusbooks.com.

Design by Jeff Williams

Library of Congress Cataloging-in-Publication Data

Novak, Michael.
    The universal hunger for liberty / Michael Novak.
        p. cm.
    Includes bibliographical references and index.
    ISBN 0-465-05131-6
    1. Liberty. 2. Economics. 3. Islam.   I. Title.

JC585.N693 2004
    320.917'67'011—dc22

                                                                2004009040

04 05 06 07 / 10 9 8 7 6 5 4 3 2 1

For Frederick Hart
(1943–1999)

Sculptor

who out of chaos
out of night
created
a new era in the world of art
brought back
a taste for being
beauty
truth

and opens the 21st century
hopefully

CONTENTS

INTRODUCTION

The Universal Hunger for Liberty

It would be nice to think that, in the war against terror, our side, too, speaks of deep philosophical ideas—it would be nice to think that someone is arguing with the terrorists and with the readers of Sayyid Qutb. But here I have my worries. The followers of Qutb speak, in their wild fashion, of enormous human problems, and they urge one another to death and to murder. But the enemies of these people speak of what? The political leaders speak of United Nations resolutions, of unilateralism, of multilateralism, of weapons inspectors, of coercion and non-coercion. This is no answer to the terrorists. The terrorists speak insanely of deep things. The antiterrorists had better speak sanely of equally deep things.

But who will speak of the sacred and the secular, of the physical world and the spiritual world? Who will defend liberal ideas against the enemies of liberal ideas?

—PAUL BERMAN

(Source: "The Philosopher of Islamic Terror,"
New York Times Magazine, *March 23, 2003)*

Bring Down Western Civilization!

World War III ended with the fall of the Berlin Wall in 1989 and the collapse of the Soviet Union in 1991. The ideas, strategies, and institutions that had guided the West after World War II proved quite flexible and powerful, and the free nations emerged from nearly a half-century of on-and-off bloodshed (the long twilight of the Cold War) as battered but grateful victors. We were glad to rest a bit.

Then World War IV began with the failed (but deadly) underground bombing of the World Trade Center in 1993. Alas, we took that blow as a crime, the deed of a nutcase, not at all as a declaration of war. Much else had been planned for New York during those days, as we later discovered, but it failed to happen: the bombing of the Federal Building and the UN building, and the blowing up of the Holland and Lincoln Tunnels.[1] We didn't grasp the full war we were in until the smoky inward collapse of the Twin Towers on September 11, 2001.

The target of the 1993 and the 2001 attacks on New York was exactly the same: the World Trade Center. As we will see in the final chapter, the two quite different attacking groups used language borrowed from the same Islamic heresy, a politicized 20th-century version of a sect founded about 1750 in Saudi Arabia. According to this doctrine, the whole world was made so that it might bow to Allah, under the sword of political extremists of Islam. Far from accepting the separation of church and state, these extremists insist that the unity of religion and politics is simpler, purer, better—and mandatory.

Far from honoring the conscience of the individual, this twisted political sect (a perversion of Islam) reduces human beings to self-destructive instruments of a cause. They use to their own purposes the submission of all humans under Islamic law (the sharia law of early Islamic centuries), such as the law enforced by the Taliban in Afghanistan. Far from seeking to bring Muslim populations under the protection of the Universal Declaration of Human Rights and into the vortex of the economic development that is rapidly removing poverty from other regions, these extremists want to bring down the decadent West.

On September 11, 2001, the United States decided almost instantly that the best defense against terrorism is a good offense. In a lightning war, the same U.S. military that Arab extremists had come to ridicule, saying that it always lost heart when blood was shed, took just 40 days to remove the Afghan regime that had mothered the hijackers of 9/11. Eighteen months later, Coalition forces took 42 days to sever the regime of Saddam Hussein from its bloody and barbarous rule over Iraq.

A bold (and much-criticized) U.S. administration had risked its entire future, including its hope of reelection in 2004, on doing what it judged necessary, even after France, Germany, Russia, and China refused to join hands. It judged that Iraq had not kept its solemn obligations to disarm under the Peace Conditions accepted in 1991. It judged that Iraq was deeply involved in sustained support for many terrorist groups[2] and may even have been implicated through at least one Iraqi secret service agent in the first bombing of the World Trade Center in 1993.[3] (There was no equivalent evidence about the attack of 2001.[4]) It judged that there was an unacceptable risk of Saddam Hussein colluding with Al Qaeda by secretly supplying an active cell with small quantities of biological or chemical agents or a suitcase of "dirty-bomb" nuclear material.[5]

President Clinton's defense secretary, William Cohen, had spent his last years in office warning against a horrific chemical or biological attack on American cities, put in place by lone agents carrying small but deadly quantities. By 1998 he was warning against the dangers of Saddam Hussein as a supplier of just such agents. The year before, in a television interview, he held up a five-pound bag of sugar, saying, "This amount of anthrax could be spread over a city—let's say the size of Washington. It would destroy at least half of the population of that city." Then he pulled out a small vial, enough to hold a small amount of the nerve agent VX. "VX is a nerve agent. One drop from this particular thimble as such—one single drop—will kill you within a few minutes."[6]

Many in the Arab world both dreaded and cheered the removal of Saddam Hussein, an anti-Islamic dictator who had slain more Muslims than any man in history. He had killed, in total, more than two million, not only in his long, bitter, incompetent war with Iran but also through the torture, murder, and massacre of his own people in Iraq. Some dreaded this event because outsiders had to do it, but cheered it because it had to be done.

And so the United States embarked upon an almost impossible task, certain to require decades—the task of raising the sights of the nearly one billion persons concentrated in the fifty-six Islamic countries of the world so that they might live in greater dignity and freedom than ever before. President George W. Bush encouraged them to envisage Islamic societies in which individuals might begin at last to live under the protection of something like the Universal Declaration of Human Rights. "Surely," the proposition was put forward, by many Islamic voices as well as by the president, "a modern and faithful Islam is consistent with individual dignity and political liberty. Surely, a modern Islam is consistent with nonrepressive, open, economically vital societies." Much evidence has emerged since 2001 of turmoil deep in the soul of many serious women and men in far-flung Islam. For them as for us, there is reason for anxiety and reason for hope. The outcome is in doubt.

In the West there is also much uncertainty. Ideas, strategies, and institutions that served the West well from 1945 until about 1991 are no longer fully functional. The United Nations has proven to be severely flawed, particularly in the composition and workings (or failures to work) of its anachronistically constituted Security Council. NATO, while in somewhat better condition, is also creaking and oddly out of shape. The World Bank and the International Monetary Fund seem to do much harm, as well as some good, in bettering the condition of the world's poor, and both need serious reform.[7]

France, Germany, and Belgium are going one way, the United States and its friends another. Nervously serene in their rich social democracies, France and Germany are experiencing unprecedented declines in their birth rates, at the same time as the ranks of Muslim immigrants within their borders mount upward, thousands upon thousands. (Germany already hosts 3.2 million Muslims; estimates for France range as high as 6 million.)[8] Meanwhile, France and Germany have benefited enormously from the huge expenditures for defense borne by the people of the United States, who have provided Europeans with a security blanket ever since 1945. Safe behind that American shield, Europeans have built up popular wealth that exceeds the dreams of any generation of their ancestors.

To satisfy their voracious need for welfare benefits, however, Europeans must severely limit the funds they set aside for military research, development, and ready forces. Accordingly, their militaries are not prepared for international combat. For this reason, Europeans are constrained from thinking in terms of power and might, which they no longer possess. Not surprisingly, they entertain the dream of a law-like international order, managed by diplomacy and state-supported commercial deals. They would prefer to deal with terrorism by a judicious mixture of hardheaded intelligence services, rational negotiation, and appeasement.

Outside Europe, however, the world is not law-like. Nor is reason according to Western modes of thought the rule. Ideological forces such as the Tamil Tigers (Hindu) and Islamic extremists like Al Qaeda, Hamas, and Hezbollah assign a preeminent role to disciplined bands of warriors who are highly trained, technically proficient, and completely disposable. They have studied Western terrorists and totalitarians (Hitler, Mussolini, Stalin), at the same time as they have declined to study Western democracy and human rights.

Their understanding of religion and politics emphasizes unity between faith and politics, not distinction, and on this point they claim an advantage over the West: their approach is neater, cleaner, and more highly motivating.

Unlike the Jewish and Christian traditions, political Islam does not go on to apply such notions as *sin* to the need for limited government and the division of powers; to apply the *development of doctrine* to progress in penetrating and more fully understanding original fundamentals as these meet new circumstances in history; and to reason from the inalienable *duty* of each single human being to thank his Creator to the inalienable *right* of each individual to do so.

Just the same, any religion that promises reward or punishment after death for actions performed during life, as Islam does, embodies a theory of liberty, even if that theory is tacit and undeveloped. Historically, Islamic theologians have scarcely lingered on this premise, the workings of human liberty. But those who bet that the hunger for liberty burns as much in the bosom of Muslims as it does among Christians and Jews are not likely to be wrong. The theme, implicit in doctrines of reward, is just below the surface in all Islamic life and practice.

Whereas for Jewish and Christian traditions and their secular outliers, *liberty* is the crimson interpretive thread of history, a major theme in all writing for hundreds of years, the hunger for liberty has only slowly been felt among Muslims and many other peoples. That hunger is universal, even when it is latent, for the preconditions for it slumber in every human breast. Every woman and man *reflects*; each *chooses*; each one on reflection *repents* or *approves* of some of those past choices. These preconditions of a theory of liberty are universal.

Yet only slowly has the plow of history begun to break up the thick crust of earlier institutions and ossified customs, so that air and sunlight might fertilize the seeds of liberty. I have heard it said in my wife's home state of Iowa that, before the plow of the European settler could reach the rich black Iowa loam, sometimes more than two feet of matted and tangled roots of wiry prairie grass had to be hacked through. The loam below may be very rich, but in most cultures stiff tangles of convention and contrary habit suffocate the seeds of liberty for a very long time. But not forever.

For liberty may begin as an internal power, an internal power to reflect upon the past (to see what might have been different in it) and upon the future (to see alternative courses of possible action). And liberty may also depend upon an internal power to choose (both to repent of some things in the past and to select and choose a new course in the future). But to flourish and break into blossom, liberty needs the sunny warmth of culture and ideas and the nourishing rain of favorable institutions of politics and economics. The inner power to act freely and the hunger to exercise liberty may be universal, but the cultural and institutional ecology of liberty may for millennia be unfavorable to its exercise. These interior powers may therefore slumber in the patience of evolution, until conditions are right. The blossoming of liberty has in fact required many centuries to unfold. Only two centuries ago, the Americans of 1776 and 1789 were poignantly aware of their own uneasy originality. They rejoiced at casting their very first votes as a free people. They made their breakthrough early and remained anxious for its future.

The world of Islam these days is experiencing profound inner turbulence. An aggressive minority is prepared to enforce an extremist politics. Meanwhile, a far larger proportion of Muslims around the world would love to remain faithful to Islam to the depths of its teaching about God and the soul. *At the same time* they yearn to live in this world in prosperity and liberty, without repression or secret police, with freedom for all to inquire and to speak, and in tolerance for others. Yet many who share such twin longings are not sure how to reply when they are accused of being bad Muslims, since there are texts in the Koran that block that desire and demand of them something more militant, including behaviors repellent to the modern conscience.

"Why," a Muslim professor from McGill University in Canada asked me in 2002 in his current role as a guerrilla fighter against the evil and repressive government of Sudan, "why must we accept an eleventh-century interpretation of the Koran (which imposes upon a petty thief the amputation of the right hand, or on an adulteress, death by stoning)? Why must twenty-first-century Muslims turn to the eleventh century, instead of the twenty-first, for a sensible reading of the Koran?" He paused to get his breath, and then clarified. "I want to be a devout Muslim, but I do not want to go back to the eleventh or even the seventh century to do so."[9]

How might one become today a Muslim at once devout and committed to democracy, human rights, and the dynamism of prosperity, especially for the poor?

◁◦▷

In France today, I am told, Islamic mosques are fairly well attended, while Christian churches are nearly empty. (The French Catholic Church speaks of its own nation as "mission territory.") Moreover, the number of Muslims migrating to France keeps growing, and their families grow large, whereas the families of those genetically French by birth and culture are small, and their numbers as a whole keep spiraling downward. The boldness of Muslims in France grows, as does their political power. Some of the seats on the City Council of Paris are already theirs. Muslim participation in street demonstrations (against the 2003 war in Iraq, for instance) deeply affects the public life of France. The ethnic situation in Germany and Austria is equally complex.

What, then, shall we imagine for the 21st century? One era is plainly receding behind the curtains, and a new one is rising. Of what shape and what form? And what is the sound of its inner music?

The Sack of Rome: 410 A.D.

My mind these days has again and again been thrown back to the year 410 A.D., when the formerly impregnable Rome was sacked by the Gothic hordes under their fierce and bearded leader, Alaric. The blow to the self-esteem of the City of Rome was fatal. Rome lost its power for nearly a thousand years, and Byzantium rose in power and glory.[10] The humble town of Ravenna on Italy's northern Adriatic coast came to dominate Rome for over a century. And yet, during the 16 years following the Sack of Rome, before all these dire events saw their full issue, Saint Augustine wrote away in his small room, trying to imagine the fate of the human civilization to come.

In *The City of God*, Augustine describes a global civilization hungering for the universal love that the Creator has poured out from His own nature into His creation.[11] He uses images that remind me of nighttimes in my childhood in the steel city of Johnstown, Pennsylvania, when I saw white-hot ingots drawn slowly from the bright light of the blast furnace: as white heat fires the ingots, so does God's love suffuse the world (on condition that we say "yes"). Augustine sees a real worldwide community sharing in God's friendship, which he calls the "City of love," a foretaste of the full communion to which humankind aspires. In part of their hearts, those who seek to do God's will live even now in that City, warmed by God's love. In another part of their hearts, each lives also in the colder "City of Man," that city of ambition, cruelty, quarreling, backbiting, gossip, envy, murder, avarice, and all the rest of the deadly sins, injuring one another and jockeying for position. In each of our hearts is a war between Two Cities.

Augustine draws up no blueprint for utopia. He imagines no such thing, choosing instead to warn us about the persistence of dystopia—that is, of the evils that lie uncorrected in our own breasts and that in fetid environments fester and multiply like smallpox, botulism, and plague. He tries to draw us beyond this half-lit world by hope and by striving, reaching for the hand that the Creator and Redeemer has extended to us in our miseries. The struggle between the Two Cities, he warns us, will go on until the end of time. Its battlefields lie within each of us, far more vividly present there than in the "outer" world of enemies and friends.

With sufficient self-reflection, therefore, the lineaments of those Two Cities may be discerned by each of us in our own experience. That we are sinners requires no special revelation. Our own self-deceptions, insecurities, lashings-out, and other quirky ways are in self-reflection all too painful to us (which is one reason we search constantly for diversion, picking up the car keys, looking for something to do, trying to escape thinking).

That we cannot by the work of our own reason come to know the inner nature of God, or His intentions in creating this universe, is equally clear in our own experience. Many, using reason, are not even sure that there *is* a God, let alone what His intentions are. The efforts of our minds to penetrate to where God dwells always fall short, like arrows shot into a pale blue sky, which then drop back to Earth. And yet we see signs. There are traditions of friendship as old as Aristotle and Cicero. There are age-old arguments about nobility of soul, and liberty, and truth, and giving one's life for the commonwealth, as did the brave young men at Thermopylae. There are even signs of what a genuine Republic of Humankind—universal and respectful of variety—would look like. In every civilization there are stories of such a golden age, as if human hearts hunger for such a time.

Moreover, the extreme edges at least of what may be taken as universal prohibitions are constantly being learned (and relearned) through bitter experiences and may thus be sketched out in certain "Thou shalt nots" and tablets of universal rights. But the living, daily shape of this longed-for Republic's common life remains to be worked out by trial and error, bloody mistake, and painful drawing back. Building the City of Man so that it comes to resemble, at least distantly, the City of God is a task to last for all time.

We can hardly help feeling its attractive power. And yet we have seen, especially in the 20th century, that premature attempts to announce "It is here!" have invariably led to murder. This City is always, therefore, not-yet, while making us restless at finding ourselves where we still are.

"Our hearts are restless, Lord," Augustine prayed some 16 centuries ago, "until they rest in Thee." He wrote those words in Africa, near what is today Algeria, and those words were as true for Christian and pagan breasts in those lands then as they are today in Muslim hearts in those same lands. And in our own hearts.

Will the Future Be Secular?

In the 21st century now beginning, we are feeling our way into a new world taking shape around us. In which direction shall we turn our own efforts? To which causes shall we put our shoulders? What shall we cheer along, and in which direction purse our lips in lusty disapproval? What shall we try to imagine up ahead? What shall we try to build?

This is a book about a vision for the 21st century. Now that I have finished it, I find it surprisingly upbeat, more so than when I began.

We have heard from learned authors in recent years that the rapid spread of free market capitalism will create massive income inequality while the spread of democracy can aggravate ethnic conflict or place tyrants in office. We have heard that global capitalism is indifferent to democracy, déclassé, and destructive of culture. And we have heard that Islam implacably and irretrievably opposes the principles of liberty.[12] I am quite willing to concede that none of these three—political Islam, global capitalism, and democracy—soars up over the walls of the City of Man; none represents the fullness of the City of God. All are fairly humble things. Islam is far from being at present the most powerful and advanced civilization on Earth (although it once was); global capitalism is not always pretty, only far better for the poor than its known alternatives; and democracy is the worst form of government, except for all the others. *Concedo.*

Augustine teaches us realism. He teaches us not to expect too much from this vale of tears, while yet expecting everything of it. He sets before our eyes a vision of enormous tension, worthy of that creature—you, I—who is "a little lower than the angels, a little higher than the beasts." A vision both of faith and of commonsense observation. To show how imperfect this world is, Augustine suggests concentrating our attention on the two best of our human institutions—in the civic order the courts, and in the domestic order the family.[13] What judge, he slyly asks, knows for certain when the witnesses who appear before him are telling the truth (not even Solomon knew that, until he ordered the sword drawn over the infant [1 Kings 3:16–28]). What wife or husband knows at all times what is in the mind of the other, or in the hearts of their children? If there is so little truth and transparency in the best of institutions, he quietly asks, how dark are all the others?

For reasons having to do with self-knowledge, then, I must forewarn the reader, in addition to chapters on Islam, in which I am an outsider, I am going to deal extensively in what follows with the Catholic people on this planet, the single largest organized group of human beings—numbering at present just about one billion—and the fastest-growing. The limitations I discern in where the Catholic people are today will easily be matched by divers readers through reflection on the grouping to which they belong. Atheists, for instance, constitute, according to *The World Almanac*, a very small minority of the Earth's population.[14] They seem also to have been disproportionately represented (and highly advantaged) in the two most awful totalitarian regimes of the 20th century, Nazism and communism. For the latter, indeed, atheism was the official creed, and it was brutally enforced.

On reflection, all of us have enough to attend to in our chosen (or merely inherited) communities.

The world as a whole needs an idea about how to structure a universal civilization that will respect all its inner varieties and different civilizations and make some sort of unity out of its inherent, rich, and valuable diversity. This future structure, of necessity, will have to give broad scope to the world's great religions. To suggest mere "secularization" as a model will not do.

First of all, secularization was the model embraced by most Western social scientists—and many leaders outside the West as well—during the 20th century, and it did not work. According to the secularization thesis, advanced societies become ever less religious, ever more this-worldly, ever less in need of God.[15] There is a fairly broad consensus among social scientists today that this thesis of the 1950s did not in fact explain what happened during the next 50 years, since such supposedly atavistic energies as ethnicity and religious fervor seemed to be enjoying a vigorous revival by the end of that period, while the reputation of the merely secular had declined.

As things worked out, secularism as a moral and spiritual ideal—the doctrine that faith in God is unnecessary, even an impediment to human health, a vestigial sign of immaturity or neurosis—appeared to more and more people to be empty of spiritual substance. Secularism seems to have no corrective for a whole society's rapid slide into decadence—on the part of the massive, worldwide entertainment industry, for instance. It appears to have no answer to moral relativism. Committed to being (or seeming to be) "nonjudgmental," secularism seems to apply no brake to cultural and moral decline, and it boasts few capacities for cultural reawakening, conversion, and renewal.

Further, secularization has pitifully little to say about the most important things, such as death, suffering, weakness, and moral failure. It says even less about nobility of soul, the love of God, the "nothingness" and "darkness" in which God is found, the universal phenomenon of prayer, or a profound and widespread sense of an inner human unity. It seems not to recognize the 20th-century rediscovery of the importance of "truth," and even the rediscovery of God, in the concentration camps of our time. These discoveries took place by a sort of *via negativa* of deprivation, experienced by the multitudes who endured the exquisitely applied pain of the Gestapo, the NKVD, the KGB, and others. Secularization is too "thin" an interpretation of human life to be widely credible, outside of special hothouses. That is why, in fact, it appeals to so few.

In its mildest form, secularization demands the privatization of religion (as in the United States), and at its worst demands its eradication (as in France: "Écrasez l'infâme!"). Let us discuss first the American model of reducing religion to a private matter. To cleave a human being into "public" and "private" is not here done with a sword. It is done by the privatization of religion—removing every vestige of religion from public life, confining religion to the private recesses of the heart. This too is an unwarranted persecution. It is an invitation to the disappearance of religion by degrees. First be silent and invisible, then dissolve into the ether.

There is a reason why it is wrong.

"Man," wrote Aristotle, "is a political animal." Humans are public, civic animals, and at times their very nature urges them to express their thanks to the Creator and Governor of the universe, as a social body, in public. "It is the duty of all Nations to acknowledge the providence of Almighty God," George Washington wrote—*nations*, not only individuals.[16]

Since questions like these are of the utmost importance to the Islamic world, let me dwell on them just for a moment.

American public ceremonies have always accommodated the exercise of the natural duties owed by each to our Creator. Such accommodation to human nature, in both our public and our private roles, is fully compatible with the functional separation of *church* and *state*. The state does not perform the church's duties. The church does not perform the state's duties. State is separated from church, but religion is not expelled from society.

The American arrangement is in this respect quite different from the French system, the naked lay state. In America no one church is the established church. Yet religion of many varieties flourishes in social and political life. High state functions are not denuded of religious exercises.

"Secular," of course, is a mischievous term, with more than one meaning. It can mean the wholesome separation of church and state, as just described, along with the relaxed accommodation of the need to exercise religion throughout the life of society. But let us turn now to the French meaning— the severe French allergy to *any* public expression of religion, that French *laicisme* that saw the wholesale government seizure of churches, schools, monasteries, libraries, seminaries, and convents, and the banishment out into the night of hundreds of thousands of clergy and nuns. In the exercise of such secularism in France, the streams of rural France "flowed red with the blood of victims of the Revolution."[17] At the French extreme, "secular" signifies nothing less than the wholesale banishment of religion by the state.

In not a few Islamic lands during the past century, in the name of secularization, religion has also been brutally suppressed. Westerners often ignore this systemic repression. Yet this enforced secularism did much to turn devout Muslims away from the secular Arab state and to inspire political radicals to cling like ticks to religious Islam—which they then twisted to their own political purposes. Thus did extremists draw upon the widespread resentment of Muslim peoples against enforced secularization, with its cruel repression of beloved traditions.

Secularization Has Already Failed

In sum, religious vitality looms as a salient characteristic of the 21st century. The decline of the prestige of the secular appears to be a secondary characteristic. Of course, the separation of mosque and state, but not of Islam and public life, may be described by some as a "secular" arrangement (given the ambiguity delineated earlier). In that meaning, the term may retain a good ring depending on the fruits it produces: if religious vitality, yes; if decadence, no.

If one regards only the long years of vulgar Super Bowl halftime shows, which in recent years have been watched by peoples in over 21 nations, the reputation of the American solution is likely to plummet. Unfortunately, the American experience has been so demeaned by our entertainment culture that the originality and luster of our free exercise of religious liberty have also been dimmed. Who would guess from watching our cinema and television that ours is one of the two or three most religious nations on the planet? In a line commonly attributed to the great sociologist Peter Berger, the two most religious nations in the world, in actual practice, are India and the United States, while the most irreligious are Scandinavian. Our misfortune, he adds, is that we are a nation of Indians ruled by an elite of Swedes.

Because of the growing salience of religious striving in the 21st century and the widespread sense that secularization has failed to satisfy the human heart, a merely secular response in the war on terrorism is not likely to succeed. To be convincing, proponents of the free society will have to give a religious as well as a secular interpretation to democracy, and also to an open, dynamic economy that steadily raises up the poor. That is why the effort to remake the future, after terrorism, must be cultural first of all, and then also political and economic, in order to be grounded well in all three dimensions of liberty.

For hundreds of millions of persons on this Earth, how a free society stands in the eyes of God matters even more than how it succeeds in worldly terms. It is crucial to show Muslim and Catholic peoples in particular, but also Hindus and Buddhists and others, the (so to speak) "sacramental" dimension of the free society. Why is democracy pleasing to God? Why is a dynamic economy pleasing to God?

However useless such questions may seem to secular persons, they are a necessary *removens prohibens*—they remove otherwise insurmountable obstacles—for many millions of people who seek before anything else to commend themselves to God.

That is why I find Saint Augustine such a useful guide in trying to imagine a planetary civilization of the future. He sees the transcendent Beauty that is the source of the real beauties of worldly cities and its magnetic power to pull them toward transcending themselves, so that in self-transformation and self-renewal they can live on in ever-new forms. Yet he does not expect too much justice, or too much goodness, from worldly cities; he has a sharp eye both for their passing beauty and for their inner corruption and defects. He sees that cities and civilizations advance through history by profound inner changes, throwing off their old skins, as serpents do, renewing themselves, living in new ways. Where there is no self-transformation, there is death.

For Augustine, all creation has at its heart a white-hot source of energy driving it forward, like an oak tree from an acorn, like bread from yeasted dough, like a waving field of wheat that in time emerges from seeds scattered on the fields. Creation springs from the insight and the outward-directed Love of God, pure Act, pure Energy, eternal, intelligent, purposive. Nothing on Earth happens but God wills (or permits) it so. With humans, God is no puppeteer but rather something like a dramatist, a great dramatist whose characters spring to life with a mind and will of their own. Human beings actually do have a mind and will of their own, and God made them that way—that is precisely what is "in His image."

In that way, God fashioned the human world to work on the principle of liberty. The Creator wanted to make at least one creature in the cosmos, male and female, capable of responding to Him with awareness, insight, and love. "The God who gave us life," Thomas Jefferson wrote, "gave us liberty at the same time." To that creature, male and female, He offered friendship. Not wishing the friendship of slaves, He made humans free—free like Himself, capable of insight and choice, self-determining, provident of their own destiny. "God created man in his image. . . male and female he created them"

(Genesis 1:27). He offers them his friendship. Whether to accept that friendship is their choice. He would not make them friends by slavery. But to make that choice is their inalienable duty and (as we say after 1776) their inalienable right. Neither mother nor father, brother nor sister, can make that choice for me or you. Only each one of us alone.

I confess that this is a Christian and Jewish way of looking at the world, a Jewish metaphysics, if you will, a biblical vision, the essential thrust of the people of Abraham. But Muslims too are children of Abraham, and to the extent that they tell this fundamental narrative differently (and they do), we are at least in the same conversation. Not all Muslims, for instance, want to say that humans are made in the image of God—that strikes most as blasphemy. Before God, we are too puny for that. *Nothing* is in the image of God. God is too great, too transcendently beyond all our categories, for that.

Nor do Muslims often talk about human freedom or about what in the philosophical tradition are called "secondary causes" or "secondary agents." Muslims concentrate on stressing the greatness of God; they fix their attention on the First Cause (as our common tradition puts it), the dynamic Source of all things and all energies. No wandering of attention from that. Muslims rush right past secondary causes, contingencies, probabilities, and liberty, and right into the necessary, irresistible actions of Allah on Earth. The actions of Allah spring from His almighty will, not from intellect. That is part of the force of their necessariness. They are Necessary causes. Unbrookable. Irresistible. Not at all easy to comprehend.

To find peace, for Muslims, is to submit to Him. Peace and Submission go together. In fact, these two are expressed in one word: Islam. In Him, at intervals all during every day, heads to the ground, Muslims do rest.

In a practical sense, Muslims have often lived in considerable toleration of Jews and Christians. I have read Jewish writers who say that, over all, the relations of Jews may have been better down the centuries with Muslims than with Christians. Both Jews and Muslims are strict monotheists, one such writer noted, and from their shared point of view they regard Christians, who believe in a "Trinity," as polytheists despite themselves. Other such thinkers find repulsive the notion that a mere man (such as Jesus) could be taken to be "God."[18] I have also read Muslim writers who denounce both Judaism and Christianity as false religions that botched the first revelation of God so badly that God later had to make a true and clear revelation to

Muhammad. Perhaps I am wrong, but it seems more difficult for Muslim writers to find an honorable place for Judaism and Christianity in their theory than in their practice. During long stretches of history, Muslims have been tolerant in practice, without ever coming to a theory of religious liberty and religious pluralism. Sometimes what seems like toleration may be an inability to coerce. But in those places where toleration was genuine, we are likely to find the rudiments of a new theory of religious liberty within Islam.

Yet some less hopeful strokes must also be added to a just portrait. In Islamic thought, the truth of God's revelation to Muhammad trumps everything, including the conscience of those who do not accept this truth. Although there are texts in the Koran forbidding it, forced conversion of Christians is not just a matter of ancient practice but has been happening on a fairly large scale in recent years, in such places as Egypt and the Sudan.[19] Even on certain campuses of universities in Iraq today leaflets have been handed out to Christian students that insist, in so many words, that they convert to Islam or die. (These leaflets may have no official approval and may in fact be a provocation meant to inflame and contribute to antidemocratic unrest.) Christian Arabs by the thousands are being driven out of Muslim lands in the Middle East today.[20] Moreover, the hatred for Jews and Israel taught in schools today and broadcast afar on television and in newspapers throughout the Middle East is at an unprecedented peak.

Throughout Afghanistan and Iraq the term "warlords" is used by journalists today in a shorthand that disguises the extent to which such ancient lands are still ruled locally by clans and tribes whose lineage and local cultures go back undisturbed for centuries. The leap of vast populations from the mental patterns of those earlier times into the categories, ideas, and symbols of the contemporary age will of necessity be a very long jump—and perhaps more than one such jump, accomplished in stages. Intricate contemporary systems such as democracy and the entrepreneurial economy require whole sets of new (and often counterintuitive) insights. They also require new habits of thought and action.

Ideas such as religious pluralism and individual liberty of conscience take time and effort to master and to assimilate, especially when they must be meshed seamlessly with more ancient doctrines. It has taken Catholics, and for that matter Protestants, centuries to learn the "new science of politics," the new science of economic growth, and the new science of religious liberty.

The Point of Unity Must Be Transcendent

Yet my point in this book is even more fundamental. I do not see on the horizon a theoretical framework for imagining a *universal civilization*—that is, one that would in fact be composed of quite different civilizations, constructed along different spiritual axes and nourished by quite different historical faiths. The paradigm of most secular thinkers seems to be: "Abandon faith, all ye who enter here." In other words, jettison your traditional religions and ethnicities, become enlightened, and allow yourself to be swept out to sea on the tide of secularization. This paradigm won't work. It will be rejected, and it ought to be rejected. Humans cannot live by the secular alone. At least, most cannot. As President Washington argued in his Farewell Address:

> And let us with caution indulge the supposition, that morality can be maintained without religion. Whatever may be conceded to the influence of refined education on minds of peculiar structure, reason and experience both forbid us to expect, that national morality can prevail in exclusion of religious principle.[21]

That is why I have made strenuous efforts in chapter 2, under the title "Caritapolis," to draw a first draft of what such a vision might look like. That term owes a great deal to Saint Augustine's vision of the City of God, which he defines as that City hidden in the interiority of human souls, composed of all those who allow themselves to be moved by God's own inner life, that is, by the love of God. Dante describes this love as "L'amor che move il sole ed altre stelle" (The Love that moves the Sun and all the Stars). In Augustine and other classic writers, there are at least six different terms for love, indicating different types of love, and one of these terms is reserved for God's own self-constitutive love, *caritas*.[22] Thence, the City of Caritas, or Caritapolis.

Even for the atheist, the term "Caritapolis" has merit, for it allows one to imagine that every form of human civilization is inadequate, especially from a transcendent point of view beyond all existing civilizations. Yet this conception does not implicate one in saying that every civilization is equally as good as every other, nor that there are no standards at all. Professor Roderick Firth, professor of ethics at Harvard, used to love the theory of the "ideal observer," a theory developed to fill the place that God once occupied and to cover such cases as actions taken in secrecy, or telling lies when there are no other human witnesses.[23] Another parable: as a painter can imagine an invisible point in the background of a painting, in whose light everything else is in perspective, so the concept of Caritapolis affords us a distant standpoint for perspective upon civilizations. In this view, civilizations are distributed in the light shed by a friendship mutually offered to all humans by their Creator, along axes of two constitutive parts of love, reflection, and deliberate choice. Even for those who do not believe in God, an ideal of universal friendship (or at least universal respect), as well as the undeniable fact of reflection and choice among human beings everywhere, might well have transcultural validity and therefore a very high value in ethical reflection.

To envisage civilizations as potentially connected by friendship, without asking any of them to submit to any other or to lose any of their own distinctness, is no small gain. To grasp how certain ideas and institutions in the political order might be designed to enhance among humans ever more frequent acts of reflection and deliberate choice is to gain a fresh insight into the human possibilities of the free society. The same is true in the economic order.

That the hunger for liberty is in fact universal is seen most vividly, and in a sense for the first time, when one by one peoples have been freed from ancient repressions and find themselves living within the orbit of institutions that call upon them to take responsibility for their own reflections and deliberate choices to a degree they have never experienced before. The fire that breaks from them then!

> *. . . Blue-bleak embers, ah! my dear,*
> *Fall, gall themselves, and gash gold-vermillion.*[24]

An Outline of the Book

I have organized the rest of this book in this fashion: First come two chapters on the culture of liberty. The first of these opens with the concrete question we are bound to address after the beginning of the war on terrorism: what shall be the nature of our long-term conversation with Islam? The second sets forth the main theoretical focus of this book, the transcultural concept of Caritapolis. Perhaps I have not here succeeded—or have not succeeded well enough—in setting forth a concept that allows the many human civilizations to be engaged on the long path toward friendship, at one stage or another, with others who are radically different. But if I have written enough to suggest to another thinker, perhaps in another civilization, how to do it better, then I will consider myself a fortunate author. I only know that the task needs to be done. Normally, civilizational advancements must first be thought out before they can be achieved.

Part 2 addresses certain economic conditions of liberty, against the universal cry of pain that some two billion of the Earth's six billion population still suffer under poverty, which is nowadays (as never before) unnecessary. By now, the secrets of how to create enough new wealth so that a firm material base can be put under every family and person on Earth are well known and have in fact been reduced to system and practice. If whole peoples are content to remain in poverty, of course they may do so—so long as they do not blame others for their plight. But if they wish to exit from poverty in a sustained and systematic way, over a period of 20 or 30 years, they can certainly follow the examples, say, of China and India, which are taking great strides in that direction today, just as the nations of East Asia did earlier, and others before and after them.

The topics treated in part 2 include: a philosophy of economics; economic realism, as in China and India; the third wave of capitalism (in Catholic nations); and—as a bridge from economic to political questions—environmental realism, or what I call "blue environmentalism."

Part 3 addresses the political ideas, habits, and institutions required by the free and virtuous society. I conclude this part with two chapters on two major religions of the world, Catholicism and Islam.

The first of these, chapter 8, describes the long struggle of Catholic peoples to come to terms with the principles and institutions of democracy—and in the end to lead the third wave of democratization around the world.[25]

The last chapter describes the turmoil at the heart of Islam these days: the struggle between the politicized heresy that some call "Islamism" (as distinct from the noble religion of Islam) and that far larger majority of Muslims who wish to live in dignity, free from the oppression of secret police and unchecked tyrants, in societies of economic opportunity and prosperity. It is a struggle whose outcome deeply affects us all.

After September 11, 2001, we are all—we Americans especially, but all the free world—implicated in that struggle. For 9/11 was a barbarous, misguided way of announcing: "See, political Islamists can be technically proficient and strike a professional 21st-century blow to prove that we are not a people of the past." Yet if political Islamists truly wish to enter into the 21st century on equal terms, why can't they master the secrets of democracy and universal human rights, rather than the horrid earlier-century secrets of terrorism and assassination?

There is an alternative to terror. It is called, in the political order, democracy. In the economic order it is called the dynamic enterprise economy. Also called, by Guy Sorman of France, "barefoot capitalism," and by others "the ownership society," it empowers poor people from the bottom up, as in China and India and a hundred other places.

Since the heart and dynamism of this new, nontraditional economy is insight—a creative idea for how to develop a new product or a new service—I prefer to name it after a word signifying the human head: in Latin *caput*, the root for the word that Karl Marx spent a lifetime denigrating, capitalism.

By whatever name you call it, a dynamic economic sector is the poor's best hope of escaping the prison of poverty. It is the only system so far known to human beings to take poor people and make them, quite soon, middle-class and some of them even (horrors!) rich.

Some will take this as a too-optimistic book. Well, optimism can be a very creative force, and I am not opposed to it. But Saint Augustine was no optimist; he was the father of political realism. He had far too keen a sense of human sin and duplicity and inconstancy—including his own—to be an optimist by a kind of cheap grace. He had enough realism to be wary of optimism, even to expect the worst. But he also had enough respect for the power among humans of the City of God to be ready always to be surprised by real grace—by, as George Washington had many occasions to remember with gratitude from his many long months of retreat after retreat, the "signal interpositions of Providence in our feeble condition."[26] To those who do all that is in them, even in the darkness of discouragement, good things often enough draw them closer to what they most love. The sometimes obscured, patient power of the Creator draws all things to Himself.

As we come forth from Him, so we are drawn back to Him. It is not only Muslims who believe that. Jews and Christians do too. And if the truth be told, so do most secular liberals, who regularly evince much more optimism about the possibilities of "progress" than anything in their metaphysical commitments entitles them to.

"The God who gave us life," as we have already quoted Thomas Jefferson, "gave us liberty at the same time." The Creator values liberty mightily and ranks it next to life itself. The universe He constructed through the mechanism of evolution contrived, at every one of the millions of turning points in the eons after the Big Bang, to form this fair Earth and make it habitable by human beings capable of human liberty. The slightest changes in the Big Bang's carbon content, or in a million other hazards of evolution, would have made such beings inconceivable.

These breathtaking facts allow us (it would seem) some faint reason to believe that this narrative of liberty will not be finished until it has suffused every society on Earth. And since the point of giving us freedom was to give us friendship, it would seem that the possibilities of Caritapolis—the City of Friendship—are still calling out to us from up ahead, in the gloom, in the wind, and for the whole world.

PART ONE

THE CULTURE
OF LIBERTY

Culture Begins with Cult

Chapter One

ISLAM

The Early Conversation, 1150–1300

DURING THE GREAT GOLDEN AGE OF ISLAM, from the 9th through the 11th centuries, Jews, Christians, and Muslims were engaged in a powerful debate about three axial ideas—God, truth, and liberty. Arguments over these three ideas exposed a radical parting of the ways.

Until the 13th century, Islam had seemed to be the superior civilization— its cities were wealthier and more splendid, its learning was more informed by the ancient world, and its armies and navies were mightier and more numerous. Then Europe took a decisive turn toward a more empirical, less mystical intellectual method. Beginning with the work of Saint Thomas Aquinas (1225–1274 A.D.), the European intellect turned decisively toward the scientific, empirical, probabilistic habits of Aristotle and away from the more poetic Plato, as vividly described by Richard Rubenstein in *Aristotle's Children*:

> Farsighted popes and bishops therefore took the fateful step that Islamic leaders had rejected. By marrying Christian theology to Aristotelian science, they committed the West to an ethic of rational inquiry that would generate a succession of "scientific revolutions," as well as unforeseen upheavals in social and religious thought.[1]

This turn put the West on the way toward a new organon of knowledge and a new politics and new ethics.

3

My theme here, however, is the greatness of Islam, the attraction of Islam, the beauty of Islam. I want also to describe a centuries-long weakness of Islam, growing out of its strength, namely, the neglect by Islamic scholars of one of the great riches of their own faith, the role of human liberty. The task ahead for persons of goodwill is to form a circle of discourse within which Judaism, Christianity, and Islam may learn again to speak coherently, together, about God, truth, and human liberty. We will now be obliged to do so in an age of pluralism and mass communications that is equally new for all of us.

The Golden Age of Islam

So let me plunge in. I begin with the high development of Islamic civilization nearly a thousand years ago, when it was in extraordinary dialogue with Christianity and Judaism, of a sort we haven't experienced in hundreds of years since. Even then, Islam took a distinctive approach to human liberty, through submission to the greatness of Allah. Consider an everyday image in which the drama of this theme is reflected in often-repeated prayer, on one's knees, head to the ground in submission to the Almighty will. Submission is a predominant theme; the very meaning of Islam is "Yes." Muslims say yes with their bodies bowed toward God, bowing in the direction of Mecca more than once a day.

May I propose a contrast? Consider the traditional portraits of Joan of Arc (c. 1412–1431). She stands erect in armor, with her face tilted upward. Her image is also a symbol of a human yes, but standing erect. Hers is a rather different sense of obedience to God. She too is in prayer and disposed in an attitude of obedience. Yet her lightsome, upward-looking face also radiates freedom and responsibility. This contrast in imagery exemplifies part of the theme I mean to pursue with you. Islamic warriors may also radiate confidence and élan. But Islam emphasizes the greatness of Allah; Christianity and Judaism highlight human freedom in response to the Almighty.

At the time of the Edict of Milan in 313, Christianity enrolled—scholars are divided—perhaps one-tenth of the population of the Roman Empire.[2] Mostly it thrived in urban pockets: in the centers of Alexandria and Antioch, Edessa, Jerusalem, Damascus, Constantinople, and some of the cities of Greece, Italy, southern France, and Spain. There were missionary outposts (even bishops) as far north as Britain. Contrary to careless descriptions of the "Constantinian" age, the Edict of Milan did not mark the "establishment" of Christianity in a modern sense, but rather the cessation of legal penalties against it. Most citizens of the empire remained non-Christians.

In 410 (not a hundred years later), Rome was sacked by the barbarians. Saint Augustine (354–430), a mature man at that time, was a Christian, in fact one of the most articulate and brightest students of Latin literature. But the majority of scholars in Rome were not Christian, the elites were not Christian, the schools were not Christian. Augustine was trying to create a Christian voice, an alternative philosophy in a pagan world. Indeed, the Sack of Rome was blamed upon the advent of the Christian faith. Rome had never before been overrun, and now walls were pulled down, aqueducts were torn up, arches were thrown to the ground. Grass grew over the ruins of Rome for several hundred years. Its population declined until it was hardly more than a large village.

A few dates are instructive: It was only in 355 that Hilary (c. 315–c. 367) was made a bishop of Poitiers in the center of France. It was only in 432 that Saint Patrick (5th century A.D.) went to Ireland. In 596 Saint Augustine of Canterbury (d. 607) was sent by Pope Gregory the Great (540–604) to become the great missionary charged with Christianizing England. In 563 Saint Columba (c. 521–597) landed at Iona and began the Christianization of Scotland. Saint Boniface (c. 675–754) began the Christianization of northern Europe, beginning with Germany in 750.[3] During this period Christianity was a struggling, fledgling, hard-pressed, scattered, and fragile flock. It was already an intellectual and cultural force to be reckoned with, beginning to inspire great new cathedrals and a new set of humanistic schools in the shadow of their bell towers. This new humanism drew on the pagan masters of Greece and Rome to fashion a fresh reading of the Bible. But the political unity of Europe was exceedingly fragile.

Into the vacuum left by the promotion of Constantinople as the capital city of the Roman Empire in 359 and by the humiliation of Rome in 410 swept both a new religion and a new army, rising like a sunlit sandstorm out of the deserts of Arabia. This movement was led by the new young genius the Prophet Muhammad (c. 570–632), who by the year 630 had conquered Mecca and begun the establishment of the vast empire of Islam. By 622 he had moved to Medina, where he died in 632. Within 11 years his successors, the Caliphs who followed him, pursued the purpose and thrust of this religion, which was to conquer for Allah all of Asia Minor, then forge onward. Swiftly taking over Palestine and Jerusalem, victorious Muslim armies swung to the north into Persia and to the south into Alexandria. They next began to conquer the whole western end of the Mediterranean.

It is difficult to describe the thousand-year conflict between Islam and Christendom (630–1683) in impartial terms, for Muslims and Christians experienced this long kaleidoscope of events in different ways. Muslim students in the West must feel terribly outnumbered, even overwhelmed, by Western biases. Yet many Protestants are predisposed to think ill of "the Catholic centuries" and thus to look with disdain on the Christian forces in the Crusades. The secular thinkers who call their own circle "the Enlightenment," in contrast to the preceding "Dark Ages," consign the Crusades to those murky shadows. For that reason, today we need to overcome centuries of prejudice to regain the view of the Muslims and Christians of that time, each of whom felt aggrieved by the other. Each side gave the other acute alarm. And the one-on-one brutality of warfare at that time inflicted indelible memories of the other's cruelty upon nearly everyone on both sides. Captivity and consignment to rowing the warships of the other, poorly fed and under the lash, left little room for happy memories. Although to many that thousand-year warfare seems long ago, to the Catholic and Muslim descendants of the participants those memories, once again stirred, are painful.

Some of the ancient fear comes back. Some dates will live forever in memory—later I will mention Lepanto (October 5, 1571) and Vienna (September 12, 1683), but there are also others, such as the fall of Constantinople, Jerusalem (twice), Tyre, and the siege of Malta. By the year 709 the Muslim armies had entered Spain—less than 80 years after Muhammad's death. By 732 they had marched up over the Pyrenees into southern France to begin an encirclement of Italy, but at Poitiers they were defeated by the Franks. That advance to the north of Spain was halted, so that from then on the concentration of Islam lay in consolidating the whole southern arc of the Mediterranean, from Spain through North Africa and then back up through Constantinople and on into southeastern Europe. By the year 1000 the Islamic Empire presided over the whole eastern, southern, and western Mediterranean, with a pincer grip on both flanks of Europe.

At this time, the cities of Islam were glorious and wealthy, monumental, filled with beautiful tile and marble. Philosophy and schools of translation flourished, while the city of Rome, broken in spirit by the barbarians, was still overgrown with weeds, and Paris, with few noble buildings and muddy streets, was essentially a farm village, a poor medieval town, and nothing like the ornaments of scholarship that, say, Damascus, Baghdad, Edessa, Toledo, and Cordoba were. By the year 800 the Christian monks were in many dispersed locations teaching new skills to the formerly barbarian tribes of northern Europe. To hunters and gatherers, they taught such arts as how to farm for a profit—that is, how to grow more than they needed to live on so that they could sell the surplus. From the proceeds, Europeans began building great new cities. In that year Charlemagne (742–814) became the Emperor of the West, and there appeared the beginnings of the Carolingian Renaissance—the first extensive building of schools, the creation of splendid churches, the early collecting of paintings and mosaics.

If you examine the contemporary "Medal of Europe" awarded each year to the person who does the most for European civilization, you will see that the figure embossed on it is Saint Benedict (480–543). This tribute is given to honor the Benedictine monasteries, established in place after place from Italy northward (notably the three cornerstone monasteries of Saint Michael in Italy, Spain, and Mont Saint-Michel, France). Around many of these monasteries gathered Europe's new cities. The monks built schools and workshops for hand-copying ancient manuscripts—there weren't yet printing presses. (Imagine the tens of thousands of men and women who spent their whole lives copying manuscripts so that other people could share the treasures of the past—imagine the dedication that took, and how many decades of careful, loving labor were required.) Libraries were built to house these treasures, then schools of music. The beginnings of modern Western civilization lie here: the beginnings of cities based upon prayer and learning, gathered around the monastery walls. Poor little cities, compared to those of the Islamic world.

Islam and Human Liberty

Next I must mention four great Islamic scholars during this period: the first, who died in 950, al-Farabi; 90 years later, a second, in Persia, the Arabic-speaking boy genius, Avicenna (980–1037), who at his death distributed abundant alms and freed his slaves; 70 years later, al-Ghazali (1058–1111); and another 90 years later, Averroes (1126–1198) of Córdoba in Spain, the most famous and most influential.

During the various wars and conquests of the previous one thousand years, most of the manuscripts of the Greek philosophers had been lost—many thousands, for example, in the fires that had ravaged the library of Alexandria. In particular, most of the Greek manuscripts of Aristotle were lost. Most of these had never been translated into Latin; they were not available in the West. During the sixth century, some of these (especially in logic) were translated into Syriac at the school of Edessa founded by Saint Ephrem of Syria (c. 306–373), and later into Persian. Al-Farabi (870–925) was one of the first scholars to have in his hands the *Posterior Analytics* of Aristotle. Then came the unexpected discovery of nearly 3,000 pages of Aristotle's "lost" Greek manuscripts in Toledo, Spain. A truly remarkable Catholic bishop, Raimondo, immediately summoned teams of Muslim, Christian, and Jewish scholars to examine them. This joint undertaking is one of the most exciting chapters of intellectual history, and we are all indebted to Professor Rubenstein for grasping its significance and telling its tale so well.

Aristotle's texts had not been in Western hands for hundreds of years; Saint Augustine, for instance, had commented mostly on Plato, not on Aristotle. Yet Aristotle was the one philosopher who had systematically thought through logic, laid the foundations for biology, collected all the constitutions of all the city-states in the region, traveled with the army of Alexander the Great, and established what we now know as political science. He had begun to organize what became the study of rhetoric and poetics. He wrote the first two systematic treatments of ethics. Aristotle's writing lies at the foundation of many modern empirical sciences, but Aristotle also thought about metaphysics, that is, about how a human being comes to understand the whole world of being, everything that can be inquired into, and how we ought to think in the largest terms about what can be true and universal across tribes and across ethnicities. His was a really extraordinary achievement. Almost all his work had been lost, except in Syriac and in Arabic.

Al-Farabi's commentary on Aristotle's works enlightened generations of Islamic scholars after him. There is a well-known story of how Avicenna, a hundred years later, "sought in vain to understand Aristotle's *Metaphysics*, and it was only through a book by al-Farabi on the intentions of the *Meta-physics* that understanding finally came to him."[4] Then, in opposition to the views of al-Farabi and Avicenna, arose al-Ghazali, who in a book entitled *The Incoherence of the Philosophers* warned of the danger to Islam if the philosophers were to become dominant forces.[5]

Avicenna had tried to show how one could think through Aristotle, follow Aristotle's arguments, and come to a much richer understanding of the world than ever before. Aristotle's achievement need not interfere, he argued, with our reverence and adoration of the infinite, transcendent God. On the contrary, it can enhance our reverence for God. However, Avicenna continued, one must note the difference between philosophical thinking and theological thinking. Philosophical thinking follows the evidence. Theological thinking is allegorical, metaphorical. It tells stories. So one ought not to hold the two in contradiction to one another; one ought to recognize their different styles.[6]

This tactic didn't save Avicenna from some of the contradictions that are apparent between what's in the Koran and what's in Aristotle. And so Avicenna was under attack from more literal-minded Muslims well before his death in 1037. His work was translated into Latin, and through his writings people in the West began to read long-lost commentaries on Aristotle.

It was a little hard to tell what Avicenna quoted accurately from Aristotle and what was Avicenna's; commentary and text were sometimes intermixed. I don't want to complicate the story unduly, but Avicenna had a somewhat more mystical than empirical interpretation of Aristotle. He was more influenced by Plato and Plato's visions of forms, his sense of beauty, his idea of the "participation" of one being in another, as when to a degree we "become one" with those we love, or those we know well. Avicenna cared less for Aristotle's down-to-earth distinctions than for a kind of inward sense of unity and oneness.

A great painting of Plato and Aristotle by Raphael hangs in the Vatican museum. Aristotle and Plato stand in togas against a background of Greek temples, Plato pointing to the heavens, Aristotle pointing to the ground. It's a very nice way to visualize the difference in sensibility and outlook of these two Greek philosophers. Plato—the divine Plato, the Medievals used to call him—and Aristotle, the earthy one.

Avicenna adopted a rather heavenly interpretation of Aristotle. Some of the Medievals, the first ones who dealt with Avicenna (William of Auvergne and others), began to think, "There's something wrong here," and raised questions. But it was Averroes, who came along a hundred years later, who wrote the most penetrating commentaries on Aristotle—three different sets of commentary. In one of those sets, he gave great chunks of Aristotle pure and straight. Granted, his version of Aristotle had passed from the Greek to the Syriac to the Arabic and then (for the Europeans) into Latin, so some accuracy was lost in the multiple translations, but still, he presented the text of Aristotle, not commentary. Through Averroes, the West gained a better grasp of Aristotle. Indeed, Averroes won the sobriquet "The Commentator" (on Aristotle).[7]

Then, gradually, through the activities of the Crusades from 1095 to 1270, new manuscripts of Aristotle's were discovered and brought back to the West, and in that way a connection was reestablished with the early Greek manuscripts. In particular, there was the great cache of papers found in Toledo, mentioned earlier. These Greek originals were translated speedily into Latin. Absorbing the earliest of these fresh materials became the work of Maimonides (1135–1204), the Jewish scholar in Spain in the 1100s, and thinking through the later caches became the work of Aquinas and others after about 1255, in Cologne, Paris, and Italy.[8]

At last, the Muslims, Jews, and Christians were all dealing with the same body of work. It was an extraordinary moment. Islamic scholars, Jewish scholars, and Christian scholars were discovering a large, secular body of reflection on what it means to be a human being, written by a nonreligious person who was nonetheless not an atheist. Aristotle had come to a sense of God through his own philosophical reflections. But he was not Jewish, not Christian, not Muslim. Nonetheless, religious thinkers were heartened: we can't be so far wrong if even a man who knew nothing of the prophets, nothing of Jesus, nothing of Muhammad, also came to a vision of God and of fundamental human ethics. It seemed quite remarkable that Aristotle's ethical doctrines were not so far from the Ten Commandments, not so far from what Judaism, Islam, and Christianity taught in practical life. The scholars felt reassured.

My aim is to emphasize this great moment of conversation, dialogue, and mutual learning. It was a conversation in which the Islamic scholars began with a great sense of superiority because for some time they had had contact with sources that the Christian and Jewish world didn't have. They had been extraordinarily brilliant in handling it. They were greeted with great esteem by those who considered themselves to be their pupils.

But there were some things that bothered Jews and Christians in what the Islamic scholars were writing. Maimonides, the great Jewish thinker, died in the year 1204. Aquinas, the greatest Christian thinker of the time, died in 1274. The latter often quotes from Maimonides, as he often quotes from Averroes and Avicenna, and occasionally from al-Farabi. The secular thinkers at the University of Paris and the lawyers—who were especially anticlerical, even in those days—particularly loved the work of Averroes. They were delighted to read in his work that you can think one way in philosophy and another way in theology. And while neither the secular thinkers nor the lawyers, who came to be known as "the Latin Averroists," in all probability entirely supported the two-truth theory—that you can hold one truth over here and a contradictory truth over there and not let it worry you—they certainly flirted with that thesis.[9] And when criticized, they sometimes dodged behind it. They used this device to break the connection that Judaism and Christianity wanted to establish, between the fact that there is one God, one Creator, and the result that there is only one standard of truth.

You can't have two truths, most Jews and Christians insisted, one for theology and one for philosophy. You can't have double-think. If faith tells you some things theologically that contradict what you think philosophically, something must be wrong. They can't both be true. You have to go back to the drawing board to see what you did wrong. There's only one Creator. And what we learn in faith cannot contradict what we learn in philosophy. If it seems to, we have to rethink. That principle has been a source of enormous vitality in Western thought.

Because there often *are* contradictions, scholars often are sent back to the drawing board. (Even John Locke, more than 400 years after Aquinas, spent a disproportionate number of pages commenting on and analyzing passages from the Bible.) And that is why in the Jewish and Christian world, new questions arise. Technology has continued to develop. New words arise. For example, the word "Trinity" never occurs in the Bible, but you can hardly talk about Christian beliefs today without using it. The word "rights" is another word that doesn't occur in the Bible, and yet you can hardly talk about rights without seeing the roots of the concept in biblical language. It may be a long, tortuous route from one to the other, but that route is there to be traced.

Thus there came to be a *principle of development* in Judaism and Christianity, made necessary by the conviction that there is only one set of truths.[10] If we discover new things in the world, we have to go back again and reread our Scriptures, reread our tradition, in the light of these new things and see how to evaluate our beliefs afresh.

Nowadays, even in the Muslim world, the unicity of truth has come to be a basic principle. The Islamic scholar Ismail Raji al-Faruqi writes in his introduction to Islamic life and thought in 1992:

> The same is valid when contradiction occurs between revelation and reason. Islam not only denies the logical possibility of such contradiction, but it furnishes in the second principle under discussion a directive for dealing with it once it occurs in the understanding. Neither reason nor revelation may lord it over the other.

When there is a contradiction, al-Faruqi writes,

> Islam declares the contradiction is not ultimate. It then refers the investigator either to review his understanding of the revelation, or his rational findings, or both. . . . There must be an aspect which had escaped consideration and which, if taken into account, would compose the contradictory relation.[11]

That bodes well for a fresh Islamic theory of the development of doctrine over time.

The Parting of the Ways

Let us return now to the three axial issues on which, in this great conversation of the 13th century, the Islamic world went one way and the Jewish and Christian world went another way—the parting of the ways. Again let me repeat: the greatness of Islam lies in this—Islam has a uniquely powerful sense of the transcendence of God, the majesty, the greatness, the solitude of God, including His incomparability with anything else. One sees that in the Muslim's abject bow at prayer, head lowered to the soil.

A sentence in the Jewish Book of Psalms says that the whole world, the whole vastness of the stars and everything else, is to God but a grain of sand. The whole world is insignificant. That's a way of saying how great God is. The purest single note in Islam gives an even starker sense of the greatness of God, and a conviction that the only appropriate human response to Allah is "yes." "Islam" means submission—"yes."

T. S. Eliot says that the most beautiful single line in all of human poetry is in Dante: "E 'n la sua volontade è nostra pace"* (In His will, our peace). That's a perfectly Christian and Jewish expression of the relationship of humans to God, and it also sounds like Islamic "submission," doesn't it? "In His will, our peace." Sometimes we are told that Islam means "peace." It does mean peace, *if* you submit to His will. Is that meaning similar to the Jewish and Christian "In His will, our peace"? Let's begin from there.

The difficulty arises because, in the way they interpreted Aristotle and Plato, Muslim scholars put so much emphasis on the greatness and transcendence of God that they gave too little credit to the causative power embodied within creatures. In all things, they tended to see God-who-acts more vividly than the active power of earthly things acting upon each other. This gave them a vivid sense of God's activities in history, but a lesser sense of human freedom and responsibility.

Being above all influenced by neo-Platonic ideas such as necessary causes, emanations from the First Cause, and the eternity of the universe, some of the Islamic philosophers (Avicenna, Averroes) ran afoul of Muslim belief in God as the Creator in time. The historian of philosophy Frederick Copleston writes: "Avicenna's idea of necessary creation and his denial that the One has direct knowledge of the multiplicity of concrete objects set him at variance with the theology of the Koran; but he tried, so far as he could, to reconcile his Aristotelian-neo-Platonist system with orthodox Islam."[12] Avicenna also failed to persuade Jewish and Christian defenders of human liberty and responsibility, such as Maimonides and Aquinas.

Apart from making *to be* everything that is, and executing His will moment by moment in history, the Islamic God seems far more impersonal and remote from the play of concrete things than does the God of the Jewish Passover, or the Christian passion and death of Jesus Christ. I do not mean to understate the importance of the Islamic insight that every act of exis-

---

*Archaic Italian of original.

tence—every bright day, cool breeze, singing bird—exhibits God's power making it *to be*. But to think of Allah as a person in the way that Jehovah is described in personal terms, or as capable of sending a "Son" who is "equal" to Him, indeed One with Him, and vulnerable to suffering, crucifixion, and death is to stray very far from the Muslim God.

In short, it is true that Judaism, Christianity, and Islam claim to share common roots in "the God of Abraham." But it is not true that in each of these traditions God is conceived of in the same philosophical terms (even admitting how poor and limping such terms are bound to be). The philosophical concepts are very different.

In one strain of Islamic medieval thought, God is too great to be affected by this moment in time, this grain of sand, this changeable world, in which there are seasons, upheavals, erosions, historic transformations and individual contingencies. Of Himself, God is concerned with necessary things, the things that are eternal, the things that stay the same. His eternal will overrules all the things that happen on lower levels. The greatest difference between Islamic thought and Jewish-Christian thought is that the former has no patience for "secondary causes," the links and patterns of causes and conditions in the created world. Islam does not wish to see *anything* as an image of God. Allah is too great for that.

Perhaps this Islamic instinct arose in this way: Nowhere else but in the desert do you see God's greatness with an almost painful clarity. In the enormity of the skies, in the feeling of nakedness on the desert, without protection, and in the fragility of human life itself, the sense of God's greatness is especially acute, and maybe that was the inspiration that led to the rise of Islam early in the seventh century A.D. This view of God is lovely and compelling. It is good when people come to a sense of God's greatness.

One of the most sensitive of American scholars of Arabic philosophy (or, perhaps better, "philosophical theology"), David Burrell, shows in *Knowing the Unknowable God* how both Maimonides and Aquinas learned some important lessons in how to approach the reality of God from Avicenna (Ibn-Sina), in particular the distinction between *essence* and *existence* and the distance between God and the created world.[13] So it must be said that both Maimonides and Aquinas were open enough truly to learn from their "conversation" with Islamic scholars. Their physical location assisted them: Maimonides in Muslim Spain, alive with scholarship, and Aquinas in Naples, closely tied to the Kingdom of Sicily and its thriving Muslim intellectual life. The entire *Summa Contra Gentiles* of Aquinas is a kind of catechism in direct dialogue with Avicenna, Averroes, al-Farabi, and others.

God's transcendence is Islam's great strength. Its weakness is that it can say little about human liberty and about how human choice affects the will of God. How can God allow for human freedom? How can God permit human choice? It's as though medieval Muslims imagined liberty to be a zero-sum game. If humans have it, God doesn't. If God has it, humans don't. Liberty was a philosophical problem they couldn't see their way to solving. The minimum one can say is that liberty is *not* an important item for reflection in the Islamic tradition. But it is the essential preoccupation of Jewish and Christian thought, along three dimensions.

First Jewish, then Christian and Muslim, writings were divided over the role of liberty as between God and man. So great is God that in the Islamic view He overpowers human liberty. There is a kind of determinism. What God knows and does is eternal and necessary and can't be changed, and thus no individual will, no knowledge of singulars or contingency is even possible to God. Allah doesn't concern Himself with our liberty, only our obedience, and it is unthinkable to talk about human beings as images of God. Allah is too great for that.

"Man and woman he created them." That much is clear in Genesis (1:27)—"in his image He made them." For Jews and Christians, human beings are made in the image of God. For Islam, to conceive of an image of God is to fall very short of, even to falsify, His Greatness. To speak of images of God is blasphemy. It marks one as a man who has not seen the point, a man in denial of the inconceivable greatness of God—an infidel.

I've already mentioned the second of the three partings of the ways of Islamic and Christian thought: the tendency toward the "two truths" view. God is light, unchanging, eternal. Muslim scholars couldn't discern a way, philosophically, to deal with contingency and changeable things, such as human beings changing their minds and following their own vocations. How does that have anything to do with God in His unchangeable nature? Islamic scholars, as we have seen, were tempted by a "two truths" theory: the urge to develop one set of truths for what philosophy led them to and another allegorical set for talking about reward and punishment as the Koran does. Where the Koran seems to talk about the ethical life and to allow for a certain degree of human liberty, scholars said, "That's allegory," or, "That's story"—that can't quite be said philosophically. Their way of solving the problem was not to solve it, just to say it was insoluble. We have stories about human liberty, they argued, but their philosophical theory about God didn't quite allow for a theory of liberty.

Christians and Jews adopted a different solution. God knows necessary things necessarily, but contingent things contingently. To know contingent things contingently is to know them in this formal mode: "*If* contingent event X occurs, *then* God knows it." God does not have "fore"-knowledge; his knowing is outside time, simultaneous to everything that happens. It does not "predetermine" events, but knows them if and as they occur. He sees our whole lives, from beginning to end, in one simultaneous knowing, whereas we, creatures of time, experience them moment by moment. For us, singular surprising events occur every day, not by some necessity but according to sets of probabilities, and some of these singular events set in motion other chains of possibilities. In all this, there is immense room for human liberty.[14]

Moreover, the Creator made humans capable of *reflection* and *choice* so that they might be free to accept His friendship or not, as free women and men. Thus, He placed humans within schemes of emergent probability, with plenty of room for contingency, singularity, and chance. Yet none of this complexity, taken as a whole, escapes His knowing or His willing. He knowingly empowers us to be free.

The third way in which Islam went in one direction and Judaism and Christianity went in another regards the *unicity of intellect*. Islamic thinkers thought they were following Aristotle, but they were not. With Aristotle, they had come to believe that each of us has two kinds of intellect. One is the "potential" or "passive" intellect, by which we are open to understand all things. We receive impressions of the world, we take things in. The fact that some people are much better listeners than others indicates different levels of potential (passive) intellect. But then there is an active, questioning, almost aggressive intellect that raises questions, deploys logic and calculation, thinks abstractly, asks more questions. And again, people have varying levels of inquisitiveness. This drive is called the "active intellect."

Some Islamic scholars took the view that while each of us seems to have a potential intellect—we are all receivers—there is really only one potential intellect in the world: the Divine intellect.[15] They observed that when we arrive at an insight, as a fruit of inquiry or investigation, we come to share in an understanding that others have shared before. (That's often true, by the way. Education often entails coming to fresh insights in books and simultaneously recognizing that other people have had these same insights before. With each advanced level of achievement, a student feels as if she is coming to participate in smaller and more select circles. That's the experience that the Islamic scholars were trying to interpret: the experience of unity with others in the act of understanding.)

One difficulty with this interpretation is purely epistemological. If there is only one potential intellect for all, it possesses all sciences and knowledge and no individual has to study—which is completely contrary to experience. All one would have to do is "tune in," without the effort to understand. Another difficulty is that this way of analyzing the act of understanding diminishes human liberty. It deprives human beings of their own personal acts of understanding. We are no longer creatures capable of individual insight and choice—the kind of creatures that the stories of Judaism and Christianity require.

Every story in the Bible is a story of how human beings use their understanding and their will. Sometimes they say yes to God, sometimes no. King David, in one chapter, is faithful to his Lord, and in the next he is not. The suspense lies in always wondering, "What will he do next?" And so the axis of every story in the Bible is the arena of human will. The most important theater of action in the world is what is happening in every man and every woman in their will. In this arena, God is offering humans friendship; do they accept it or not? That's the drama of history. That drama hinges on human liberty, our capacity to say yes or no. The Jewish and Christian story is that God created the whole cosmos so that somewhere in it would be a creature with whom He could share His love or His friendship. And to human beings He offered His friendship, as to no other creature. That's why human beings have a dignity beyond any other creature. That's why the death of a cockroach or a fly presents no moral crisis—no wrong against the natural order, in which all things come to be and then perish. Yet the untoward death of humans is somehow a violation of due order.

It is a hopeful sign that in modern times the famous Islamic professor al-Faruqi writes in a similar vein:

But man. . . is capable of doing as well as not doing the will of God. Only he, therefore, of all creatures, satisfies the prerequisites of moral action, namely freedom. Moral values are. . . the higher part of the divine will which necessitates the creation of man and his appointment as the vicegerent of divinity on earth.

It would indeed be a poor, uncoordinated work on the part of God if He had created such a cosmic creature as man without enabling him to know His will; or placing him on earth which is not malleable enough to receive man's discharge of his ethical vocation; or one where the doing or not-doing of that will would make no difference.[16]

This passage from al-Faruqi seems to me (but perhaps I am not learned enough) an abrupt but fruitful adaptation of medieval Muslim writers, in the direction taken earlier by Maimonides and Aquinas. For the latter, in any case, God wants the friendship of *free* people, not slaves, so we are *free* to say yes. "The light shines in the darkness, and the darkness grasps it not," the Christian Scripture (the Gospel of Saint John) begins. So freedom is at the heart of the Jewish and Christian story, as it may well be—but did not seem to be—at the heart of the Islamic story.

You can see the dynamism that this Jewish and Christian story begins to unleash in the 11th century through industrial inventions and new social institutions.[17] The strength of horses is in the shoulders, not the neck or the head, so the invention of the shoulder harness was tremendously important for civilization. There was also the invention of the rear rudder for steering ships; the invention of mariners' tools for plotting one's position on the Earth, which enabled men to go out on the ocean; eyeglasses and magnifying glasses; the cogs and wheels that made watches and clocks possible. This sudden explosion of innovations—what's called the first Industrial Revolution of the 11th century—started making Western civilization the equal of Islam.[18]

And it was in that era that the Crusades began (1095), seven Crusades in all, lasting over a 200-year period, to try to recover the Holy Land, which *had* been Christian but then was conquered by Muslim armies. The aim of the Crusades was to make the holy sites accessible to Christians and have the Gospel preached in the land of Christ. Whatever the judgment we make of those wars, they marked a point at which we can begin to see the reversal of the advance of Islam. By 1099, Christians dwelt freely again in the Holy

Land. Less than a hundred years later, the Muslim advance started again: they drove the Christians out of Jerusalem in 1187 and out of the Holy Land in 1244 and 200 years later reconquered Constantinople, in 1453. Their massive fleet began closing in on the shores of Italy in 1571, when they were struck by preemption and defeated at the battle of Lepanto. A century later, their overland advance was halted by the Polish cavalry in 1683 at the outskirts of Vienna. (Otherwise, Europe would have fallen under the Turkish Empire.) By the skin of Christians' teeth, the two crucial battles for the heartland of Europe, at Lepanto and at Vienna, ended happily for the West. And perhaps also, in the long run, for the eventual history of liberty in the Islamic world. I am thinking here not merely of certain pioneering discoveries in the West, but preeminently of internal momentum within Islam itself. For deep in the bosom of the Islamic world, does not a theory of liberty still lie buried, undiscovered and struggling to emerge and to prevail?

More importantly, because Jews and Christians held that humans are made in the image of God—the Creator of all things—they felt called to create, to invent, to discover, to figure out how all things work. The great thrust of modern science and modern technology, the invention of a new form of political science, the huge gathering process of "modernization," the invention of economics—all were in due course launched in history, impelled by the West's empirical and experimental temper. The dynamism of the West began to grow, partly under the influence of the Bible, as David Landes, a nonbelieving historian, has written in a recent, most marvelous book, *The Wealth and Poverty of Nations*. Jews and Christians took joy in discovery, in being like God in fresh discovery. They also took joy in discovering by the sweat of their brows that work is a vocation; that to work is God-like.[19] "To work," as Saint Benedict put it, "is to pray."

And finally, the exercise of liberty. The task Christians faced was to create a world in which liberty would be possible in more and more areas—in politics and economics and daily life. These ideas gave a powerful dynamic to civilization.

The Task Ahead

The third part of my inquiry concerns the task ahead for Christians, Jews, and Muslims of goodwill. The United States is now home for a great many

Muslims. Muslims are our fellow citizens. All of us have been thrown into a worldwide struggle for our own survival. That's a fresh reason—but not the only reason—why it's our vocation to revisit those three ancient problems—the transcendence of God, human liberty, and truth—to see whether, after all, there aren't in our three closely linked religions, in Islam, Judaism, and Christianity acting together, resources for coping with human liberty, pluralism, and the free exercise of faith in the God of Abraham.

Is there not a principle of doctrinal development in Islam that explains how Islam in actual fact has been found to be different in different civilizations? History shows that there's a certain freedom within Islam to adapt to different cultures and climates, to experiment, to change, and to develop. Isn't it possible for those developments to occur, specifically, in Islam's interpretation of human liberty? In chapter 9, I present some authors—Muslim and non-Muslim—trying to precipitate precisely those developments.

On America's part, since the 1949 Universal Declaration of Human Rights, we have not paid much attention to human rights in the Islamic world. We were preoccupied with the Soviet sphere, with Latin America, with Africa. We let the whole Islamic world go without examination.

Who today is going to speak for the rights of women in Islam and the poor within Islamic countries? Who is going to speak for the opportunity for economic prosperity? For the dignity of individuals? For human rights?

We need to give voice to the rights of all humans, including the rights of Muslims. We would be unfaithful to ourselves unless we did. I believe, and the evidence supports my belief, that there's a great echo to that voice in the Islamic world. The world saw the joy in Afghanistan when people were liberated from the Taliban. In Iraq there was joy and celebration at the fall of Saddam Hussein, and there has been quiet persistence in trying to erect a freer society than ever before, despite exceedingly violent terrorism sustained in significant measure from abroad. The world saw in Iran—that other regime that was taken over by a highly politicized version of Islam and placed under great internal repression by the Mullahs—that as many as 100,000 young people took to the streets every weekend during January and February 2002. As the 21st century begins, there's great restlessness in Iran. And armed rebellion in the Sudan.

There seems to be a widespread desire everywhere to have human rights declared, protected, and advanced, and for economic opportunity to be

opened up for all Muslims, as it has begun to be for the other poor people
in the world.

In a word, there are four universal liberties, which are also Muslim liberties.

First, the liberty of Muslims to worship the Almighty (Allah) without terror or coercion, according to conscience and tradition, so that the praises of
Allah may be sung freely in every part of the world, with the same freedom
that others enjoy in praising God as conscience directs.

Second, the liberty to study, learn, and inquire and the liberty to write and
speak from the honesty and purity of one's own heart, docile to the light that
the Almighty (Allah) sheds in all.

Third, liberty from poverty and freedom from want, for Muslims everywhere in the world.

Fourth, liberty from torture, tyranny, and arbitrary, autocratic government, so that all the human, civil, and political rights of Muslims are respected—everywhere in the world.

Liberty of worship, liberty of speech, liberty from poverty, and liberty
from tyranny. Basic human liberties. Simple things. Basic things. Fundamentals.

We Americans claim no rights that are American rights only. All our rights
are also Muslim rights at the same time. Every right endowed in us is endowed also in every Muslim, and by the same Creator.

There is, I think, a vision of the world in which the profound pluralism
that separates people and also the profound unity in basic rights and dignity
that holds us together can be formulated in terms that make cultural, economic, and political sense. I call this imaginary City, to which human imagination always draws us, Caritapolis. With perhaps more boldness than
wisdom, I try next to present a sketch of it, an outline, a conceptual frame.

Chapter Two

⟡

CARITAPOLIS

A Universal Culture of Mutual Respect

WHEN ROME WAS OVERRUN BY GOTHS IN 410 A.D.—men dragged away in captivity, women raped, statues overturned, walls torn down, buildings gutted, treasures carted off—desolate Romans in the provinces blamed the Christians. None of this would have happened, they said, if Rome had remained faithful to the pagan gods of ancient Rome. In rebuttal, the most probing Latinist of his day, a Catholic bishop in northern Africa, Augustine, felt obligated to develop an account of how God works among men that would end these accusations and chart a new future for the Earth. The Roman Empire of the time had fashioned the nearest thing to a "global empire" the world had yet seen, extending westward, eastward, and especially northward, much farther than Alexander's empire several centuries before and embracing a pluralism of peoples never before administered from one center. And now it was breaking apart. A new civilization would have to be formed. Saint Augustine was trying to inspire its inner dynamic.

The fruit of his analysis was *The City of God*, set forth in 22 long chapters ("books"). After the Bible, Augustine's writings were the most influential works of the next thousand years, both for medieval Catholics and particularly for the Protestant Reformation. By their unflinching realism, they to some extent anticipated Machiavelli, but in a larger context. Augustine's work, especially *The City of God*, sheds much light upon our contemporary situation, because we are again struggling for a vision of unity in the midst of a necessary pluralism and in a time of much turmoil.

For something new has again arisen in our midst—the first outlines of a truly global, planetary civilization, after the breakup of the old order. An inner dynamic again seems to drive all nations toward some sort of universal culture of human rights and some form of economic intertwining. Nations may not be becoming *identical* (far from it), but they are at least developing "family resemblances." Analogous pressures bear upon all, from certain prevailing directions. These pressures are today called "globalization." What are they? How they can bridge radically different religions and civilizations?

The Three Dimensions of Globalization

Globalization has at least three dimensions: political, cultural, and economic.

The Political Dimension of Globalization

Political expressions of globalization are multiplying, beginning with the world wars of the 20th century. In the 1920s Stalin, Mussolini, and Hitler burst upon the world stage, shouting that dictatorship was the most efficient form of government for fulfilling the general will and lifting up the poor. But the world learned bitter and unforgettable lessons from the age of dictatorship. Democracy has many faults, but no system yet invented better protects the human rights of minorities and individuals, both from single tyrants and from the tyranny of the majority. Thus, nearly everywhere around the world dictatorship is failing people, and those who can are striving to develop the political parties and coalitions that lead to government based on the consent of the governed under the rule of law. "The rule of law" is a system of law that looks upon all as equals, and on none with special favor.

After World War II, the Universal Declaration of Human Rights broadcast a condemnation of certain evils (genocide, torture, etc.) to all nations and awakened virtually all peoples.[1] Outside the United Nations building in New York City stands a statue of Francisco de Vitoria (1486–1546), the great Christian thinker from Spain who is regarded as "the father of international law." Judaism, Christianity, and Islam see all the world's people as one. International law seems a natural expression of this vision. All have been given a vocation to "build up the kingdom of God" on Earth, a kingdom never finished but before the last day always partial, incomplete, and flawed.

A second political expression of globalization, devising national systems of positive law that guide, teach, and shape peoples in ways worthy of the destiny their Creator intended for them, has entailed long struggles of trial and error in the face of human ignorance, unreliable passion, and willful blindness. The struggle for an international rule of law is an uncertain historical adventure.

Two simultaneous movements against the hegemony of the nation-state, one from "above" and one from "below," constitute a third political expression of globalization. In Europe, for example, individual states are yielding some of their sovereignty and prerogatives to the European Community. They are forming new realities larger than the nation-state. At the same time, many nation-states are under pressure to grant new autonomy to internal regions within their domain. Thus, the former United Kingdom is today ceding more and more autonomy to Scotland and Wales; Lombardia is pressuring the Italian central state for greater recognition and autonomy; and in France and Germany, constituent regions of these nation-states seek ampler room for local self-government.

This double movement toward larger units "above" and smaller units "below," even though it arises from many mixed motives, including unworthy ones, is anticipated by the principle of subsidiarity: some problems are best solved on smaller and more local levels, while others require larger, cross-cultural entities.[2] The practical tendency of contemporary thought favors decisions made at the most concrete and immediate level consistent with practical wisdom; the "universal," utopian tendency favors more extensive organizations and institutions, ultimately on a global scale.

The Economic Dimension of Globalization

Before 1989, few thinkers predicted the sudden collapse of socialism as an economic system. Right up until that time, many still saw socialism as the wave of the future, and others were arguing for a "third way" between socialism and existing capitalist societies. The collapse of socialism as an economic idea eliminated the socialist alternative and cast doubt on a main pillar of "the third way."[3] For one thing, welfare states have promised greater benefits to future retirees than they have any prospect of paying, since their populations are rapidly aging and younger workers grow ever scarcer. Both because of abortion and because of a lessened willingness of young couples to have large families, many nations have been experiencing a "birth dearth," or the opposite of a population explosion—a severe population contraction.[4] Thinkers around the world who once depended upon socialist ideas—or at least on the ideas of social democracy and the welfare state—are only now awakening to this portending financial crisis.

A second implicit assumption of the welfare state—namely, that the central state is relatively protected from the world economy and able to dictate its own course alone—is also no longer secure. Like gale-force winds, the international forces of invention and discovery, global trade, open market exchange, free capital flows, and labor mobility across borders rush right through the individual welfare states. The tidy and self-enclosed social systems of these nation-states, locked into the forms of social welfare developed in the early 20th century, are under sudden and intense stress. Such stress might well provide a favorable new opportunity for the renewal of civilization, if it leads to new ways of thinking and new social institutions.

Some of the global pressures from outside are as follows: In 1965 gross world product was $1.7 trillion; by 1999 it had leapt to $30.2 trillion. In part, this tremendous increase in the wealth of the world during a mere 35 years was due to new inventions and discoveries and to the millions of new small businesses put into operation by poor peoples who had never had the chance to become entrepreneurs in the past. In part, though, this immense growth in wealth was also due to an even larger increase in world trade. Between 1965 and 1996, world trade from one country to another skyrocketed from $186 billion to $6.37 trillion.[5]

The kind of goods exported by the less developed countries also changed dramatically. In 1963, 85 percent of the total exports of such countries were in the form of commodities, usually basic commodities. By 1998, 79 percent of their export had shifted to manufactured goods, and only 21 percent was still in commodities. A great deal of the new manufacturing in the world is now taking place in countries where just a few decades ago there was practically no manufacturing. As we shall see in chapter 4, this has been a great boon to the poor of China and India. While still only a relatively small percentage of workers in the developing world work in manufacturing industries, these few are now drawing income and benefits far superior to any that their families knew in the past. They are also learning new skills and aptitudes.

In the last 30 years, moreover, just as gross world product and world trade exploded, so also did foreign direct investment, which leapt to $400 billion in 1997, 14 times the level in real terms of two decades earlier. The daily turnover in foreign exchange markets increased from around $20 billion in the 1970s to $1.5 trillion in 1998. International bank lending grew from $265 billion in 1975 to $4 trillion in 1994.[6]

These indicators shed light on why we find ourselves living in a very different world from the world of just 30 years ago. The world today is far richer, more interconnected, and more dynamic. Each nation is more interdependent with other nations than it was then. Some find this new global interdependence frightening and claim to prefer the security of isolation. Yet the interdependence of one country with another better exemplifies the solidarity of all human beings than did their earlier isolation. As Saint Ephrem of Syria and other fathers of the Church in the Near East pointed out in the fourth and fifth centuries of the Christian era, international commerce gives practical expression to the need that the different nations have of one another—this one producing wine, that one wool, another grain, and still another lumber for ships—and in this way international commerce testifies to the fundamental unity of the human race.

On the other hand, these relatively sudden transformations exact heavy costs. Local industries, for many generations protected from the larger world, now face the stiff winds of competition from other peoples who can manufacture the same goods more cheaply, more efficiently, and sometimes with higher quality. Dozens of sources of strain and friction have been brought about by the emergence of the global economy from the global wars that wracked the 20th century. Not the least of these is the lack of a hospitable philosophy of globalization. Most ideologies of our time (fascism, socialism, Third Worldism, etc.) have been hostile to the new sources of economic dynamism and have long repressed the forces of individual creativity, initiative, and imagination that make possible the open entry of the poor and the marginalized into the "circle of development." Most advanced thinkers, whether for traditionalist or socialist reasons, have been radically anticapitalist. Thus, they find themselves ill prepared for the present sources of dynamism, invention, and growth.

The Cultural Dimension of Globalization

Globalization has also brought us the experience today of an unprecedented network of contacts between peoples and cultures. Television images from one part of the world now reach families in another part of the world almost simultaneously. All can be watching the same images at the same time, or at least as the waking day turns around the globe. Between 1980 and 1998, the number of television sets per 1,000 people worldwide nearly doubled, from 121 to 247, and the number keeps growing.[7] Sitting in our own homes or offices, we watch weather reports on television describing temperatures and changes of climate in a long list of other cities on every continent around the world. Ideas of human rights and democracy also spread rapidly around the world, as do images of suffering and injustice. So also, alas, do images of seduction, hedonism, and rebellion against the good and the true.

Again, more people than ever before are traveling today from one country to another. Traffic by airplane today has become so cheap and convenient that the crowds who go to London, Rome, Paris, and other great cities are no longer merely aristocrats or the learned, as in earlier times, but from among the far more humble. On a more permanent level, many families today have members who are living in other countries in far parts of the world—even our families have become planetary.

But that is not all. Multiple lines of international commerce and trade are weaving a single circle of exchange. More and more people today spontaneously begin their thinking by trying to imagine the needs and wants of people on the far side of the planet. Thus, the American writer Thomas Friedman describes a Jordanian political journalist who tells him with satisfaction that CNN has just begun to include Amman in its reports on the day's temperatures and weather forecasts. For him, Jordan now exists in a way it had not before; it counts for something in the eyes of others. And shortly thereafter, an Israeli businessman explains to Friedman that he and his associates no longer think first about local economic conditions and what they will produce for those, and then about some possibilities for export. Rather, they now find themselves thinking about the whole planet and about what they might be able to export, and then they think about how to produce it. We have become different sorts of persons, the man explains; we think of ourselves in a new way. A planetary way.[8]

Consider a few other indicators:

- International travelers doubled between 1980 and 1996, from 260 million to almost 600 million—one-tenth of the world's population every year.
- Between 1990 and 1996, time spent on international telephone calls more than doubled, from 33 billion minutes to 70 billion minutes.
- In constant 1990 prices, the cost of a three-minute telephone call from New York to London fell from $245 in 1930 to almost $50 in 1960, to $3 in 1990, to 35¢ in 1999.[9]

Profound changes are occurring in the ocean depths of cultures as well. In Indonesia and Burma and Burundi and Ghana and in all corners of the world, one hears more and more people appealing to the same universal ideas: human dignity, the right to personal economic initiative, liberation from poverty. As one observer from Africa has written:

In the days when governments were the only source of information for the ordinary citizens, the government could, through propaganda and censorship, get citizens to believe that conditions in their countries were not much worse than those obtaining in other places. With the improvement in the global communication system, large proportions of the populations of Africa have come to know much more than their governments would have wished them to know. In this way they have learned much more about the achievements and failures of different forms of government and economic systems in other parts of the world and the standard of life in countries with different political and constitutional systems. They have also become aware of the growing interest of the international community in democratic governance and sound economic management, and the international support for democracy and human rights in the continent of Africa and elsewhere. This development has not only undermined the previously successful propaganda of governments, but has also given very potent incentives and encouragement to those who fight for democracy in these countries. In the past these persons were often discouraged by the fact that there was not much support at home for their efforts or much interest in their struggle internationally.[10]

Certain ideals for society and the individual appear to have universal force and are now inspiring people everywhere. If the nations of the world ever do come to a universal culture of respect for human rights, it will be a world much closer to respecting the dignity of the individual person than it was only a generation ago. In important aspects, the entire world is now living through a common cultural drama—the attempt to build societies worthy of such ideals as individual dignity and universal solidarity.

The Crisis in Moral Ecology

Liberty, political and economic, depends upon a supportive moral ecology. The American founding father James Madison once observed that a people incapable of governing their passions in their private lives can hardly be capable of practicing self-government in their public lives. Human beings are capable of reflection and deliberate choice, yes, but it takes some training and work over a lifetime to develop the habits of temperance, equanimity, courage, sobriety, and the other virtues that enable them to make cool and collected judgments and to keep their course steady under heavy fire. The practice of liberty is protected by a bodyguard of sound habits. As the great American hymn puts it: "Confirm thy soul in self-control / Thy liberty in law." For human beings as individuals, liberty is a form of self-control, placing as many actions as possible under the domain of sober reflection and deliberate choice. Most people are capable of self-government only when the surrounding society supports them in that difficult task by shaming them when they stray too far and encouraging them with noble examples and daily inducements of praise.

The Great Global Transformation, 1900–2000

It is doubtful that the world ever went through so great a transformation in one single century as it did during the 20th century—the century whose first half was wracked by two world wars that cumulatively swept more lives away in violence (more than 200 million) than had in some earlier centuries constituted the entire world population. Nonetheless, because of the immense tide of invention and discovery that sprang from the development of a new type of economy (the capitalist economy), and because of new levels of health care and physical plenty that resulted, the population of the world leapt from 1.6 billion in 1900 to 6 billion in 2000. In significant measure, this increase in population was due to the fact that children, once born, were living far longer lives by the end of the century than at the beginning: average life expectancy around the world shot up from about 47 to 65. It jumped from 44 to 80 in one of the nations most developed in this respect, Japan, and from 31 to 44 in one of the least developed, Ethiopia.[11] From the time of Christ until about the year 1820, the world's population grew at a relatively minuscule rate, rising from 231 million to 268 million in the year 1000, to just over 1 billion in 1820. From then on, it began a rise so steep and sudden that it shot almost straight up, increasing to 6 billion in 2000.[12]

There are some other fascinating indicators of the Great Transformation. The number of automobiles sold worldwide in 1900 was 4,000; in 1998 the number had risen to 54 million. In 1900 the average number of hours of work per week in Britain was 52, but it had dropped to 36 by 1998.[13] In 1950 (the first year the UN compiled such data), the average infant mortality rate was 157 deaths per 1,000 live births; by 2000 this had been lowered to 60. (In India, for instance, the rate fell from 190 to 73.)[14]

What Is Moral Ecology?

Moral ecology is the sum of all those conditions—ideas, narratives, institutions, associations, symbol systems, prevailing opinions and practices, and local dispensers of shame and praise—that teach us the habits necessary for human flourishing and support us in their practice. The families, neighborhoods, schools, churches, associations, and other institutions that affect our daily lives, especially in our younger years, establish the "climate" in which we are reared. An honest, truthful, and straightforward culture makes it much easier for us to mature as moral beings, to develop sound habits and good characters, and to conduct ourselves with candor, honesty, and truthfulness. Growing up in a culture that is devious, corrupt, and hostile to truth-telling makes such development not only difficult but also far less frequent. For in addition to these immediate institutions, the ecology in which we live out our moral lives is also either polluted or invigorated by the narratives, symbols, images, ideas, solicitations, and songs exhaled by such modern broadcast media as television, radio, cinema, and other instruments into the minds and souls of modern societies.

Allen Hertzke is one of the first to have offered a sustained presentation of moral ecology as a testable intellectual concept, in an article called "The Theory of Moral Ecology."[15] He shows its parallels to, but also differences from, the concept of biological ecology. His approach is to employ the concept of "threshold" to designate that point at which the relative frequency of some sets of moral acts within a limited "ecosystem" causes deterioration or "degradation" of the context for subsequent human actions by others. Such degradation, in turn, makes sound decisions by other agents far more difficult to sustain and inflicts heavy costs (such as necessary defensive actions) on yet others. He notes that there are both left-wing and conservative uses of "moral ecology," so that the concept itself is ideologically neutral. Moreover, there are forms of degradation to a given moral ecological system about which all can agree.[16]

When human beings can expect others to deal with them honestly and in nonthreatening ways, they do not have to take defensive precautions. Everyday transactions support a high degree of openness and amiability. It is quite otherwise when sudden acts of violence begin to appear, cases of robbery or burglary, a higher incidence of rape, more frequent acts of extortion, growing disbelief in the effectiveness of justice, the pervasive practice of cynicism. The widespread painting of graffiti on public buildings, the breaking of windows, the vandalization of public telephones and restrooms, public urination in the streets, the scattering of garbage—all these acts are signs of individual freedom and lawless impulse run amok. They are signs also of profoundly violent and anomic passions ready to erupt at any time in spasms of destruction. The frequency of such behaviors can be measured, and hypotheses about their significance can be tested. So also can hypotheses about their causes and preconditions.

On the more positive side of the ledger, such ideals as "the free society," for instance, have their own proper narratives, a history laden with heroic and symbolic figures, seminal ideas, special disciplines and asceticism, and visions of the good life that drive us onward and inspire us. All this too is part of moral ecology.

The Crisis of Moral Ecology

A free society is constituted by three interdependent and yet independent systems. It is constituted by a *democratic republic* in its political life, based upon the consent of the people, the division of powers, and the rule of law; by an *inventive economy* in its economic life, based on personal initiative, personal property, and open markets; and by a *culture of self-government* in its moral-cultural life, based upon the widespread practice of the virtues required of a free people: self-mastery, respect for others, law-abidingness, public-spiritedness, and the like. All three of these systems must be functioning in some measure of mutual balance, each checked and modified by the other two.

A healthy economic system is indispensable if the love of the people for the system, especially the least fortunate, is to be maintained. But the good order of the political system is more fundamental, since without the rule of law a proper economy swiftly degenerates into mutual destruction. Most fundamental of all is the culture of self-government, for citizens who cannot govern their passions in their private lives cannot be relied on to practice self-government in their public lives either. In our time, the secrets of a sound economy and a sound polity being fairly well understood, *the single most severe point of crisis* lies in our uncertain understanding of the moral ecology of the culture proper to freedom, both on the national and the global scale.

In Eastern Europe after 1989, for example, cries for "freedom" and "democracy" were on everyone's lips. But after two or three years of open elections, during which time economies had not yet begun to improve, people learned that free elections are not enough. Unless the economy is growing and the lives of those at the bottom are showing at least some tangible improvement, people will not love democracy. Then people learned another lesson: passing laws permitting economic prosperity—free markets, private property, and the financial improvement of one's own condition—does not of itself produce wealth. With intellect and will, citizens must breathe life into the bones of the law. Economic prosperity depends on the subjective commitment of millions of individuals to a new way of life: they must look around, see what needs to be done, and take the initiative to do it themselves. They must work, invest, take risks, solve day-to-day difficulties, and bring new realities into being—that is, they must practice economic creativity. They must also learn to work well with others—with workmates, customers, suppliers, and all those on whom their success depends. In other words, they must learn a new morality. They must put in place a new moral atmosphere and new habits, practices, and expectations.

To live well in a free society is morally far more demanding than to live in a socialist or traditionalist society. One must reach deep into oneself to find new moral resources. One must summon up initiative. One must take prudent risks and be prepared to lose everything in order to create something new that did not exist before. Only thus is new wealth produced. To be a self-governing people in a free society is morally more demanding than to live in subjection under a Communist state or in a traditional dictatorial society.

Mastering the virtues required by a vital democracy also demands significant personal effort and institutional support. Some have called the requisite political virtues, generically, "civic republicanism," but the name for them is not so important as the daily practice. Among the requisite virtues are such habits as civility, personal responsibility, cooperativeness, a spirit of compromise (through which everyone, faced with as few zero-sum choices as possible, gains a little), and the habit of "loyal opposition" rather than mutual ill will. We would be well served by a written guide to all the required good habits, political, economic, and cultural, such as Aristotle provided Athens in the *Nicomachean Ethics*. At present, we do not have one.

Analytically, in all three of its constituent systems, the free society is driven by the *open, unrestricted drive to question*, to inquire, to better understand. The free society, then, is also "the open society," as Karl Popper named it.[17] It is driven by two different sets of questions: questions seeking understanding ("What is it?") and questions building up to judgments about the preponderance of evidence ("Is that so?"). Questions of the first type seek insight; questions of the second type seek a grip on reality. The free society craves both and needs both to prosper—and if it is to survive.

The crisis of moral ecology occurs today because prevailing ideologies and practices demonstrate that *inadequate self-knowledge* eats at the heart of the free society. Three examples: Too many theories about *economics* stress the centrality of "self-interest" and "the bottom line," as expressed in predominantly material, even narrowly monetary, terms. Too many theories about *politics* pretend to a realism based upon "power" and "interest." Too many theories about *culture* select relativism, subjectivism, or license as foundational principles—such as the idea that freedom means "do as you wish" and "construct reality as you choose."

But all these forms of self-knowledge suffer from premature closure. They cut off inquiry before all-important questions have been asked. The fact that a company has a healthy bottom line does not obviate further questions as to whether its business activities are honest and just. The fact that a nation has particular interests and the power to secure them does not still all questions about the justice or decency of its actions. The fact that an individual (or a culture) chooses a particular construction of reality raises a further question: Is that construction illusory? Self-mutilating? Destructive of others?

The ongoing emergence of a single world, under pressure from prevailing political, economic, and cultural winds, now confronts us with the need to think through an adequate *human ecology*. What are the common (perhaps not yet fully imagined) narratives, symbols, ideas, and habits that are emerging from global human experience and that in the future could lead us toward a flourishing world culture? Ideally, such a culture will not be homogeneous, but diverse. All parts of it will prosper. No parts will be left behind in the misery of the prescientific, precapitalist, predemocratic past. The human rights and human potential of all will be respected, institutionally and culturally.

These are large questions, and the outline of a plan of action will require the common labor of many minds. As a small contribution toward that large work, I would like to propose a modest point of departure.

The Four Cardinal Virtues of Human Ecology

Consider for a moment four vices that would poison any hope of a global ecology of amity, let alone of free cooperation among peoples and nations.

Were any people or nation to *proceed with arrogance*, as if they were all-seeing and all-knowing, others would be repulsed and driven into stern resistance. Were any people or nation to *suppress questions, inquiry, or the gathering of evidence*, others would rebel. Were any people or nation to *enslave, demean, or use others as mere means*, it would win the contempt of onlookers and the fierce resentment of those so demeaned. Were any people or nation to *treat other peoples highhandedly, doing to them what it would not tolerate being done to itself,* other peoples would look on with disgust.

No doubt there are other vices destructive of an amicable world order. Let us begin with these, however, and then turn them into their opposite virtues. From these vices, we may derive four cardinal virtues, hinge virtues, on which at least a rudimentarily sound moral ecology for the human race might turn. I call them (but the names are not nearly so significant as the realities) cultural *humility*; respect for the regulative ideal of *truth*; the *dignity of the individual person*; and human *solidarity*.

Cultural Humility

A proper sense of one's own fallibility, past sins, limits, and characteristic faults does not require the embrace of cultural relativism. To see one's own faults and limits, and those of one's culture, it is not necessary to hold that all cultures are equal. The reality of the world is so large and the universe of being so immense that it is foolish to imagine that all of it can be grasped and comprehended by any finite body. Moreover, every culture is implicated in certain specific historical sins, omissions, even horrific deeds. Every culture has characteristic blind spots. Every culture suffers from the illusions that false pride engenders. Every culture overestimates its strengths and underestimates the depth and reach of its weaknesses. Every culture is led by self-love to pay far too little attention to the cultures, needs, and achievements of its neighbors. Every culture looks with humorous disdain on the mannerisms, tastes, and proclivities of cultures different from its own; comedians of one culture mock the idiosyncrasies of others.

All these characteristic faults are reasons for leaders and individuals in one culture to lean over backward in trying to be fair to people of other cultures, recognizing that they may well be mistaken in their initial perceptions and judgments. They need to warn themselves about the potential distortions introduced into their perceptions by their own self-love, self-preoccupation, and habitual inattention to others.

On the other hand, it is obviously true that some cultures have more rapidly achieved economic growth than others. It is also true that some better practice religious liberty, freedom of the press, and the rule of law. Neither political nor economic development has proceeded at the same pace in all nations. Nonetheless, without embracing cultural relativism and without bad faith, one may recognize the limits, sins, and characteristic blind spots of one's own culture, even while remaining grateful for its worthy achievements. No one culture represents the dazzling fullness of the whole human race.

Humility means being aware that no one possesses the whole truth but that all of us stand under the judgment of truth. In my truth there is some error, and in the error of others (in those of my adversary, for instance) there is bound to be some truth. In short, the humble man knows that he needs the help of others to see events and circumstances truly, and so he watches carefully to detect what his enemies may be seeing that he doesn't. Aware of his past errors of judgment, mistakes, and misperceptions, as well as of the potential distortions introduced by his passions and urgent interests, and recognizing from past experience his limits, he shows his adversaries and weaker allies a serious and genuine respect.

Truth

It was one of the great discoveries of the peoples of Eastern Europe, living under the oppressive daily presence of engines of what came to be called The Lie, that many of them learned to *refuse under any condition to cooperate with The Lie.* Perhaps it was not clear to them what "the truth" might be, but they had become quite adept at recognizing the lie.[18] Lying took place even in the reporting of weather predictions; when there was to be a great Communist parade or festival, such predictions were invariably favorable. In addition, under torment or torture, many who suffered in prison camps, people like Anatoly Shcharansky and Mihajlo Mihajlov, reported that they learned an important lesson.[19] As long as they were faithful to their own sense of truth, they retained a power that their jailers could not take from them. As long as they were determined not to be complicit in The Lie, they felt an integrity of soul and a certain inner, virtually indomitable power. Of course, their liberty could be taken from them by mind-altering drugs or even by certain tortures beyond their power to retain consciousness and to endure. But up to those levels, they became painfully aware of the sheer moral power of their own inner determination not to lie.

This awful experience may have been a backward way of coming to the concept of truth, but it was altogether appropriate. Such men and women came to think of "truth" not as a proposition imposed upon them but rather as a kind of inner light and imperative to fidelity. In this light, maintaining fidelity to truth as opposed to lying and falsification was crucial to their individual moral survival. But the same fidelity, they could see, is exceedingly important for a civilized society. It is a necessary condition for a free society. For if there is no such regulative ideal, then human relations do not fall under the authority of truth and evidence but answer only to authoritarian will and power. If there is no truth, then there can be no just claims against tyranny and no evidence of violation of rights, one way or the other. Appeal to truth is an indispensable condition for the practice of liberty. The old adage "The truth shall make you free" was lived out in the experience of many dissidents behind the Iron Curtain. In fact, in the concentration camps and torture chambers, fidelity to truth was sometimes the only form of liberty to be enjoyed.

Those in the West who play with the idea that relativism is crucial for liberty are playing with fire, since regimes built solely on the principle of lying, without any possibility of appeal to evidence and fair judgment, dwell under the sign of stark naked power. Under that sign, thugs move into positions of leadership, and the finer spirits concerned about such niceties as evidence and argument are driven first to the periphery and eventually to prison. Against false imprisonment, one cannot shout, "Injustice!" For to that, thugs reply, "Says who?" And one cannot say, "Those charges are false!" For there is no longer any such thing as "true" or "false." It is now power, power alone, that speaks.

Truth as a regulative ideal is, in this sense, a crucial concept for a civilized society. It is the necessary concept if people are to have respect for one another's fairness in reasoning and judgment and to submit opposing judgments to the light of evidence. Only such a regulative ideal makes conversation in the light of evidence possible. Civilized persons converse; they reason with one another; they argue. Barbarians club one another. Barbarians live under the sign of naked and unadorned power. The free live inside the gates within which evidence is respected.

The Dignity of the Individual Person

What, after all, is human dignity? The English word "dignity" is rooted in the Latin *dignus*, "worthy of esteem and honor, due a certain respect, of weighty importance." In ordinary discourse, we use "dignity" only in reference to human persons. Both Aristotle and Plato held that most humans are by nature slavish and suitable only to be slaves and that they lack natures worthy of freedom and proper to free men. The Greeks did not use the term "dignity" for all human beings, but only for a few. By contrast, Christianity insisted that every single human person is loved by the Creator, made in His image, and destined for eternal friendship and communion. Following Judaism, Christianity made human dignity a concept of universal application. "Inasmuch as ye have done it unto one of the least of these my brethren, ye have done it unto me" (Matthew 25:40). Christianity made it a matter of self-condemnation to use another human as a means to an end. Each human being is to be shown the dignity bestowed on him by God because each is loved by God as a friend. Each has God as "a father." Obviously, many students of economics are neither Christians nor even believers in God. They therefore do not look at the world in this way. Nonetheless, as a matter of intellectual history, it is of some utility to discover the origin of concepts and to observe how its secularized equivalent took shape.

As every tree in the world is an individual with its unique location in space and time and a shape all its own, so it is with every member of every species of plant and animal. To speak of the individual in this sense is to speak of what can be physically located, observed, seen, and touched. In this context, the common good would be either the sum of the goods of each individual member or "the greatest good of the greatest number." A purely materialistic conception of the individual, like Thomas Hobbes's, is compatible with a high valuation on each individual. But it is also compatible with the view that the whole is greater than any part and ought to take precedence over any part. It is this latter view that George Orwell satirizes in *Animal Farm*. In this view, the human being in the social body is like the steer in the herd, the bee in the hive, the ant in the colony—an individual whose good is subordinated to the good of the species.

A person is more than an individual. Aquinas points out that, as the concept of *individual* looks to what is material, so the concept of *person* looks to intellect and will: the capacities of insight and judgment, on the one hand, and of choice and decision, on the other.[20] A person is an individual who is able to inquire and to choose and therefore is both free and responsible. For Aquinas, the person is in this sense made in the image of the Creator and endowed with inalienable responsibilities. The good of such a person, who participates in activities of insight and choice (God's own form of life), is to be united with God, without intermediary, face to face in full light and love. The ultimate common good of persons is to be united with God's understanding and loving, the same activities of insight and choice coursing through and energizing all.

Analogously, on Earth and in time, the common good of persons is to live in as close an approximation of unity in insight and love as sinful human beings might attain. Since this requires respect for the inalienable freedom and responsibility of each, and since human beings are imperfect at best and always flawed in character, it is by no means easy at any one historical moment either to ascertain the common good or to attain it. To solve both these problems, even approximately, persons need institutions suitable to the task.

But what sorts of institutions are likely to raise the probabilities of success in identifying and achieving the common good in history? These must be invented and tested by the hazards of history. They are not given in advance. Human beings proceed toward the common good more in darkness than in light.

Two fundamental organizational errors are ruled out, however, by an accurate judgment about the requirements of the human person *qua* person. The specific vitalities of the person spring from capacities for insight and choice (inquiry and love). From these derive the principles of liberty and responsibility in which human dignity is rooted. The human person is *dignus*, worthy of respect, sacred even, because he or she lives from the activities proper to God. To violate a human person is to denigrate the Almighty. It is an error to define individualism without reference to God and without reference to those other persons who share in God's life. A self-enclosed, self-centered individualism rests upon a misapprehension of the capacities of the human person, in whose light each person is judged by God, by other persons, and by conscience itself (whose light is God's activity in the soul). The person is a sign of God in history, or to speak more accurately, the person participates in God's own most proper activities, insight and choice. The person is *theophanous*: a shining-through of God's life in history, created by God for union with God. This is the impulse in history guided by Providence and discerned by the authors of the U.S. Declaration of Independence when they spoke of human persons as "endowed by their Creator with certain unalienable rights" and strove to invent institutions worthy of human dignity.

On one side, then, a self-enclosed individualism falsifies the capacities of the human person. On the other side, so does any vision of the common good as a mere sum of individual goods (or the greatest good of the greatest number). Even if it were true (in some dreadful utilitarian calculus) that a hundred persons would experience more pleasure from torturing one person than that person would experience pain, such an action would be an abomination. The person is never subordinate to the common good in an instrumental way. Persons are not means but ends, because of the God in Whom they live and Who lives in them, and because of their nature as rational beings capable of reflection and choice. The common good of a society of persons consists in treating each of them as an end, never as a means. To arrange the institutions of human society in such a way that this happens without fail is by no means easy.

The human race has so far only approximated the achievement of such institutions. Over most of the planet's present surface, including most of the world's peoples, persons are still conceived of as means to the ends of the state. Their personal liberty is not respected. Every form of collectivism, in which each member is treated as a means to the good of the state, violates the dignity of the human person.

Among the figures of the Enlightenment, Immanuel Kant (1724–1804) is probably the one who spoke most clearly to the concept of human dignity. He did so in the light of a categorical imperative that he discerned in the rational being, and he made famous this formulation of the principle of human dignity: "Act so that you treat humanity, whether in your own person or in that of another, always as an end and never as a means only." This is not, of course, a description of the way in which humans always (or even mostly) treat other human beings. It is, in the Kantian scheme, a prescription, an imperative, a duty. (In other schemes, it might appear as an aspiration, a good to be pursued, an ideal for which to strive.)

Still, it is not difficult to see in Kant's formulation a repetition in non-biblical language of the essential teaching of Judaism and Christianity: "Thou shalt love thy neighbor as thyself" (Leviticus 19:18). "And this commandment have we from him, That he who loveth God love his brother also" (1 John 4:21). This interpretation of Kant seems correct for two reasons. First, the ancient philosophers of Greece and Rome, before the contact of those regions with Christianity, did not reach this principle. Second, one must note the quiet but strong culture of German pietism in which Kant grew to maturity.

From the point of view of modern history, of course, it seems absurd to say that humans are not means but only ends. In the 20th century, more than a hundred million persons in Europe alone died by violence, often in a way they could not have foreseen even in their worst nightmares. In the last century history has been a butcher's bench, and the words "human dignity" have often sounded empty.

Solidarity

When Leo XIII described in *Rerum Novarum* (1891) the tumultuous changes then churning through the formerly agrarian and feudal world of premodern Europe, he saw the need for a new sort of virtue (a reliable habit of soul) among Christian peoples, laypeople especially, and he wavered between calling it "justice" or "charity," or "social justice" or "social charity."[21] By the time of *Centesimus Annus* (1991) one hundred years later, John Paul II had brought that nascent intuition into focus in the one term "solidarity." By this term he did not mean the great Polish labor union that contributed so much to bringing down communism—although no doubt the worldwide fame of the term "Solidarnosc" added helpful connotations to what he intended—but rather the special virtue of social charity that makes each individual aware of belonging to the whole human race, of being brother or sister to all others, of living in *communio* with all other humans in God. Solidarity is a deeper concept than "globalization," for it adds the dimension of communal interiority and personal responsibility. Solidarity is not an impersonal habit of losing one's self in groupthink, disappearing into a collectivity. Solidarity points simultaneously to the personal responsibility and initiative of the human subject and to communion with others. It is exactly the reverse of what socialists meant by collectivization. Solidarity does not lull individual conscience but rather awakens it. Solidarity evokes responsibility, enlarges personal vision, and connects the responsible self to all others.[22]

In these days of "globalization," even as described in merely economic terms, it is almost impossible for any intelligent human being to imagine the self as an unencumbered, detached, solitary individual unlinked to others.

Interdependence so forces itself upon the world's consciousness, in fact, that most attempts to define globalization fail. There are at least five standard definitions of globalization, each one inadequate standing by itself:

1. Globalization is not merely a dramatic drop in transportation and communication *costs*.
2. Globalization is not just the shrinkage of a formerly vast realm of distant and remote nations into one small "village," linked in instantaneous *communications*.
3. Nor is it merely the centripetal energies of a single global *market* interconnected by the Internet, satellites, cellular phones, and television.
4. Globalization is not the mere geometric increase of "foreign direct investment" and cross-border *trade*.
5. Although, of course, globalization today is all these things,[23] globalization also has an *interior dimension*. External economic globalization has changed the way individuals experience themselves and the way they think.

All these are steps toward the interior realities of solidarity. Are human beings not planetary creatures, one another's brothers and sisters, members of one same body, every part serving every other part?[24] These are the best of times for those committed to solidarity, and pinching times (as in wearing shoes that do not fit) for those committed to a view of themselves as solitary individuals.

It may be useful to remark at this point that the imperative for globalization began with the commission to all Christians, "Go preach the gospels to all nations," which turned Christianity away from being the religion of one tribe or one people only and toward seeing the whole human race as one people of God. But that is only its historical genesis. This global viewpoint is the natural ecology of the human race as a whole today. Secular reason is now global too, not merely tribal. However, it is in fact only so when "reason" is practiced on a very large, supple, and sympathy-infused spirit. In this new ecology, it is not sufficient to respect the other as like oneself—one needs also to respect the other as other. Such respect goes far beyond "tolerance." It seeks to learn from—to be enlarged by—what is other. It is willing to argue respectfully with the other by presenting evidence and attending to the evidence presented by the other. Such respect is based on a mutual reverence for the truth that neither one wholly possesses.

Specific sets of virtues need to be learned within all the component peoples of Caritapolis if such a community of respect is to be practiced. Specific institutions also need to be developed. We will put off discussing these until later chapters in parts 2 and 3, and again in the Epilogue.

Caritapolis

In *The City of God*, Saint Augustine differentiates between two different cities, the Earthly City (the one with which we have been primarily concerned in this chapter) and the Invisible City, which is made up of those who love God and who experience God's love within them. The invisible filament of divine love that encircles the world bears warmth and light to the Earthly City, drawing it onward to be better than itself. It invites humankind to be moved by a law of amity, respect, and cooperation higher than its own.

During the past century the formerly separated peoples of the world have grown greatly in number and physical interaction, until the whole planet now seems abuzz with activity. All peoples are coming into frequent contact with one another. All are interpenetrated by new media of communication such as television, the Internet, and the cell phone.[25] We have become aware of one another's concrete reality as never before in history. People in one part of the world can see with their own eyes how people in other parts of the world live. They hear ideas formerly unheard and discern currents of passion and emotion of which they were formerly unaware.

Saint Augustine observed that the Earthly City was everywhere a world in conflict, racked by injustice and scarred by some truly unacceptable practices such as slavery and torture, which he saw no possibility at that time of removing from the world. But nowadays the move to eliminate slavery and torture, like the move to respect individual and social rights, has gained moral power around the world. Even if these movements have not been everywhere successful, they have transformed a significant number of societies. Simply to survive, other courses of action now are thrust upon the human race that were hardly imaginable before.

Whereas Saint Augustine suggested that the best we could do in the Earthly City was to reach a tentative balance of power, a balance of fear,

today necessity imposes upon us a universal relation more vitally interconnected than that. It is not enough today for citizens not to fear each other,
although I am far from denying that fear plays an important role in human
affairs even today. It is not enough merely to "tolerate" each other. Slowly but
surely, it is becoming necessary to respect one another, to pay one another
the honor of taking each other seriously. This is at least an approximation of
the friendship with one another that remains, as it were, a gravitational pull.

The founder of my native state, Pennsylvania, conceived the idea of establishing a new commonwealth based upon friendship. His name was
William Penn (1644–1718), and he had been imprisoned in England for belonging to a dissident church, the Society of Friends (Quakers). Penn often
pointed out that, in offering His friendship to human beings, God founded
this world upon the principle of freedom, which is the air and the aliment
of friendship: without freedom, there is no friendship. The Pennsylvania
model of religious liberty, for instance, having brought reasonable social harmony, became the closest model for the U.S. Constitution of 1787. A later
example: when firemen and policemen in the Twin Towers in New York City
gave their lives for their fellows on September 11, 2001, they showed the
greatest of all loves. That a polity needs to be founded to some degree on
friendship therefore has some basis in fact.

Many hostilities today are rooted in caricatures and false information
about the other party. Campaigns of hatred and vilification are reported to
be taking place in schools and houses of worship, in newspapers and on television stations. Given the power of contemporary weapons systems and the
vulnerabilities of modern urban life, creative individuals and institutions
need to strive mightily to overcome the envies, hatreds, and hostilities that
set people against people. The tyrannical architectonic of societies that op-
press their people and keep them in misery are breeding grounds of resentment, and such regimes, above all, need exposure to sunlight.

Caritapolis is the City of Communion, that is, participation in the love of
God that the Christian gospel announces.[26] It is not solely a City of human
communion, one human with another, but of humans also with God; love
shared among all. If there is one Creator of all human beings, His love for
humans (in Judaism, Christianity, and Islam at least) is the magnet toward
which creatures are pulled, the Origin to which they return, the Measure by
which their own poor efforts are judged.

Nowadays, world relations based on fear of one another, resentment, envy, or lack of respect would be, even if long merely smoldering, ultimately explosive. In a complex world civilization such as ours, with so much potential for disaster, working toward a set of relations that command mutual respect is the only prudent course. The realism demanded by Augustine (and seconded by Reinhold Niebuhr[27]) remains obligatory. In the meantime, every step taken toward a global vision in which all human beings receive the honor due them by their nature advances the shabbier, much battered, but still stumbling-forward Earthly City. Its aim: a faint approximation of that "city on a hill," *Caritapolis*.

We shall inquire further into the politics of Caritapolis in part 3 and in the Epilogue.

Conclusion

It is not only amity and cooperation among ourselves that shape our guiding vision. It is also that form of love for our surroundings, for the planet that is our carrier, that the ancients expressed as "stewardship."

Now that the human race has learned at last "the causes of the wealth of the nations" and with this knowledge has broken the chains of poverty for two-thirds of its members, a new challenge looms into view: how to care for the natural environment of the human species. For the triumph over poverty led to both the trebling of the average life span and the growth of the world's population from less than 1 billion in the year 1800 to more than 6 billion by the year 2000.

During the last third of the 20th century, the "greens" brought about a revolution in moral consciousness unprecedented in the scope and swiftness of its success. But much still remains to be done, particularly in bringing clean water to the scores of millions of human beings who suffer for not having it. We will come to that task in chapter 6.

Meanwhile, we need a dose of the realism that a practical experience of the free economy normally teaches humankind (except those protected from it by a cocoon of gifts from others, such as professors). Lunch does not come free, everything has to be paid for. And yet invention and ingenuity keep expanding the scope of new possibilities. Today it is no longer true that one man's gain is automatically another man's loss, not when both men together are creating new wealth never seen before. The most common situation under the new rules—and the situation to be striven for and multiplied millions of times over—is win-win.

Even the poorest and most recent immigrants living in America have medicines, income, housing, and opportunities in the top fraction of 1 percent of the estimated 60 billion humans who have ever lived on Earth.[28] Given this initial lift, and the lessons concerning how it is done, virtually all other economies on Earth are also ascending.

When wealth is no longer finite and fixed forever, when new and unprecedented wealth is being created every day, a new form of common sense comes into being. I call it the "blue revolution"—the systematic awakening of human reflection and choice, the stirring of universal liberty, the acceptance of adult responsibility for one's own fate, the increasingly visible gait of the free and the brave, the emergence of a family of peoples you can count on. The people of the emerging Caritapolis, when you come down to it, have learned to respect one another, and will have done so (when the process is complete) universally.

PART TWO

THE ECONOMICS OF LIBERTY

Capitalism Lifts the Poor

Chapter Three

A PHILOSOPHY OF ECONOMICS

THIS SHOULDN'T BE SHOCKING but it probably will be, so let me blurt it right out: *Business is a noble Christian vocation, a work of social justice, and the single greatest institutional hope of the poor of the world. If the poor are to move out of poverty, no other institution can help them as much as business, especially small business.*[1] Despite the strong prejudice against business in literary studies, the humanities, and social studies, as well as among the clergy and the artists, a hardscrabble truth needs to be faced. No other institution creates new, progress-generating jobs that bring the poor income, the opportunity to develop their talents, and independence for their families, as small business does.

In Latin America, Africa, the Middle East, and Asia—to the one side— are an immense number of poor people either *under*employed or *un*employed. To the other side is an immense amount of work to be done. There are homes, clinics, and schools to be built; sanitation to be supplied to villages and cities; and lights and refrigerators and ovens to be manufactured for those who lack them, so that their children can live decently.

All that work to be done, all those good people looking for work—who will bring these two elements together, like two live wires now held apart? Who will bring these two wires together to generate the spark of development? That is the role of entrepreneurs: to put people seeking work together with all the work desperately needing to be done.

The vocation of business is the single most strategic vocation in the work of social justice. It is the vocation most necessary for lifting the poor out of poverty. Business creates jobs where jobs did not exist before.

Yet as a recent issue of the *Religious Studies Review* demonstrates, many scholars in this nation's divinity schools nurture disdain for business corporations and even for the business vocation.[2] After the fall of socialism in 1989, what is left on the left? Well, anticapitalism is left. Anticapitalism is the single broad cause that has for generations united both the Leninist and the social democratic left. It has put the entire left in bed with the traditionalist, agrarian, aristocratic right. From the right as from the left, there are century-old arguments against business and (nowadays) "neoliberalism."[3] The collapse of socialism did not make hostility to capitalism go away. That hostility, which is older and deeper than socialism, is not hard to understand; I once shared it myself. Poets, romantics, and mystics have long been hostile to vulgar, grubby, "selfish" capitalism. Aristocrats hated it too. Capitalism is rejected, not as less practical or less effective than other systems, but as corrupting, even *evil*. And also successful—the unkindest cut of all.

Many Catholics, left and right, hold the view that the very motor of capitalism, which some economists say is "self-interest," is only a form of primordial selfishness, directly contrary to the two Great Commandments: to love one's neighbor and to love God. They say that the "profit motive" is an expression of one of the seven capital sins, greed. They insist that capitalism benefits only the rich and grinds down the poor. They say that capitalist individualism turns each man into a solitary atom, *homo homini lupus*. They say that capitalist advertising breeds hedonism, envy, greed, lust, a love for luxury, and moral vacuity. They argue that capitalism makes buying and selling into the organizing principle of virtually every sphere of life, even the churches and the universities and hospitals. They insist that capitalism destroys leisurely meals and delicate cuisine in favor of fast foods and a hurried, frantic lifestyle and that it brings about a severe flattening of good taste. Capitalism, they add disdainfully, breeds vulgarity of every sort. It puts up ugly, boxy buildings and disfigures highways with omnipresent billboards and neon lights. When they compare capitalist buildings to the beautiful tastes and high styles of aristocratic cultures, and even to simple peasant life, they find capitalist living hateful. They actually believe that capitalist wealth arises from exploitation of the immiserated poor both overseas and in capitalist urban centers.

The source of this hostility lies in a philosophical error, not an empirical survey. Even when any factual objection is rebutted—even when it is conceded that capitalism *is* in fact more productive, efficient, and economically creative—still, it is argued, capitalism is immoral. This judgment seems to flow from a certain habit of wishfulness, dreaminess, or, perhaps better, utopianism. In that light, the humble realism of capitalism appears to be a surrender to vulgarity. On the right, the source of hostility to capitalism appears to be nostalgia for the high courtesy, chivalry and *noblesse oblige* of the aristocratic, land-based order of the precapitalist regime. On the left, capitalism is compared to the never-realized dreams of socialists. Both left and right compare capitalism, not to any historical system that has actually existed, but to an ideal of perfection that they imagine. A more just and realistic assumption would be this: just as one should not expect too much from democracy, so one should not expect too much from capitalism. Both are flawed systems.

Perhaps I am wrong in this diagnosis of the sources of hostility to capitalism. If I am, the larger point stands forth all the more starkly: simply in order to *understand* the vocation of business in the highly ideological world of Western elites today, a young woman or man about to make crucial life choices needs to engage in a decent amount of philosophic inquiry.

In fact, there are at least three levels of discourse in which a philosophy of economics is both necessary and useful. This is true not only for those about to choose a career but also for those already engaged in business, who need from time to time to explain themselves to their own children. I hope that putting my points in autobiographical terms will help the reader to follow along with me. I begin with the first level of inquiry.

Adjudicate Among Economic Ideologies

At some point at the end of my graduate studies, I decided that I needed to turn my philosophical and theological interests toward the study of economics. Practically every aspect of my education had accustomed me to thinking in an anticapitalist vein. Nearly everyone trained in the humanities learns to abjure "bourgeois" tastes and to admire the aristocratic manner. Who as a young humanist does not want to be described as a "prince of a man," and to be thought to belong to "an aristocracy of the spirit"? What young woman fails to suspect that, if people could but see it, she is a "princess"?

But think about this a little. How odd is it that humanists disdain "bourgeois" tendencies and "philistine" habits when in fact nearly all the beautiful lace, millinery, tapestries, clothing, and nearly all the most elegant wines, best cheeses, and most beautifully wrought swords, cutlery, and woodwork of the West have been executed by the bourgeoisie? For the bourgeoisie are precisely those who are neither lords nor serfs but skilled craftsmen, living independently, by their wits. By contrast, real princes and princesses in centuries past seemed to spend an undue amount of time murdering their own relatives or sending them to the Tower. Few aristocrats produced a beautiful object of art.

In other words, the humanities teach most of us an aristocratic ideology rather sharply at variance with the real world. The aristocratic ideology carries with it a profound contempt for business, businessmen, and a capitalist way of life. It inculcates *ressentiment*. The rise of the businessman in recent centuries has been accompanied by a decline in the wealth, status, and self-importance of princes, dukes, counts, lords, and barons—and those they support.

From the left, I was instructed by Paul Tillich at Harvard (and not by him alone) that a Christian theologian *must* be a socialist.[4] It went without saying that capitalism is not aristocratic but vulgar and ethically corrupt. No theologian whom I encountered supposed, even as a hypothesis, that capitalism could be a *moral* system. Its immorality (or amorality) was a given.

As a young man, I was fairly easily persuaded by the aristocrats and the socialists. My own family had been born quite poor, and in Johnstown, Pennsylvania, the mill-owners lived on the hill up above the workers. On the other hand, a question nagged at me. I could not help remembering that a part of my family had *not* emigrated to America when my grandparents did, separately, from the mountain regions of Slovakia in Central Europe, just before and just after 1900. Our European relatives were then living under Soviet socialism—not under that tepid sort that Engels called, with disgust in his voice, "*Christian* socialism," but the kind that later writers liked to call, referring to the Soviet Union, "*real existing socialism.*"[5] The rolling Soviet tanks that had crushed the Prague Spring of 1968 were a vivid reminder to me of what my European relatives lived under.

Therefore, I had mixed feelings about socialism—and also about capitalism. I was strongly pulled toward socialism, but something warned me to hold back. And that is why I decided to begin my study of economics. Both of necessity and by choice, my study would be that of the philosopher and theologian, and neither that of the graduate student who wished to become a professional economist nor that of the student in a school of business who aspired to a career in business. I wanted to reach a point of view that would allow me, on some valid independent grounds, to reach a decision between rival ideologies.

Is it more reasonable, I was asking myself, to commit myself (like so many of my confreres) to a career of promoting a mild form of socialism and denigrating capitalism, or to a career, unlikely as it then seemed to me, of taking a stand *against* socialism? It is important to note that these alternatives, as I saw them, were asymmetrical: I could oppose socialism without really embracing capitalism. Without being a socialist, I could look upon capitalism with irony and with disdain. Many academics did that in those days, and still do. I could also embrace socialism and, *along with it*, its explicit and intense opposition to capitalism. At that time, actually *praising* capitalism from a moral point of view was not a possibility I could easily imagine.

I need to mention that along with the internationally acclaimed sociologist Peter Berger, for two summers I spent two weeks or so in Cuernavaca, Mexico, teaching in Father Ivan Illich's Center for Intercultural Documentation (CIDOC), and my subject in one of those years was something like "The Theology of Revolution." The problem of the poor of Latin America and elsewhere worried me very much, but my point of view was not economic, but political. Even then I could feel in every strain in my argument the need for greater economic knowledge. In fact, I was deeply impressed that Berger, for whom I had (and still have) much admiration, was just then discussing his own first researches in economics.

Berger had been making a sociological study of economic development, and although he had begun with a socialist paradigm in mind, he had become fascinated by the surprising empirical picture emerging from economic statistics in South Korea, Taiwan, Singapore, and Hong Kong. It was from him, I believe, that I first heard the term "the Four Little Tigers" of Southeast Asia. He had begun a book, *Pyramids of Sacrifice*, in which he was arguing that both capitalist and socialist systems seemed to be abandoning huge swathes of people to unnecessary and uncalled-for poverty.[6] His attitude at that time was, "A plague on both your houses!" Later, sustained exposure to

East Asia made him begin to reconsider. He encountered unassailable evidence that capitalism has the capacity to transform economies from extreme poverty to rather stunning development, even in a short span of 20 years.

From Aristotle I had learned in my early years of philosophy a deep respect for collecting specimens, whether of botanical, biological, or political forms of life, before attempting to make evaluative judgments. That seemed to me the right way to proceed in trying to adjudicate the question between ideological points of view.

To begin with, it was clear to me that socialists explicitly proposed an *ideology*, because when they began they had not a single existing example of socialism to point to. By contrast, liberals (those in favor of free markets) claimed to be practical, not ideological, and argued from the success of existing practice.

In reply, socialists countered that, even though capitalists may not think they have an ideology, they act from a false consciousness, in line with their own interests, but out of kilter with reality. In fact, they said, capitalism is doomed to self-destruction and will soon be swept into the dustbin of history. Inexorably the world is moving toward collectivization, they said, and the most rational and scientific organization of that world collective will be socialist. As late as the early 20th century, they called their viewpoint "scientific socialism," and this magnetic North Star pulled on the minds of many of the most influential social thinkers and intellectuals of Europe and America. By the end of World War II, even those who were not out-and-out Marxists adopted an anticapitalist tendency, along with an economic outlook that, within the limits of their own pragmatism, measured progress from the socialist point of view: "More active state = forward! Free private enterprise = backward!" Communists spoke glowingly of the "progressive forces" of the world, in which they included those who adopted more or less pinkish shades of the Marxist worldview: anticapitalist, antibourgeois; a division of the world into the oppressors and the oppressed. That was about where I was in those days.

Beginning to Fashion a Philosophical Point of View

But I also knew I needed to step back a little, to gain a deeper point of view. Looking back on it, I can see now how much I relied upon scholars with far larger sets of empirical tools than I possessed for discovering the concepts, criteria, and methods to apply. I found most useful those scholars who had some serious commitment to socialist views themselves, for they had a knack of taking socialist claims seriously enough to reformulate them as empirical hypotheses. Although Sidney Hook's main interest lay in the area of political and civil freedoms rather than in economics, for instance, he was one of the first of the major American philosophers to move away from Marxism for clear practical reasons and with a profound tragic sense.[7] To a lesser but still useful extent, Irving Howe and other writers in *Dissent* helped too, if only by spelling out their own version of socialism (famously described in *Dissent*'s first number as "the name of our dream").[8] In Britain, Stuart Hampshire edited a splendid volume of essays in which a variety of socialists addressed the question: "What went wrong?" That is, why wasn't socialism working out anywhere as described in its theories?[9] Michael Harrington, in his earnest American love for concrete cases, also provided much that was empirically testable.[10] I also learned to admire the intelligence and, in a large sense, fairness (he could be quite polemical but was willing to admit mistakes) of Robert Heilbroner.[11]

But without question, for me the single best aid was the sustained work of Peter Berger over many years, first in a set of two books he edited on empirical studies of equality around the world, and then most convincingly of all in his small masterpiece, *The Capitalist Revolution*. In that book, Berger formulated the 50 empirically testable propositions most commonly advanced to demonstrate the superiority of socialism over capitalism and then assembled the evidence for assessing them.[12]

This is far from a complete inventory of the studies I eagerly sought out. Friedrich von Hayek's and Ludwig von Mises's books on socialism opened my eyes to the epistemological deficits of socialism.[13] Without a price system, national commissars were simply blind to the strength and frequency of choices and desires, wholly without crucial information, limited to guesswork. Igor Shafarevich taught me the sources of the socialist passion for equality and uniformity and its dread of choice and difference.[14]

Socialism, I concluded (you can see the argument in *The Spirit of Democratic Capitalism*), grows out of a great number of philosophical assumptions and radically erroneous ways of imagining the world that go far beyond its mistaken economic theories.[15] This is why many on the left, after the humiliating collapse of socialism in 1989–1991, did not give up being left-ists. The chairman of the Socialist Party of Chile told me, after asking for permission to publish *The Spirit of Democratic Capitalism* in Spanish under the Socialist Party imprint, "I would like to demonstrate to Chileans that so-cialism is not exhausted by the mistaken economic theories of the nineteenth century." In his hands in Chile, and in many other places, socialism mutated into a theory of culture and politics. It became a radical revolt against the Jewish and Christian view of the human body and human sexuality; it re-belled against Western culture's hard-won realism, prudence, and sense of limits. The left is not bounded by economics: it has an appetite for the un-limited, the utopian, the dream.

In ethics today, therefore, the style of the populist left is largely undisci-plined by economics. It prefers rebellion, a flare for surrealism, and mockery. The left today expresses itself in massive protests, such as those of the antiglobalization protesters in Seattle, Genoa, and Johannesburg, whose style always includes angry lawlessness. Its preferred philosophy today is "post-modernism," a radical reduction of human reason to questions of power and interest. This deconstruction issues in nihilism, whose lightly disguised im-plication is that only the will to power matters. (Paul DeMans's postmod-ernism, not surprisingly, has the same roots as Nazism and Stalinism.) Mussolini defined totalitarianism quite simply as "La feroce volontà!"

All these post-1989 developments show that it would have been a grave mistake to understand socialism as merely a theory about economics. That was only a fraction of its appeal. One must approach questions such as cap-italism and socialism on a plane deeper than economics. One must take care to attend to both the cultural *and* the political dimensions usually beyond the ken of economics.

Capitalism and Socialism Are Not Symmetrical

On this plane, it turns out that capitalism and socialism are not symmetri-cal concepts. One can speak abstractly of capitalism in more or less purely economic terms, with relatively little reference to questions of culture and politics, and still make limited sense. (I do not believe that capitalism can be wholly captured or explained in this way—hence my own tripartite schema for talking about the three parts of the free society: economic, political, and moral/cultural.[16] Still, the thriving libertarian movement shows that mine is not the only alternative.[17])

By contrast, socialism is a far more sweeping and unitary system than capitalism. Politics and culture are as much a part of its essence, under its single collective system of control, as economics. Not for nothing is the primordial socialist flag one single color, red, without division. (Recall Victor Hugo's rationale for its design in Paris in 1831.)[18] Under socialism, all things are pulled into one. It constitutes a religion, an ethic, a cultural force all its own. It has its own distinctive mystique, scorning the self-imposed limits of classic Western politics. Socialist man is and intends to be a *new man*, and to understand socialism adequately, scholars have been forced to turn to philosophy and theology, beyond mere economics.[19]

By the same measure, economics alone turns out to be inadequate for understanding the success of capitalist economics, although for quite different reasons. Prior to 1989, in the Soviet Union, China, and other broad regions of this planet, capitalist acts among consenting adults were treated as crimes against the state, punishable by death. Business corporations operated solely at the sufferance of the state, with no right to exist independently on their own. In this respect, too many economists and businessmen in the United States forgot how much they *depend upon a political regime* of a certain type, one that is respectful of three basic human rights among others: the rights of association, private property, and personal economic initiative.

While one can make sense of a capitalist economy in its own terms, with relatively little intermixture of political control or interference, nonetheless a capitalist economy is a fairly rare growth in world history. Few are the regimes that have allowed it the liberty to thrive, and even fewer have nourished the specific cultural habits required for its flourishing—until very recent centuries, none did. Even where its fragile life seems to flourish, significant parties and interests within the state work relentlessly to submerge a free and creative capitalist economy under political domination.

More than that, large governmental systems and welfare agencies in modern states suffuse the thoughts, desires, and habits of entire peoples. Two debilitating features of democracy thus come into view, exactly as Tocqueville predicted a century and a half ago: the drift downward toward materialism and mediocrity, on the one hand, and on the other hand, the taste for surrendering liberty to the paternal state in exchange for a reduction in the uncertainties of life and in pursuit of greater "equality." (Many foolish initiatives are undertaken in our times in the name of equality, but their issue is almost always a more oppressive subservience for all.) Thus, Tocqueville pictured the future, or present:

> I am trying to imagine under what novel features despotism may appear in the world. In the first place, I see an innumerable multitude of men, alike and equal, constantly circling around in pursuit of the petty and banal pleasures with which they glut their souls. . . . Over this kind of men stands an immense, protective power which is alone responsible for securing their enjoyment and watching over their fate. That power is absolute, thoughtful of detail, orderly, provident, and gentle. It would resemble parental authority if, fatherlike, it tried to prepare its charges for a man's life, but on the contrary, it only tries to keep them in perpetual childhood.[20]

In Sweden the great Gunnar Myrdal eventually admitted that despite his earlier, angry denials that this would ever be the case, social democracy in the end made new generations of Swedes malingerers and fibbers, lying to their doctors in order to obtain written medical excuses and calling in sick to their employers.[21]

In addition, experience shows that the social democratic state better rewards the middle-class custodians of welfare benefits than it does the unemployed and the very poor, whom it thrusts into psychological dependency, helplessness, and *ressentiment*.

Such experiences demonstrate that political regimes can powerfully alter cultures. Moreover, certain changes in a people's culture deeply affect their economic behaviors. A capitalist economy depends heavily on work habits, family patterns, and metaphysical or religious energies of particular sorts. That is why it fares far better in some cultures than in others.[22] Time and again it will fail to function in cultures that lack the necessary cultural habits. It will fail again and again (in Latin America, for instance) under insufficiently rigorous moral systems.

The range of cultural and political systems within which capitalist systems can thrive is fairly narrow. Certain cultural and political preconditions must be met or else the economic system goes awry. *Culture and politics are prior to economics and supply necessary preconditions for it.*

For the philosopher and the theologian, to sort out the chief cultural and political prerequisites of capitalist and socialist systems is a fairly daunting task. But it is also a richly rewarding one, and of considerable use to economists to the extent that it throws new light from new perspectives upon perplexities they face every day, especially those involved in dealing with questions of development in a global framework. A philosophy of economic life, moreover, illuminates the cultural and political terrain for practical men and women, who must try to decide which economic system, and which form of it, they wish to throw their weight behind. To identify and promote those economic systems best suited to human flourishing (I am not supposing at this stage that there is only one), practical people need all the philosophic and critical help they can get.

Sorting Out the Necessary Concepts

In *The Spirit of Democratic Capitalism*, I set forth three different disciplines within the new *theology* of economics for whose development I call. The same three disciplines are relevant for the new *philosophy* of economics, which in some ways is more urgent. The first level of discourse in a new philosophy of economics is the one in which we have so far been engaged—the comparison of alternative systems of economic organization (such as socialism and capitalism). As we have seen, that set of inquiries soon leads us to prior and more basic questions having to do with cultural and political questions that must be faced in any and all economic systems. These inquiries constitute the second level of discourse in a new philosophy of economics: inquiries into the basic concepts that cut across *all* economic systems or help to shed light on the differences among them.[23]

The third level of discourse, to which we will turn in the final section, takes up special ethical dilemmas that arise *within* particular economic systems. For example, why are there firms (or corporations) in capitalist systems, and what is their nature and function? Should there be limits on the amount of compensation to chief executives of corporations? How were prices set by national planners in existing socialist systems, and with what results?

To sum up, there are three realms in which questions about economics tend to fall: questions involving *comparisons between or among economic systems*, such as between market and nonmarket systems, capitalism and socialism, and the like; *perennial economic questions* in all historical systems of human economic life, such as scarcity, constraints of various kinds, supply, demand, prices, and risk; and questions regarding *particular institutions within economic systems*, such as corporations, inventions, and individual initiatives (within capitalism); national planning boards (within socialism); and laws and customs affecting land ownership and relations within and among families (within feudalism).

At its first stage, as we have seen, a helpful philosophy of economics offers empirically testable hypotheses concerning the claims of rival systems. Sharp philosophical differences divide American capitalism and not only "real" socialism, such as one finds in Cuba, North Korea, and the pre-1989 Soviet Union, but also French and German social democracy. Each little boy and girl, Gilbert and Sullivan once sang to us, is born either a little liberal or a little conservative. When the hour strikes for these infants to begin to think critically, they will not want to rely solely upon family upbringing or personal temperament in choosing the economic system they support. The reasons leading up to such a choice can in principle be laid out in arguments amenable, one by one, to empirical falsifiability. Their initial beliefs can be submitted to systematic comparison with actual facts so as to test the truth or falsehood of these beliefs.

To conduct such inquiries, a broad range of considerations forces the inquirer to stretch his mind to reach a high degree of philosophical clarity about as many as *30 or 40 concepts*, which may not at first be clear in his head. These concepts are of varying sweep and breadth and draw upon many different disciplines for their clarification. Simply to set them forth in an outline is to suggest the breadth and depth that an adequate philosophy of economics must reach. In digging deeper into more fundamental questions, the inquirer will certainly need to be clear about what he means by such basic terms as:

- Time, history, progress, development[24]
- Family, association, organization, civil society, the state[25]
- Individual, person, liberty, action, habits, virtue[26]

- Insight, reflection, judgment, practical wisdom, intention, choice[27]
- Happiness, human flourishing, creativity and invention, common good, public interest, civility[28]
- Equality of opportunity, equality under the law, equality of uniformity[29]
- Political liberty, economic liberty, moral/cultural liberty[30]
- Objections against capitalism—political, economic, cultural, aesthetic[31]
- Objections against socialism—political, economic, cultural, aesthetic[32]
- Error, misinformation, evil, sin, and irrationality[33]

One will note that these are, as it were, *background terms*—belonging more to philosophy than to economics, they do not yet include such fundamental terms of economic discourse as "scarcity," "abundance," "demand," "supply," "general welfare," "self-interest," "full employment," "inevitable trade-offs," "economic reason," "markets," "enterprise," and many others.

Many arguments that *seem* to be about economic realities arise when individuals use these background terms in different ways. Some of these usages are less plausible than others, and some are flat out ill informed. Much would be gained, then, by putting together a small handbook defining the most fruitful usages of such terms and their interrelations and exemplifying them in helpful ways. Isolating where exactly disagreements actually lie is an enormous gain, since most disagreements never even get defined but go around and around in impenetrable fog.

I sometimes entertain the hope that, when confronted with evidence that disconfirms their earlier-held expectations, reasonable persons will be able to change their minds. On the other hand, after the fall of socialism few on the left admitted publicly that they had been wrong about socialist economics. Just the same, even when not everybody agrees, it is still good to have a reasonable method for clarifying *where* we do not agree. When that happens, fundamental political and economic disagreements are probably good for a free society. The competition of ideas, in any case, is essential to the free society.

Facing Particular Questions Within Capitalism

When I first began this book, I thought that on this third level I would take up some particular problem within the capitalist system today, such as corporate compensation, the 2003 accounting scandals surrounding some six to ten major listed corporations (out of thousands of firms),[34] debates about the minimum wage, or the like. All these questions deserve discussion. But I have been so struck by the sheer hostility against corporations voiced by many politicians in Washington, some journalists and TV pundits, and many professors on university campuses that it became unavoidably clear that a deeper issue must be dealt with.

Some years ago, when many intellectuals in the United States believed that some sort of socialism or social democracy was clearly the direction in which history was moving (and *should* move), their contempt for capitalism was at least understandable. Socialism was the horse they put their money on. But after the utter collapse of socialist economies, one expected these cheerleaders to emerge a little chastened, a little more realistic about what can be done and why, and in that way to come to some peace with economic reality. Instead, their underlying ire against capitalism, after being submerged for about a decade, has burst out into the open again, with a kind of hysterical passion and irrationality far less credible than before.

Even commentators inclined to the left have found it hard to see much coherence in the antiglobalization demonstrators who fly all over the world in magnificent airliners to attack with violent rage the big business, capitalism, and transnational corporations that make those airliners function. In a less violent way, even Democratic centrists seem unable to resist lashing out against "the rich" and "big oil" and "business interests." The magnet placed beneath the grid of politics by Karl Marx still draws antibusiness particles leftward with the same old potency.

Thus, in concluding these remarks, I would like to draw attention to several current accusations against the capitalist system by its university foes, particularly in departments of religion.

Accusations and Rebuttals

In a long essay on theology and economics, Joerg Rieger of the Perkins School of Theology at Southern Methodist University writes of the "newly victorious" capitalist system as though it were a *disease* expanding "into the farthest regions of the globe and into the most private realms of our lives." He voices at least 12 accusations against capitalism. Rieger worries that this destructive disease invades our worship (as in "refreshment of tired bodies and minds on Sunday morning"), our concepts of faith (as in "faith-based institutions"), our hope (as in the American determination to prevail after the first shock of September 11, 2001), and our charity (as in "compassionate conservatism").

If these complaints seem frivolous to you, Rieger is more deeply dismayed by the power of advertising, which is "geared towards reshaping our innermost desires and reaches levels of our humanity that we cannot control moralistically. . . . We are bombarded with thousands of images each day, all designed to shape our desires and to make us more perfect participants in the so-called 'free' market economy," he rushes on.

> With every breath we take we are integrated into the market, be it through the workplace, the way we relax, the way we shop, the way we save money, the way we plan for our retirement, the way we address social need, not to mention the influence of media and entertainment. During most of our working hours we are, therefore, more or less directly hooked up with the market economy. . . .[We are in a world] where even our best intentions and heroic actions are constantly being pulled into the vortex of the market. . . . Theology and the church—even where they try to resist—may be unconsciously shaped by the capitalist market economy.[35]

Stop to think for a moment. It is not only under capitalism that economic concerns press on nearly everybody. Are not the Gospels themselves redolent with the pastoral, rural economy of first-century Palestine? Are not the apostles and ordinary people preoccupied with plowing, seeding, harvesting, fishing, finding and preparing food, and seeking places to sleep? In the socialist countries under communism, every minute of every day was shaped by standing in line, hardship, scarcity, and sensory deprivation. Under social democracy, fights over subsidies and privileges, handouts and prerogatives, color every day. Every day one faces the latest in a series of strikes for higher benefits or new privileges. Fears of high unemployment and dwindling reserves for old-age assistance disturb every minute of every waking day, because everyone knows that the young generation is far less numerous than the old and that the old are living far longer than in times past. Who will pay for the benefits the state promised them?

Scarcity and want are the human condition. Moreover, there is no evidence whatever that inequalities within capitalist societies exceed the distance between the *nomenklatura* in the Soviet Union and the impecunious peasants of the vast countryside, or the inequalities of days gone by.[36] On the contrary. The Hungarian counts who dwelt in the great Castle of Spisska Podhradie in Central Slovakia inhabited realms of privilege far above the serfs (my great-grandparents, for instance) who tilled their fields and cleaned their stables. Their rank was much further removed from the common grasp than the rank of America's top CEOs is from the grasp of poor immigrants to America. Many Americans born as poor as you and I have become CEOs of America's largest companies (and will enjoy a career in that post, on average, shorter than that of an NFL linebacker).

Let me word this rebuttal another way. If Rieger wants to argue that the condition of the world's poor is worse today than in 800 A.D. or 1250, or 1650, or 1880, or 1933, or 1976, he must demonstrate that, not merely allude to it as a silent assumption. It can be shown without extraordinary effort that on practically every index of health—mortality, infant mortality, the elimination of certain destructive diseases and the discovery of cures for others, caloric intake, clean water, literacy, care for the eyes and teeth, basic democratic freedoms and elementary rights—a huge expanding circle and growing proportion of the human population is better off under capitalist systems and lives on levels higher than those even dreamed of in earlier systems.[37] Before capitalism, even kings and presidents were bled to death by unknowing doctors, and the easiest mode of transport was by horse, not a Toyota or a Ford.

Rieger describes capitalism as generating "a full-blown *repression* and the powers that cause it. . . . The fate of people *on the underside* has to do with the *repressions* by which our so-called free economy operates. Economic expansion is built, for instance, on the vast availability of cheap labor."[38] But Rieger must show that there is more cheap labor today, under capitalist systems, than there was in Egypt for the building of the pyramids, or in feudal Europe for the building of the castles, or among rural populations generally in those regions where the growing season was short. (Bishop Berkeley commended early capitalism in Ireland for bringing indolent peasants into productive labor.) Is there greater cheap labor today under capitalism than there was in Communist Eastern Europe and China? Is there a higher proportion of unemployed people in social democratic Europe than in the capitalist United States today? It is invention, not cheap labor, that fires economic expansion—the invention of computers and cell phones and other products we have not yet seen.

It is possible that Rieger has not noted the rapid rise in economic prosperity in the nations of East Asia, in Chile, in southern Europe, in Ireland, and increasingly in China and India since 1980. Extreme poverty in these regions, vast only 50 years ago, has been tremendously reduced thanks to the spread of capitalist methods and conceptions. The capitalist economy is not, as he puts it, "expanding" because it does not help people, but because it does. Those capable of comparing it to alternative systems have come to recognize that it works far better than their current systems. It is expanding by desire and by imitation.

Rieger denies that capitalism "and the desires connected with it are 'natural.'"[39] He alleges that the term "natural" points incorrectly to the vulgar desire to "[keep] up with the Joneses" and that all people everywhere "want more stuff. . . a bigger car, a bigger house, and more money *at the expense of everybody else.*"[40] But this is surely wrong. What Adam Smith posited as the two natural desires, important for economic development but too humble to have been noted by earlier moral philosophers, are these: "the natural effort of every individual to better his own condition" and a "propensity to truck, barter, and exchange one thing for another."[41] In other words, we are predisposed to self-improvement, including economic self-improvement, and to a cooperative spirit of voluntary and fair exchange. There are many examples of both these natural desires in the Bible, not to say throughout the history of *homo sapiens*, in all times and places. Markets too have been virtually universal and in the Bible are ubiquitous.

Thus, Rieger seems to have less than an accurate idea of what is distinctive about capitalism. It is neither markets nor private property nor profits, all of which existed—even flourished—in precapitalist eras (such as the biblical era). What is distinctive about capitalism *qua* capitalism is the organization of an economic system around *the human mind*—around invention, discovery, and the sort of enterprise that creates new things that never before existed. In a capitalist economy, people do not need to get "more money *at the expense of everybody else*," as Rieger falsely imagines. That was precisely the condition of the precapitalist, even premodern, mercantile economy, in which avarice was the besetting sin. In those days wealth was limited, and anyone's acquisition of it necessarily deprived others of it, in a zero-sum game. In a capitalist economy, unprecedented amounts of new wealth are created that no one "takes" from anybody else; on the contrary, new inventions increase the whole world's pool of wealth and distribute it more roundly to larger proportions of others than at any previous period of world history. That is precisely why so many of the formerly poor, including many of America's anticapitalists, are now middle-class. From this highly favored position, some can now rail against the system for not fulfilling their wishful dream of the way a society ought to be arranged.

Rieger asserts more than once in his essay that criticism of the capitalist system is stifled and that "no critique of the system is permitted."[42] His whole career and those of scores of thousands of other intellectuals show that that claim is false. It is far more rare to meet a theologian who is in favor of capitalism, for articulate and well-discerned reasons, than to meet dozens who are critical, even publicly disdainful, of it.[43]

Without elaborating on it, Rieger quotes without critical comment the opinion of a feminist theologian: "We middle-class North American Christians are destroying nature, not because we do not love it, but because of the way we live."[44] *Destroying nature?* That is a highly improbable claim. Consider the ecology of North America itself (as we shall do at length in chapter 6). If we look at the ecology of North America in the year 1450, say, or 1650, or 1850, we would find that large stretches of it were then composed of inhospitable deserts, virtually uninhabitable and untamed plains, eroding mountains, and frequently poisonous streams.[45] The ability of North America to sustain human life and the average mortality of the people who inhabited North America were by current standards very low.

As a matter of plain fact, modern North Americans have led the way to vastly improved health care, living conditions, and expectations of mortality, not only in North America but also (through the medicine, hygiene, and science that they have pioneered and eagerly shared with others) in other parts of the world. So what are we to make of the extreme claim that North Americans are responsible for "destroying" nature outside America's own national boundaries? That extreme claim is indefensible. Indeed, the opposite is closer to the truth. In some ways the ability of the Earth to sustain human life (at an ever higher standard of quality) has been lifted to a higher level than at any prior period in history. A higher proportion of people are alive, and living longer, and living better, than ever before.[46] Again, if crucially needed minerals and other "nonrenewable" resources were becoming scarcer, the laws of economics predict that they would be becoming more expensive. But the opposite is the case. In all but rare instances, precious resources are experiencing falling prices compared with earlier years.[47]

If Rieger is receiving the average professorial wage for a tenured university position, and if in addition he earns a little additional money lecturing and writing, he stands no doubt in the top 10 percent of all income earners in the United States.[48] His standing may be even higher if he is married and his wife also receives income. But it is clearly true that he does not consider "making money" the highest end of his life. Actually, in fact, a large majority of Americans do not. About 64 percent of American adults are working for income; about 30 percent of able-bodied persons between the ages of 18 and 65 are not working for income at all.

Among the 139 million civilians employed in the United States, 24 million work for the Fortune 500 companies, the largest industrial corporations, about 50 million are employed by businesses with fewer than 100 employees, and almost 10 million people are primarily self-employed. About 20 million work for government—federal, state, and local. About as many—20 million—work for nonprofit organizations such as churches, hospitals, clinics, libraries, museums, schools, universities, research institutes, foundations, the Girl Scouts, the Sierra Club, and thousands of other nonprofit associations and activist groups.[49] In sum, nearly one-third of Americans (some 40 million!) work in the not-for-profit sector (including government); the other two-thirds pay the taxes and make the donations that support them.

And most Americans, like my father, prefer time with family and a lower level of job commitment over chances for advancement that entail longer hours and continuous travel. Most prefer the kind of work that makes them happy over a more demanding kind in which they could make more money. People who are really ambitious for great wealth, or even for great achievement, are few. Indeed, my long experience with college students shows that most students are quite content just to get by.

Next, Rieger also claims that Americans are peculiarly money-driven. But that claim must be set alongside Jacques Maritain's observation in *Reflections on America* that "the American people are the least materialist among the modern peoples which have attained the industrial stage."[50] What is the evidence either way?

Finally, it must be said that Rieger's description of Americans cringing under a deluge of seductive images (presumably from television) seems preposterous. Neither advertising gurus nor retailers feel anything like the omnipotence with which Rieger endows them; they sometimes experience abject failure and most of the time barely enough success to keep going on. A great many highly touted products, like the Edsel, just die. True, some products are so good that they are smashing successes, but rarely is it the advertising alone that brought them their good fortune.

The bottom line is that many intellectuals are scaring themselves into extremist positions for which they must present empirical evidence, and they do not have such evidence. They are misled by an inner antipathy for an economic system they do not show evidence of understanding fairly, whether in itself or by just comparison with other systems. They seem to imagine some personal (or perhaps collective) vision of utopia and then compare capitalism and democracy to that, while neglecting the existing economic and political alternatives. They also fail to notice a significant clue: the long, long lines of immigrants from all over the world—at any one time millions of them waiting for their visa applications to be processed—straining to enter into the very few dynamic capitalist and democratic systems of the world, precisely because those who enter such systems poor have a very high probability of exiting out of poverty within a half-dozen years. Democratic and capitalist countries are good for the poor. They are in fact the last best hope of the poor of the world.

Conclusion

In a word, those of you among my readers who are called to vocations in business have a great chance to swell the numbers of people around the world now exiting from poverty, by means of the creative economic enterprises that will spring from your own imagination, discipline, sweat, intelligence, and hard work. Without taking money from anybody else, you are in a position to create new wealth never before seen and to pay most of it out to workers, pensioners, shareholders, suppliers, transporters, and in good value to your customers.

Create and give!

That is not a bad motto for what you are called to do. Be worthy of it.

And do not too much mind the disdainers of your work—they have been paying people in business the compliment of envy and resentment for hundreds of years. As some of Professor Rieger's comments suggest, the newest preferred tactical assault is by way of a certain utopianism about the environment. We will turn to that subject—an important one in its own right—in chapter 6. But first, one of the great contributions of the business society to human liberty is the diffusion of economic realism (except in most universities, which are by and large run on socialist economic principles). And so a few words on economic realism may not be wasted.

Chapter Four

ECONOMIC REALISM

MANY LONG CENTURIES WERE REQUIRED before human beings discovered the causes of the wealth of nations and began to achieve economic
development in whole nations. Economic life is hard, and some of its lessons
and laws do not lie on the surface but must be learned the hard way, through
experience, through rough trial and error. One might at first imagine, for instance, that the ten brightest people in the Iowa Territory about 1860 might
have been charged to develop a ten-year plan for land use, assign settlers to
it, and supervise their activities in order to coordinate them as efficiently as
possible. Rational efforts, one might imagine, require rational planning and
management. Abraham Lincoln, based on observation and a different set of
expectations about the human mind, approached the problem of development quite differently. He proposed giving any homesteader who promised
to farm it about as much land as a family could handle, allowing each family to do what it thought most intelligent, and allowing communities to set
up their own marketplaces. He judged there was more practical rationality
in thousands of free people meeting in open markets than in even the thousand smartest brains in the Territory meeting on some government board of
management. I have asked a number of professor friends about free markets,
and it is not intuitively obvious to them that markets generate a larger fund
of practical intelligence than smart planners would. But practice confirms
that they do.

Thus, a key cultural problem in our day is that most of those who work in our systems of higher education work in an environment that is antithetical to markets. They tend to look at markets as inferior orders of existence. For instance, they strongly resist the importation of "market tests" into university procedures. Moreover, the admissions brochures of their universities announce to the world that they are training "the leaders and managers of the future." The not-so-noticed implication of this claim is that the population that these "leaders of the future" will "lead" and "manage"—that is, the herd about to be led and managed—are all those poor people outside the university. What if those who are supposed to be led and managed do not have enough respect for the universities to accept so passive a role?

There is considerable tension between town and gown. On a voting map of the nation, the university towns generally stick out from the surrounding counties, little red patches in a sea of blue. The difference in voting patterns and ideological leanings is usually quite marked. Much of the difference lies in a different experience of markets, business corporations, taxes, the role of government, and the capitalist ideal. University communities typically pride themselves on being rather to the "left" regarding big business. During the Depression years of the 1930s, that was more or less understandable. After the fall of the Berlin Wall and the revelations about the dismal record of real socialist economies, it is not so intelligible. After the flood of new technologies whose invention and marketing were sparked by the remarkable cuts in capital gains taxes during the 1980s—electronic and other technologies that didn't even exist before then, such as the Internet, biomedicine and genetic medicine, cell phones, laptops, computer networks, and digitized libraries—continued leftishness seems positively perverse.

One would have thought that the collapse of socialism, both behind the Iron Curtain and in the practical economic thinking of social democrats and democratic socialists, would have thrust virtually all intellectuals and social commentators into a realistic embrace of democracy and capitalism—these two imperfect and yet precious systems that have done so much to liberate and raise up the families of all of us who came to America dirt poor. One wouldn't have had to accept capitalism and democracy just as they now are, but only be willing to make of them the best that our finite, limited capacities permit. But rather than accepting that reality all around us—that constraint, if you will—many of the same voices that once hated America and capitalism *still* hate America and capitalism, and perhaps now even more desperately. Their lack of an alternative and the bitter disappointment of their socialist illusions seem to have deterred them not at all.

At least this much has been gained. Today these anticapitalists are no longer Communists or Socialists. They declare themselves to be environmentalists, and they vibrate with hostility against "globalization." And as in the bad old days, they want the state to command private businesses. The trouble with antiglobalizers is that those forlorn parts of the world not yet included in the global system remain today the most desperately poor, ill, and likely to die young.

To utopians, however, facts don't seem to matter. For them, the main problem seems to be that neither democracy nor capitalism provides much in the way of pure, brightly idealized outcomes, romance, poetry, or myth. Both are systems for poor and weak and largely ignorant adults who are bounded on all sides by constraints, including above all their own internal limits. Many professors, of course, try to be fairly reasonable in their idealism and struggle admirably to quell their own romantic tendencies. Sometimes they confess that socialism turned out much worse than they expected 20 years earlier and that capitalism turned out to be much more vital. And some of them manage to overcome their environment pretty thoroughly and strike out marvelously well on what seems like a much more realistic view of the world. One of those I most admire in this regard is Professor Thomas Sowell, formerly of the University of Chicago and UCLA and now at the Hoover Institute, who to my mind exemplifies the instincts for realistic constraints that the ancients used to call *phronesis* or practical wisdom (or, in some translations, prudence). On constrained and unconstrained visions—in my terms, realistic and utopian visions—Thomas Sowell has written a whole book, as he has done in a broad range of the most controverted and difficult issues of our time.[1]

The Realism of Thomas Sowell

One of the most stunning features of the work of Thomas Sowell is that he was early indoctrinated in the democratic socialist narrative of history and rebelled against it only much later. He has described the experience as an awakening from a dream, the end to a period of intellectual wishfulness. He discovered a reality principle. He came to loathe the illusions in which he had been encouraged to live. In *A Personal Odyssey*, Sowell describes those illusions as a childish evasion of hard realities, limits, and constraints.[2] In *The Vision of the Anointed*, Sowell could not wholly repress his anger at those who, while nourishing illusions that destroy so much that is good, legislate how their lessers should live.[3] Those "unconstrained" by reality set the standards for "the leaders and managers of the future." They also help to set the tone for the artists, filmmakers, and journalists.

Perhaps the most bracing feature of the work of Sowell appears—*bang!*—on page 1 of his book on the basic insights of economics, *Basic Economics*, where he immediately invokes that most central of adulthood's themes: constraints, limits, tough choices, losses as well as gains.[4] He defines economics right off the bat in the classic words of Lionel Robbins: "Economics is the study of the use of scarce resources which have alternative uses." We humans are limited in our powers. We are limited in our knowledge. We are limited in the time we have to learn, to consider, to act, to follow through. On all sides we experience constraints.

But the most significant limit to our desires is scarcity. Our desires far exceed the available goods. "People want more than there is." Because there are alternative uses, we must make choices; we cannot have all alternatives. We must deprive ourselves of many good things in order to gain an alternative few. Realism 101. Journalists for the *New York Times*, Sowell wryly observes, are continually shocked that middle-class Americans, some even with swimming pools of their own, are "Just Getting By." Some, horrible to say, are "Constrained by Credit Card Debts" and still face "Dreams Deferred and Plans Unmet." It is too bad that middle-class Americans don't just get manna from heaven. It is sad that they find the defining constraints of adulthood to be chafing. They refuse to grow up into realism.

Sowell returns often to his fundamental theme: There is scarcity, and there are alternative uses for resources. Deal with it! He presents both intelligent and unintelligent ways to deal with unpleasant choices among alternatives. He specializes in showing how most of the courses of action proposed by the most influential media outlets (he has collected some unforgettable quotations) are among the unintelligent ones, based upon demonstrable fallacies. It would be a useful exercise for some enterprising graduate student to abstract from his books a long list of common fallacies that Sowell unmasks in order to publish from it a catechism of utopian economics.

Because of recent riots in streets from Seattle to Geneva against globalization, I particularly like one chapter of Sowell's on the international economy. The fallacy with which Sowell opens comes from the economic reporting of the *New York Times* about the North American Free Trade Agreement (NAFTA) in 1993: "Abundant evidence is emerging that jobs are shifting across borders too rapidly to declare the United States a job winner or a job loser from the trade agreement." Here, Sowell notes, the *Times'* fallacies are two. First, there is no fixed sum of jobs, some of them "shifting" one way or the other. Second, trade is not a zero-sum game in which one country wins and another loses.

The reason a country engages in trade is to gain; the reason another country agrees to trade with the first is also to gain. When each country pockets these gains, new jobs are created. Through trade, *both* become more prosperous, and both gain jobs. In the six years following 1993, for example, the U.S. auto industry, which Congressman David Bonior of Michigan had predicted would "vanish" under the NAFTA agreement, actually gained 100,000 jobs. Mexico gained probably even more.

Sowell also has nifty discussions of the differences among "comparative advantage," "absolute advantage," and "economies of scale." For all human beings, time and resources are finite, so concentration of effort is a gain. It is an absolute advantage when, because of climate, geography, or the mixture of skills in its population, one country is able to produce cheaply something that another cannot produce nearly so cheaply, or even at all. Bananas can be grown in North America, but only in greenhouses and at prohibitive expense; they can be bought at a fraction of that cost from the nations of the Caribbean.

Yet even when one country can produce *practically everything* more cheaply than another, it may still find it advantageous to concentrate on those products in which its advantages are significantly greater. For example, even if the United States can produce both shoes and shirts more cheaply than Canada, the United States may find it more efficient to concentrate on producing the one in which it has a huge advantage and buying from its partner the one in which it has a far lower advantage. In that way, both countries concentrate their efforts, to the maximum advantage of each. Using very clear tables, Sowell shows that the man-hours it takes to make 500 shirts in the United States compared with the hours it takes in Canada, against the man-hours it takes each to make 500 pairs of shoes, prompts U.S. producers to concentrate on shirts and Canadians to concentrate on shoes. The result is that the two countries, together, using the same number of man-hours, produce 6,000 more shirts and 1,000 more shoes than they would otherwise have done. In such ways, both countries exercise comparative advantages. That is why all countries seek partners with mutually beneficial matches.

Economies of scale lead nations to trade too, inasmuch as some countries are so small that their internal market cannot support large expenditures of capital or labor unless they find partners whose needs complement their own. Thus, South Korea and Taiwan could not produce much of what they now manufacture without access to far larger markets outside their borders. The Dutch retailer Royal Ahold has more than two-thirds of its sales outside the Netherlands, and the Swedish retailer Hennes and Mauritz has more than four-fifths of its sales outside Sweden. The U.S. retailer Wal-Mart exports much more than either Royal Ahold or Hennes and Mauritz, but four-fifths of its sales remain in the huge U.S. market, which affords it ample economies of scale. U.S. auto companies can manufacture and export automobiles to Australia at a price far cheaper than Australian companies, facing a much smaller market, can possibly manufacture them.

Since all resources, including labor, are scarce, no country can make everything. Concentration of effort upon selected uses of resources brings higher rewards than does diffusion of effort. Economics is the science of predicting the costs and benefits of such alternative uses, given the constraints of scarcity and finitude.

The fallacy that "exporting high-paying jobs overseas" harms a nation, Sowell writes, also remains a hardy perennial. It seems like common sense, but it is a fallacy, largely because excitable commentators forget the realities of scarcity, finitude, and the need for concentration—and the advantages to be gleaned from concentration on comparative advantages. For more than two centuries now, higher-wage countries (Great Britain in the 19th century, the United States in the 20th) have been exporting jobs to low-wage countries while continuing to gain in national wealth and also in numbers of jobs and in higher prosperity.

For instance, the comparative American talent in the field of computers, which Americans pioneered, is invention and innovation, especially in software. Concentrating where Americans are strongest and rewards are greatest, Americans can easily afford to allow other peoples overseas to manufacture much of the hardware for the industry. This is not to say that adaptation within and between industries is always smooth, easy, and without cost. Economics, in whose very constitution scarcity is a dominating landmark, is not an especially rosy discipline.

Sowell is unusually good, if succinct, on "international transfers of wealth," especially in showing us how to interpret scary terms such as "debtor nation." In any given year, Japanese Toyotas or Hondas may be the best-selling car in the United States, while no U.S. car has ever been the best seller (or even remotely close to being one) in Japan. So, true enough, the Japanese usually have a huge trade surplus with the United States. As an accounting mechanism, registering only the physical things that move across boundaries, the United States is a "debtor nation." But the U.S. economy exports more services than goods, including most of the software that runs the computers in Japan and elsewhere. These exports often do not show up in the accounting tables. Meanwhile, with their surpluses, the Japanese and others build factories in the United States. They do this, among other reasons, so that they do not have to pay for shipping their cars across the ocean. They also do it because the comparative advantage of our political and civil institutions and the inventiveness of our economy make investment in the United States more secure and more rewarding than in most other places.

True, the largest share of foreign investment in the United States comes from the British, not the Japanese. It is also true that foreign investment is accounted for as a "debt." But here we must distinguish, Sowell insists, between words and things. As an accounting convention, Japan profits from selling to us, and Japanese investment of these profits over here may be referred to as "debts." But real salaries are then being paid here to Americans who are producing more things with these funds than we otherwise could. In the world of real things, the United States is not getting poorer. On the contrary. From 1980 to 1990, the United States doubled its gross national product from $2.7 trillion to $5.6 trillion. By 2001 it had nearly doubled again, to $10.1 trillion.[5] If it takes "debt" to make so much progress, some forms of debt must be pretty creative.

On the other side, in the spurious sense, the United States has been a "debtor" nation for most of its history, and it didn't hurt. During the 19th century, foreigners put up much of the money for the Baltimore & Ohio, New York Central, Illinois Central, and other railroads and otherwise helped to turn this predominantly agricultural nation into a manufacturing colossus. American jobs flowed from those investments, and so did new inventions and new industries.

Sowell also writes highly illuminating pages on remittances to foreign countries from immigrants working here, on foreign aid, and on the myth of economic imperialism. His hardheadedness in facing up to scarcity, constraints, and less than perfect choices has a refreshingly adult quality. Sowell not only covers ground but keeps his feet on it. After floating through so many visions of glorious futures in which there are no constraints, no tradeoffs, no losses, and no frustrations, Sowell's realism is a tonic. I rather like writers who deliver the bump of reality every page or so.

Economic Utopianism

Quite different from Thomas Sowell's realism is the unspoken, nearly invisible, yet omnipresent utopianism about human beings, human institutions, and their possibilities that one often meets in public policy discussions. Some set up so unconstrained a dream of "freedom," "democracy," "rationality," and "efficiency," and so pure a standard, that no known human beings are living within such luminous realms. For example, one writer expresses dismay about the deficiency of freedom in the lives of American workers, who show up daily for their factory jobs "controlled" by the incentives offered them. But to confound incentives with "controls" is to imagine so pure a state of freedom, altogether apart from costs and benefits, that one wonders if even angels could enjoy it. In real life, when the incentives are not just right, one brother says, "No, thanks," and seeks employment elsewhere, even though the other brother, for other reasons, goes ahead and enters the factory. Is that not a quite considerable freedom, imperfect as it is? "In politics," I remember Aristotle writing, "one must be satisfied with a tincture of virtue."

In ethics, it is a great mistake to expect the same clarity and perfection as one finds in logic, mathematics, and the deeper reaches of metaphysics. The range within which finite, imperfect, and largely ignorant human beings can enjoy freedom is not unbounded. Yet it is a domain altogether real and precious, and worth dying to protect.

The color chosen for itself by the international left is red: red for revolution, for fire, for the dawn of a new day.[6] The color we might as well choose for the alternative future—not backward-looking, but trying to anticipate the movement of a whole century—is blue, the color of the hopeful sky, the color also of the oceans that occupy so much of the world's surface. I have always liked blue. It has a solidity to it and also seems to say, "Lift up your hearts."

> Two men looked out from prison bars
> One saw mud, the other stars.

This childhood ditty has always pleased me. "Lift up your eyes," it seems to say, and in daylight what one most often then sees is blue sky. I like the color of the sky, its clarity, its allure, its sense of infinite distance. It seems to express exactly the way in which the so-called Augustinian realists differ from old-school conservatives. Not at all dour, sad, and distressed, we look instinctively upward, at daylight sky or nighttime stars. We also have a vision of the future—not of a world perpetually going up in flames, as in the leftist vision, but a good solid vision that offers real hopes and real achievements and has the permanence of the sky. During his first visit to Manhattan, Jean-Paul Sartre loved the fact that at any corner on the great avenues of New York one can see a limitless sky in four directions. He thought it a perfect expression of American optimism: even in Manhattan, the greatest achievement of vertical human construction anywhere on Earth, we Americans *still* want to see the sky, to be reminded that there are few limits to what we can achieve. The blue sky beckons all people upward toward the heavens; the genius of the United States is to urge its citizens upward as best they can.

To a certain extent, admittedly, we Augustinians have stolen the vision of the future with which the left has long adorned itself. We are not backward-looking but forward-looking conservatives; we admire deeply what our fore-bears have created, and we mean to carry it forward in the light of the dreams we share with them.

That is why, in a way, I prefer the name "Whig," the name the early Lincoln used for the party of which he was proud to be a member. The "Whig tendency" favors liberty and realism, commerce, progress, and humble common sense. It is the party of the counterexample and of watchfulness for unintended consequences. It is a party nowadays as outraged by the taking of helpless life through abortion as by the practice of slavery, and for the same reason: no one can choose for himself the fate (slavery, abortion) that he is thereby inflicting on another. In such matters, choice is not a moral option. A house cannot stand half-slave and half-free—or half aborting and half not aborting the helpless.

Blue is also a suitable color for truth, having the clarity of air and the breadth of the oceans. Truth is a standard very important to liberty. We hunger for truth as well as liberty for several reasons. For one thing, the standard of truth makes us listen to others and to respect them, since we recognize that we might learn from them. We listen to them because it is *evidence* that counts, and they might be in possession of important clues that we lack. We want to get to the truth of things, and to do so we need the help of many others, even of our adversaries. Respect for evidence leads to respect for persons, and respect solely for evidence frees us from intimidation by power or flattery or lies. As Thomas Jefferson reminded us: "The opinions and belief of men depend not on their own will, but follow involuntarily the evidence proposed to their minds."[7]

We have all heard it said, "It is the truth that makes you free." But we don't often think why that is so. The truth—the evidence for things—is better than power, or flattery, or favoritism, or lies. It frees us to come closer to reality itself. Truth frees our minds to disregard everything except reality.

If you have ever been falsely praised, falsely flattered, you know how unsatisfying that is and how much you value the unvarnished truth. Truth has a good clean taste, like a handful of cold water from a mountain stream after hours of sweaty hiking in the mountains. If you hunger for truth, flattery is not in your diet; it is fluff, disgusting fluff at that. And if you are unafraid before the truth, you are free from a great deal of common human stress. You are free to deal with reality itself.

As many heroes learned in the prisons of the 20th century, if you set your compass by the truth, your torturers have no power over you. If you refuse to tell a lie, they may want what you have, but they cannot get it from you.[8] They are the prisoners and you are the free man, because you live in truth.

Economic Realism in China and India

Another great lesson in economic realism was learned in Asia.

One of the most staggering facts about the end of the 20th century was "the great leap forward" of China and India, but not through the miserable socialism of Mao Tse-tung's *Little Red Book*. Instead, this unprecedented acceleration in economic development was powered by new governments running on a "blue" agenda—favoring liberty and realism. Private property, low taxes, and open markets were chosen as the institutional propellants of economic advance. The dynamic propellant, however, was the awakened human spirit: the creative, innovative spirit of enterprise, invention, practical wisdom, and the hardheaded weighing of costs. It is the drive in young fathers to better the condition of their families. It is the natural instinct to truck and barter. It is the natural instinct of human beings to serve one another by looking to what the others need and offering goods to meet that need in exchange for goods that help their own families.

These are the three fecund natural instincts to which the ancients paid too little attention: the drive to create new things; the drive to better the condition of one's family; and the drive to trade. They are such humble and simple drives. Perhaps the ancients thought them below the dignity of aristocrats, suited only to the inferior province of the worker bees. Humble these natural drives are. But in modern times they have revolutionized the condition of the poor.

Well more than half the human race lives in Asia. As the 20th century began, Asians were among the poorest of the world's poor. Just over a hundred years later, nearly a half-billion Asians along the Southeast Asian rim have joined the world's wealthiest nations. Now two great nations numbering just over and just under one billion persons each, China and India, are in full gallop out of poverty, going just as fast as their energy and ingenuity can take them. Never before in history have market systems expanded by two billion persons at one time. Never have so many people at once moved from penurious agriculture to immensely profitable manufacturing jobs. Never has exiguous poverty turned to historically novel affluence in such great numbers and in such a short time. Africa, whose tropical advantages in fruits and grains from the abundance of nature have long been legendary, used to look down on Asian misery and was in fact home to many immigrants from Asia. But Africa has now been left far behind by a supercharged Asia. It is one of the great stories of rapid movement out of poverty of all time.

Looking out on the world from the West—from London, say, or New York—it used to seem that a great deal depended upon what happened along the axis that runs straight eastward, through Warsaw and Kiev and Moscow and on out to Vladivostok. If democracy and capitalism could take root along that axis, I remember myself once thinking, we might see great pressure put upon China and then India to move in that direction. India, of course, already had democracy, but unfortunately it had inherited from the British a pale Fabianism, rooted in an aristocratic hostility to capitalism and in a hankering for the paternalism inherent in genteel socialism. The Indians were perfect in mimicking a British lord's sense of superiority, even in their economic discourse. China, at that time, seemed lost in a soup of Marxism and backward agriculture. The economic situation seemed hopeless.

When I directed the humanities program at the Rockefeller Foundation from 1972 to 1974, I met there Norman Borlaug, who was to win the Nobel Prize for his inventions of miracle wheats and rice, which saved the lives of hundreds of millions of people. In those days I remember reports from Rockefeller and elsewhere predicting famine in India in 1984. Only after 1984 had come and gone and there had been no such famine—in fact, India had during that period become a net exporter of food—did I inquire how that had happened. In simple terms, the Indian government had altered its policies. It no longer controlled the price of rice so as to keep prices low for the happiness of city people, even though farmers were driven into poverty. It cut the taxes it had placed on growers. Allowed fair market prices and tax-free product, every small farmer in India found strips of land he had never before put in production, and the rice yield soared. From the heights reached immediately after controls had been lifted, this abundance brought prices back into equilibrium. In addition, Borlaug's new seeds made each year's crop amazingly more productive.

Highly populated China next door, perpetually short of food supplies, could not but notice this sudden and immense achievement in India. Chinese leaders decided that they would rather be rich unorthodox Communists than poor orthodox ones. They set aside Mao's *Little Red Book* and went blue by allowing private property, a free rein to the practical wisdom of producers, and a favorable tax environment. Human creativity did the rest. Chinese agriculture also experienced an economic "miracle," although what happened was no miracle at all but simply the working of natural laws.

The Chinese and Indian "Miracles"

To gain a historical perspective on these two giants of the developing world, consider the following statistics that my brilliant colleague at the American Enterprise Institute, Nicholas Eberstadt, culled from Angus Maddison's latest edition of *The World Economy: Historical Statistics*:

> In 1820, China's per capita GDP is placed at about $600, India's at $533 (the numbers being "international 1990" dollars). To get a sense of how poor this is, consider that Maddison estimates contemporary (2001) Ethiopia's per capita GDP at $660.
>
> In 1950, 130 years later, India's was scarcely any higher—just $619— and China's was actually lower—$439. (Decades of almost nonstop war, revolution, and upheaval took their toll.)
>
> By 2001, however, India's estimated per capita GDP was nearly $2,000, and China's was over $3,500. To put these numbers in historical perspective: Germany's per capita GDP in 1880—i.e., the Bismarck era—is estimated by Maddison at $1,991, and Britain's estimated per capita GDP for 1880 is $3,477, about the same as contemporary China.[9]

India had 17 percent of the world's people in 2003, but only 2 percent of global GDP and 1 percent of world trade. At nearly one billion population and with a labor force of 470 million, India is the world's largest democracy by far. Although terribly divided by religion, ethnicity, native language, and caste, India somehow manages to hold precariously together almost by a common will for national greatness. The 21st century may be the century in which India truly becomes a world power—perhaps to assume a seat on the Security Council of the United Nations, and almost certainly as a great, growing economic power in Asia.

Indeed, Goldman Sachs predicted in 2003 that in the next 50 years growth will slow in the world's six biggest developed economies as well as in the three biggest developing economies—Brazil, China, and Russia—but not in India. With an average annual growth of 5 percent for the next half-century, India will have a GDP larger than Japan's in another 30 years, and in 50 years its per capita national income (in dollars) will be 35 times larger than today.[10]

It was Rajiv Gandhi, the Indian prime minister from 1984 to 1989, who quietly began moving away from Nehru socialism, with its slow rate of growth; from 1982 to 1992, GDP growth jumped to an average of 5.6 per year, and then in the next decade jumped again to an annual average of 6 percent. In 2003 annual growth hit 8.4 percent in the third quarter. With China booming next door and its own young and eager workforce (more than half of India's population is under 25 years of age) coming into the market at baby boom size, India looks to enjoy economic vitality for many years to come.

Its problems are immense. Its roads are too few and too poor, its railroads dilapidated over too many long stretches, its housing simultaneously flimsy and scarce, jammed together and too urban-dirty to be primitive.

Yet the great monsoons of 2003 ended a long drought: agricultural production soared by nearly 10 percent, and the lot of massively poor rural India tangibly improved. Meanwhile, India is beginning to expand its manufacturing capabilities, investing heavily in factories for pharmaceuticals, autos, aluminum, and low-cost steelmaking.

But where India is making the most revolutionary change is in harnessing its well-educated, English-speaking young professionals into a new powerhouse in the service sector, providing software engineers, business analysts, record keepers, technical experts for telephone online services, data-processing, and research, and dozens of other white-collar specialists for the support of businesses abroad. Naturally, most of this outsourcing is for English-speaking firms in more expensive parts of the world.

The new and creative business leaders in India's new services sector are issuing a challenge to businesses everywhere in the world: you better have an "India strategy" in your global future.

These days education for young people with good work habits pays off, and the new electronic technologies and fiber-optic networks make overseas workers seem almost like local resources. In addition, wages in the new service industries are rocketing up by 10 percent per year, and India is expanding the size and well-being of its middle class quite remarkably.

In his new book *In Defense of Globalization*, Jagdish Bhagwati notes the progress toward this destiny in both India and China: "According to the Asian Development Bank, poverty declined from an estimated 28 percent in 1978 to 9 percent in 1998 in China. Official Indian estimates report that poverty fell from 51 percent in 1977–78 to 26 percent in 1999–2000."[11]

To be sure, poverty has not yet been defeated in India. At night, satellite film shows whole regions wrapped in darkness for want of reliable electricity, even where large cities such as Patna ought to be sparkling and winking with all-night activity. Despite this darkness, the government's propagandistic motto for 2004 is "India Shines." Poverty is an old, old tale in India. What is new is steady growth, creativity, new breakthroughs, optimism, and a sense of destiny beginning to be at last fulfilled.

The story in China began a little later. Kicked off in part by close observation of the successes of its nearest great neighbor, the Chinese story is very much the same. Bitter poverty is an ancient, grinding memory in China, and after the murderous horrors of "the cultural revolution" of the 1960s, most Chinese became exceedingly cynical about the fine moralistic slogans of the Communist Party. The Communists had debunked Confucian morality and old traditions, so when their own moral pretensions burst like a soap bubble, moral maxims seemed worth no more than air. A Chinese American woman, away in America for nine years, was shocked by what she saw on her return: "A lot of people simply don't believe that things like truth, selflessness, and altruism exist," she quotes from a government researcher in Beijing. "We have a very cynical population."

As we will see in chapter 6, China faces a potentially crippling water shortage as industry and modern urban living make ever greater demands upon its relatively few river basins. Yet there is so much optimism in China about a better future that obstacles, even huge ones, do not seem to dent it. There is no doubt that the Chinese, from top to bottom, have given up on the dreams of socialism. Marx and Lenin were always foreign imports, although their vision of societies moving forward in large collective masses and with little attention to individuals as individuals had some precedent in the China of the Great Wall, in whose construction masses of coolies lived out dreary, antlike existences. More so in Asia than in Europe there was a diminished sense of individuality and a heightened sense of collective belonging to family and to ancestors, feudal authority, and state authorities.

Suddenly, in the new China even the government is celebrating individual ownership, individual initiative, and individual economic imagination. Watching what happened in neighboring India and even the immense productivity of the mere 3 percent of the land that remained to private initiative (which produced 33 percent of the food that actually reached the Soviet table), the Chinese leadership promoted the expansion of private property holdings and encouraged individual economic creativity. Indeed, Chinese leaders made a kind of Faustian bargain: they would keep total control of the political system but allow increasing increments of private initiative in the economic system. They made a wager that they could, for a sufficiently long period of time at any rate, stave off the usual consequences of such a bargain and guide China safely through a massive transition to a new sort of morality, a new way of thinking, and a new way of living. For the general law is that a capitalist economy leads, sooner rather than later, to popular demands for democratic representation. The reason is that successful entrepreneurs can scarcely help beginning to believe that they are smarter than political commissars and, with their keener sense of realism, know better how to do practical things. They want representative government that includes them. They want representation along with the taxation imposed upon them.

So far the Chinese leadership has begun to benefit from the tremendous economic growth achieved since about 1984 by China's formerly stagnant economy. By 1991 the Chinese economy had caught up to India's in total GDP, and it has been shooting past India's ever since. Growth in 2003 exceeded 9 percent in just one year. The growth in basic commodities has been spectacular. As *The Economist* reports, "China accounted for half the world's consumption of cement, 30% of its coal, and 36% of its steel."[12] China has become the second-largest importer of oil; having passed Japan, it is now gaining on the United States. Its demand for other basic commodities has also become ravenous and is pushing world commodities price levels steadily upward.

China, says *The Economist*, "aims to become the world's leading shipbuilder by 2015, displacing South Korea and Japan." As the same weekly also notes, prior to 1492 Chinese vessels, six times larger than the puny little ships of Christopher Columbus, ruled the Pacific. Again today the Chinese ports of Shanghai and Shenzhen rank below only Singapore and Hong Kong as the four busiest ports in the world. And the Chinese have only begun to build large-sized tankers and merchant ships (175,000 deadweight tons each), the first of the initial order for 25 having been delivered in February 2004 in Shanghai. China is preparing to become a colossus in world trade.

So successful have been the experiments in the free economy since the mid-1980s—the successes achieved by Margaret Thatcher and Ronald Reagan, especially as compared to the losses suffered by François Mitterrand in socialist France, did not go unstudied—that the Chinese leadership has lately moved to give private property the protection of fundamental law.[13] There have also begun to be ever more certain celebrations of hard work, initiative, and individual success.

Back in 1989, in the famous scenes from student rebellions in Tiananmen Square and Shanghai, the Shanghai students, challenged by foreign journalists to state what their revolution was for, fashioned a papier-mâché Statue of Liberty. When asked why they had mischievously given the statue Western eyes, they responded, "Because that's the liberty we mean."

The problem for China in the future, if our hypothesis about the three-sided interdependence of the free society is correct, is that its moral culture has been gravely wounded by the long, torturous Communist experience and its Communist political class is not yet training itself in the insights and habits required for making a democratic system work well. Without the background embrace of a strong moral structure, such that people will not do some things that the law would permit them to do, out of deference to supervening moral principles of a transcendent nature, a free economy is likely to self-destruct. For those individuals with no fear of the law and no allegiance to any moral code deeper than the written law will seek advantage after advantage, force others to take defensive actions, and bring the whole system into contempt.

In the end, an economy depends for its efficiency and its human satisfaction on trust in one another. Its currency, for one thing, is no better than the trust people put in it. Their trust depends not only on how the letter of the law is observed but also on the spirit in which all players honor the law. Even more than on a good body of law, trust depends on widespread public respect for those ethical rules that are more universal in their sweep than human law can ever be brought to go. (There is a saying among financial accountants in America that it can take 14 years for special commissions to formulate a set of financial laws for certain types of transactions, and 40 minutes for sharp accountants to figure out a way around them.) The massive numbers of human contingencies run far beyond the abilities of lawmakers to cover them all.

Mere trust in one another's virtue is, of course, also not enough. Since all human beings sometimes sin, it is crucial that a democratic society able to function well maintain a strong system of checks and balances. At all times, it must be in the interest of some parties to play sentinel to the interests of others, and the reverse, so that no one is without an external guard against abuses of power. It is impossible to do without particular human interests—they are the very dynamism that drives progress forward—but interest must be arrayed against interest, so that each sees the need to keep watch on its rivals. To every interest, there must be a counterinterest. (This is the operational meaning of the American motto, "In God we trust." In practice it means: "We trust in no one else; for everybody else, there are checks and balances.")

Successful commerce, then, depends on a vital moral culture. But it also depends on good laws and on intelligent, flexible, farseeing political rulers, whose potential abuses of power are held well in check by a well-designed system of limited government, under the restraint of practical checks and balances.

Economic realism demands, in the end, clear-sighted attention to moral cultural realities—to the moral ecology of the daily life of citizens and officials—and to the design of limited but farsighted and effective government. Not even for the free economy is there a free lunch. Dues must be paid both to the cultural environment and to the political system of law within which it takes effect. All three systems, cultural, economic, and political, must each be in good health and able smoothly to act as both supports for and checks upon the other two.

Whether China can master this more complex art as its economic miracle unfolds along the lines that economic laws predict will say much about the future—happy or troubled—of the rest of this century. But for that matter, that test must also be met by India, the United States, and all other nations as well.

It sometimes seems that economic reform is easier to achieve than cultural or political reform.

Conclusion

Capitalism began slowly in Europe—in northern Italy, certain free cities in France, and especially Great Britain—then leapt across the ocean to its most spectacular experiment in the heretofore virgin and undeveloped country, the United States. Capitalism then had a second wave in Germany and other countries of Western Europe after World War II. Its third wave began with the "Four Little Tigers"—Taiwan, Singapore, South Korea, and Hong Kong—but soon also leapt to such diverse Catholic countries as Ireland, Spain, Portugal, and resurgent, entrepreneurial Italy, followed eventually by Poland, Slovakia, and others among the former Communist nations.

We need now to take a look at the theoretical underpinnings of the Catholic part of this third wave. These reflections may have some applicability for some of the non-Christian nations in the developing world.

Chapter Five

CAPITALISM'S THIRD WAVE

FROM ABOUT 1970 A "THIRD WAVE" of democratization began building (sometimes unsteadily) in Catholic cultures on several continents, as Samuel Huntington has suggested:

The third wave of the 1970s and 1980s was overwhelmingly a Catholic wave. Two (Portugal and Spain) of the first three third wave countries to democratize were Catholic. Democratization then swept through six South American and three Central American countries. It moved on to the Philippines, the first East Asian country to democratize, doubled back to Chile and affected Mexico, and then burst through in Catholic Poland and Hungary, the first East European countries to democratize. Catholic countries were in the lead in every region of the world, and the most Catholic region, Latin America, was the region that democratized most fully. Overall, roughly three quarters of the countries that transited to democracy between 1974 and 1989 were Catholic countries.[1]

More than that, something like a third wave of capitalism has also been getting under way in Catholic nations—but not without having to overcome a great deal of ancient (almost Ciceronian) and modern (social democratic) resistance. To grasp this conflict clearly we need to examine the condition of the Catholic Church today.

At the beginning of the 21st century, to the surprise of almost everybody, the Roman Catholic Church is the fastest-growing of the world religions. Numbering just over a billion members today, its numbers by the year 2025 are projected to approach one and a half billion, just about two-thirds of all Christians, and one-fifth of all living human beings (see table 5.1).[2] At that point, the Church will be the single largest institution on Earth that is worldwide in scope and embraces within itself nearly all cultures, in all their variety.

Remarkably overlooked by the world's press, most of this growth is taking place in Africa, Latin America, and Asia. Among the top five Catholic populations, only Italy, with nearly 56 million Catholics, is in Europe. The others lie along different missionary trails of the modern age: Brazil (144 million), Mexico (124 million), the United States (65 million), and the Philippines (63 million).

Also overlooked is the fearsome persecution of Christians in Africa by a newly aggressive Islam pressing downward from the North. Incited by politicized activists, Muslim mobs are burning churches, murdering, and carrying off into slavery Christian victims who now number in the millions.[3] Worldwide persecutions of Catholics during the past one hundred years have exceeded in ferocity and variety those of any time in the past. Robert Royal writes in *The Catholic Martyrs of the 20th Century*: "The twentieth century, by any measure, presents a brutal spectacle that may be remembered historically as one of the darkest periods of martyrdom."[4] Historically, a season of martyrs has been a harbinger of great growth for the Church. From present trends in both conversions and population growth, demographers are already projecting unprecedented growth.

The Catholic Cult: The Eucharist

Every culture is a distinctive answer to the riddle of human existence.[5] The cult around which Catholic cultures are formed celebrates the offer of the Creator to share with human beings His friendship, if they choose to accept it. This Lord wishes the friendship of free women and men, entered into not under duress but in full personal and political liberty. God freely made us and freely sent His Son to unite us to Himself, and His Son freely accepted the sacrificial destiny assigned Him. (He did not have to.) Correspondingly,

TABLE 5.1   Number of Catholics Worldwide (in millions)

Continent	Year 2000	Year 2025 (estimated)
Latin America	461	606
Europe	286	276
Africa	120	228
Asia	110	160
North America	71	81
Oceania	8	11
Total	1,056	1,362

the offer God makes to human beings is addressed to the personal freedom of each.

At the base of the Catholic cult, then, lies liberty. Its crown is the invisible bond among those united in the gift of God's love.[6] Catholics call their cult the Eucharist (the giving of thanks). In it, all creation is summed up and offered to the Creator in common prayer: the Eucharist is all creation, redeemed and at prayer.[7]

Of course, at the heart of the Church is the sinner. It is as a body of sinners that the Church prays. The Catholic Church is not a good home for utopians—nor for puritans. James Joyce once described it as "Here comes everybody!"

Yet another distinctive feature of the Catholic people is their cultural variety. The daily recurrence of Christ's Sacrifice at the Mass is so powerful a central cult, and the careful nurturing of the clarity of the Creed so highlights "the necessary things,"[8] that large and significant adaptations to time and place and to individual cultures are part of the normal practice of the worldwide Church. In other words, the term "Catholic" actually signifies both worldwide commonality and local concreteness. The Church in Poland is different in feeling from that in Italy, as the Church in Nigeria is different from the Church in Australia. Yet it is easy for pilgrims from all such places to come together as one in St. Peter's Square, united under the Bishop of

Rome. They also renew their unity at the one same Mass each day, wherever they may be on the globe.

The strength of this internal structure is obvious in the recent promotion and defense of *democracy* and *universal human rights*, especially under Pope John Paul II, in places as diverse as Chile, the Philippines, Eastern Europe, Africa, and (regarding the unborn) Western Europe and the United States. Its weakness becomes apparent in the relatively uneven record of Catholic cultures in adapting to a *capitalist economy*. At the highest level of the Church, Pope John Paul II produced a sustained body of reflection that gave a large boost not only to this "wave" of democracy but also to a form of capitalism disciplined by the framework of democracy and of a culture of life. He also championed three fundamental human liberties as the engines of human development: first religious and cultural liberty; then political liberty through democracy and the rule of law; and in the third place, economic liberty through the free and creative economy.[9] As beacons of a proper "moral ecology," he sent out several guiding themes: the solidarity of all humans,[10] the common good,[11] social justice,[12] the social destination of all the goods of the Earth and the origin of the right to individual property,[13] the dignity of the human person,[14] the principle of subsidiarity,[15] and the subjectivity of society (it is not a hive or a herd, but a community of free persons).[16] In a way entirely original with him, he also called attention to the *subjectivity of the person* (by which he meant the individual's capacity for understanding and choice and its expression throughout social life). He pointed out that work itself has a subjective dimension, for the steelworkers of Krakow poured their own intelligence and will into the girders they turned out, and this entire subjective dimension was an aspect of work that the Marxists completely overlooked.[17] All these, the Pope wrote, are part of the "moral ecology" or "human ecology" of a culture—that whole ethos within which humans work out their free destiny.[18]

From the point of view of its intellectual leadership, in this pope at least, the Church is well positioned to face the huge tasks of economic and political development that lie ahead in the 21st century. From having been flat on its back after the French Revolution, for some time threatened with a shrinking body of believers, the Church as the new millennium begins has rebounded spectacularly both in numbers and in intellectual self-confidence. Just a few decades ago, the French political philosopher Pierre Manent wryly observed that the future of democracy seemed assured and that of the Church doubtful. But today it appears that the Church has adapted far more easily to democracy than democracy has to its own moral and cultural disorder:

> Thus, the political submission of the Church to democracy is, perhaps, finally, a fortunate one. The Church willy-nilly conformed herself to all of democracy's demands. Democracy no longer, in good faith, has any essential reproach to make against the Church. From now on it can hear the question the Church poses, the question which it alone poses, the question *Quid sit homo*—What is man? But democracy neither wants to nor can respond to this question in any manner or form. On democracy's side of the scale, we are left with political sovereignty and dialectical impotence. On the Church's side, we are left with political submission and dialectical advantage. The relation unleashed by the Enlightenment is today reversed. No one knows what will happen when democracy and the Church become aware of this reversal.[19]

Nonetheless, in actual practice, the dispersion of the Church into many different cultures and historical streams around this planet inevitably results in uneven progress among the more or less Catholic nations. Many largely Catholic cultures aspire to *democratic* political life but are not yet prepared to understand or to welcome *capitalist* development. For many reasons, and from the residue of many different historical experiences, the Catholic people in the less developed world face at least four major streams of resistance to capitalism.

The Four Anticapitalist Traditions

It is perhaps easiest to understand, first, the anticapitalist reflexes of those cultures that lived under communism for 40, or even 70, years. But there is also, second, the resistance of those in the Holy Roman Empire who experienced several hundred years of agrarian feudalism, as in Latin Europe and across the Atlantic in the American colonies of Spain and Portugal.

Third, all through Africa, many necessary cultural and political preconditions of a capitalist economy have barely been met, if at all. Almost entirely lacking, for instance, are a stable rule of law; widespread personal ownership of property; and a male culture of work and self-improvement. (In many countries men were expected to be hunters and "warriors," while women performed most of the agricultural labor.) As mentioned in the last chapter, many Asian cultures have broken ranks with Africa and recently awakened to visions of progress and the urgent desire "to improve one's condition." First East Asia and now China and India are rapidly embracing capitalism and leaping far ahead of Africa.

Fourth, one of the least helpful inheritances from British, French, and American "progressives" during the past century has been the exportation to the less developed world of a soft sort of "Fabian socialism." This unfortunate foreign export infused Third World elites with a powerful anticapitalist prejudice and an excessive expectation of benefits from the state. Many Catholic bishops and professors in such places share in this prejudice and stubbornly resist "liberal" ideas as antithetical to their own desires for traditional "community" and "collective responsibility." They judge that their own culture, however backward politically and economically, is morally preferable to Anglo-American liberalism, which they equate with materialism, atheism, and dissolute morals.

A word on this latter point may be helpful. Early in the last century there emanated from Spain a little book, hardly more than a pamphlet, entitled *Liberalismo es pecado*, translated as *Liberalism Is a Sin* by Felix Sarda y Salvany.[20] This pamphlet distilled the long-smoldering animosity of the Iberian nobility against the merchant culture of the Anglo-Americans. As such Iberians saw it, the Anglo-Americans distorted human nature by their "extreme individualism" and their compulsive preoccupation with material progress. Claiming real moral substance, unfeigned civility, and a noble code of honor for the old order, the author of this pamphlet saw in the liberal world no more than selfishness and self-interest. Even until not so long ago, in the work of Ortega y Gasset, the Iberian world has abounded with polemics against "the mass society," "consumerism," "materialism," and the "vulgar culture" represented nowadays by McDonald's and MTV. Nonetheless, today the rise of democracy and an entrepreneurial culture is rather markedly transforming Portugal and Spain, and new arguments must be addressed. Even the Pope seems to be siding with the new order, to the extent that it is good for human rights, "ordered liberty" (the opposite of "license"), and a culture of virtue.

In Western Europe, Canada, Australia, and the Americas, meanwhile, the situation is not altogether different. Many of the U.S. Catholic clergy are the sons or nephews of labor unionists or are influenced by other family members whose political leanings are not a little hostile toward, or suspicious of, business. Among the Latin American clergy especially, these suspicions and hostilities are fairly routine. Only in relatively rare cases does a prelate or highly placed clergyman seem to have had the experience of growing up (as Pius XI did) as the son of an entrepreneur who was the owner of a small business. The result is a fairly widespread lack of sympathy for capitalist activity and an eagerness for state solutions. In a recent article, Sandro Magister reports on a study by two Italian sociologists, Luca Diotallevi and Roberto Cipriani, of the political and economic attitudes of about 1,200 members of ecclesiastical movements and institutions. They found that:

- Forty-four percent of those interviewed held that the state should provide jobs for everyone.
- Forty-eight percent held that the labor market should be made more rigid and less flexible.
- A very great number of them wanted the state to have control of the most important businesses.[21]

Thus, it can hardly be a surprise, only a severe disappointment, that during the last years of the 1990s Jesuit colleges all over Latin America sponsored essay contests on the evils of "neoliberalism." That term, not carefully defined, is loosely associated with such shibboleths as the International Monetary Fund, Reaganism, Thatcherism, and "the Chicago School." No criticisms were solicited by the Jesuits about the corruption and economic irresponsibility of precapitalist Latin American regimes, sometimes militaristic, sometimes feebly democratic (sometimes both in alternation). All the fury of the Jesuits' criticism was directed only outward, toward attempts to reform Latin American traditions on the "Anglo-Saxon" model—that is, reforms from the dreaded "liberal" direction.

Thus, even though the democratic idea has been winning favor on the Latin American left, which for a long time had shared Marxist suspicions about democracy, the conviction that *a capitalist economy is a necessary* (but not sufficient) *condition for the success of democracy* is still very far from having taken root.

Meanwhile, the Latin American right, rooted in land ownership, is often just as anticapitalist as the left, but for ancient, traditionalist reasons. The land-owning interest fears and resists a newly emerging entrepreneurial class, which threatens its own inherited sources of power and wealth.

Partly as a result of this double assault on capitalism, from left and right, democratic experiments in Latin America are likely to be short-lived. In the relative absence of such new enterprise as might generate economic growth across all social strata, popular discontent continues unabated, generation after generation.

Meanwhile, tens of millions of Latin Americans are no longer content with the bare subsistence of farming life and thus keep streaming toward the slum-filled cities to seek opportunity. But there they are often frustrated. Few are the factories to employ them. No longer *campesinos*, few have any chance to become proletarians working in industry. Most are "entrepreneurs," living hand to mouth, buying and selling whatever they can get their hands on, usually as *illegales* or *informales*, as Hernando de Soto has detailed in *The Other Path*.[22]

The culture around the Latin American poor so far offers little support, moral or legal, to entrepreneurship—neither legal status, through cheap and easy incorporation, nor accessible credit through small loans, nor secure property rights, nor education in entrepreneurial skills and economic literacy. It does not even offer them praise and honor but rather shame and legal rejection. Traditionalist mothers think working for the government bears honor but hold business and entrepreneurship in bad odor. For one thing, business is known to be highly insecure when political tides turn, and businessmen are forced by politicians to pay a constant stream of bribes and fees.

Nonetheless, by 2025, as Philip Jenkins points out, Latin America will surpass Europe as the continent with the single largest Catholic population.[23] Therefore, its lingering hostility to capitalism, which is in fact a necessary condition for the success of democracy, is a matter for grave concern.

Capitalism and Anticapitalism

Recently, the Pontifical Academy of Social Sciences completed a five-year study of democracy around the world, in the light of new perplexities that have arisen for Catholic social teaching in recent times. (We will treat of this gradual but full Catholic embrace of political autonomy in chapter 9.) Meanwhile, no similar study has been made by the Pontifical Academy of Social Sciences, or by any other Catholic body that I know of, concerning the question: if democracy is the *political system* the Church now recommends to the Catholic people as most consistent with the Gospels, which *economic system* ought it to recommend, and under what conditions?

It is true, of course, that Pope John Paul II thrice asked precisely that question in "The Hundredth Year," and the third time he asked it he finally replied in this way:

> Returning now to the initial question: can it perhaps be said that, after the failure of Communism, capitalism is the victorious social system, and that capitalism should be the goal of the countries now making efforts to rebuild their economy and society? Is this the model which ought to be proposed to the countries of the Third World which are searching for the path to true economic and civil progress?
>
> The answer is obviously complex. If by "capitalism" is meant an economic system which recognizes the fundamental and positive role of business, the market, private property and the resulting responsibility for the means of production, as well as free human creativity in the economic sector, then the answer is certainly in the affirmative, even though it would perhaps be more appropriate to speak of a "business economy," "market economy" or simply "free economy." If by "capitalism" is meant a system in which freedom in the economic sector is not circumscribed within a strong juridical framework which places it at the service of human freedom in its totality, and which sees it as a particular aspect of that freedom, the core of which is ethical and religious, then the reply is certainly negative.[24]

With the same caution that the Church showed in observing the fruits and demerits of democracy before committing herself fully to it, the social thinking of John Paul II has moved strongly, but with reservations and cautions, to state the essential understandings that lie behind a capitalist economy. As the Church did with respect to democracy, the Pope has been careful to think through these concepts within the horizon both of faith and of the long Catholic intellectual tradition, pushing the latter into new territories.[25]

Nonetheless, despite the new ground taken by the Pope, in many quarters within the Church, and even in the Vatican itself, there remains energetic resistance to capitalism. Many of the Latin clergy especially interpret capitalism as a malignant form of that much-dreaded 19th-century menace, antireligious liberalism, which (in their view) relies on an ideology of materialism, atomic individualism, and relativism. Many clerics, especially from Latin America and, indeed, from certain quarters in social democratic Europe, are positively repulsed by capitalist ideas, which they insist upon construing pejoratively. Indeed, efforts to argue against these clerical anticapitalists that "at least capitalism works to lift up the poor, look at the results," typically win the retort: "Yes, capitalism works, but the means it uses are still immoral."

Here again Augustinian realism is a better guide than utopian dreaming. "Self-interest" does not mean selfishness ("What does it profit a man if he gains the whole world but suffers the loss of his soul?"); it is a humbly neutral term. Wounded by inbred weaknesses ("original sin"), humans need humble stepping-stones, even on their way to extraordinary accomplishments. I doubt that Thomas Sowell is a devoted reader of Augustine, but those who have learned their realism from Augustine will feel at home with Sowell.

Although the two anticapitalist currents, Marxist and Catholic agrarian, rush downstream in the same direction and at some points flow into each other, the Catholic anticapitalist critique is not reducible to the Marxist critique. For instance, the Catholic left parts company with the Marxists by holding firmly to the fundamental right to private property. Just the same, traditionalists on the right have done at least as much as leftists to shape Catholic anticapitalism. The paternalism of the traditional aristocracy and the land-holding gentry dovetails quite nicely with socialist authoritarianism. Both oppose "uncontrolled" free markets and helter-skelter individual opportunity for all. The assumption of both the right and the left seems to be that the poor are not yet ready to compete on their own, without being protected by guardians. The dispute between them boils down to which guardians the poor should turn to.

To set forth a positive theology of capitalist purposes, institutions, and methods requires a large store of patience. One must be willing to meet a long series of accusations—as we saw in the preceding chapter—one by one, sorting out what is true in each from what is downright contrary to fact, or even over the top. In addition, one must patiently ask the anticapitalist critics to present their own better alternatives for lifting up the poor. For the issue is not who can imagine a prettier paradise. The question for anticapitalist Catholics is this: considering that there are still millions who do not yet share the material goods suited to their human dignity and God-given talents, what do you have to offer, in this world as it is, that will raise up more of the poor from poverty than capitalist systems regularly do?

One can read dozens of volumes of the so-called liberation theology of the 1970s and 1980s without finding a single page of concrete proposals on how to move the poor out of poverty. The traditionalist Catholic nations did not succeed in doing that, and neither did the multitude of socialist experiments in the 20th century.

Yet in Hong Kong and South Korea, Taiwan and Singapore, formerly among the poorest of the world's nations, large majorities have with impressive rapidity been lifted out of poverty by capitalist methods. The same is true of Ireland during the past 20 years, and a similar dynamism appears to be slowly but steadily bringing prosperity to most people in Poland, Slovakia, Lithuania, and some other formerly Communist nations of Central and Eastern Europe where cultural factors and the rule of law have been in favorable alignment.

By contrast, although much progress has been made in Latin America since 1989, in the shift away from traditional state-centered mercantilism to more liberal economies, reforms have been rather more halfhearted, incomplete, and lacking in full popular support. Latin American elites of both right and left remain strongly entrenched in their inherited privileges and self-interests and steeped in anticapitalist prejudices. Three major states (Brazil, Venezuela, and Ecuador) in early 2003 fashioned an informal alliance of leftist, anticapitalist government that rejects (as if it were an organ transplant from a foreign body) a short-lived experiment in "liberalism."[26]

Catholicism and Culture

There is a reason so many Catholic countries are poor, many social scientists have been saying for some time. Not only are many currents in the Catholic community anticapitalist, but many attitudes inculcated by traditional land-based, agrarian Catholic cultures are themselves hostile to economic development. In an earlier study of the cultural factors that defeat democratic and capitalist development, Larry Harrison and his colleagues developed a table of 14 basic attitudes that either facilitate or torpedo the liberation of the poor from poverty and political oppression. In later work not yet published, Harrison and his team have isolated another 10 measurable empirical factors—for a total of 24—that are preconditions of economic development.[27]

Students interested in the full panoply of the cultural attitudes that make development more probable should consult Harrison's work. The best we can do here is offer three or four examples. Cultures that are not likely to succeed in economic development evince, among others, certain cultural attitudes. In their orientation toward time, they are likely to focus on the past or the present. In their expectation of the power of personal agency, they are inclined toward resignation and fatalism. In their attitude toward wealth, they tend to think of it as a fixed sum, already given, and in need solely of redistribution. And in their attitude toward inquiry and dissent, they are likely to prefer repetition, doing what has always been done and thinking what has always been thought.

By contrast, societies that are likely to experience economic growth display a focus on the future; confidence in being able to affect their own destiny and a can-do attitude; a view of wealth as virtually unlimited, depending on human creativity, good habits, and well-designed institutions; and a conviction that questioning is not a threat but a source of creativity, insight, and progress.

Empirical research has turned up some negative findings too. The good news is that two Catholic jurisdictions in particular have shown spectacular economic growth during the past two decades: Quebec and Ireland. From being the poor, backward child of Canada, Quebec has become an economic dynamo. Ireland's millennial poverty has given way to entrepreneurial wealth that has rocketed its per capita income above that of many major European states. The bad news is that church attendance by the Quebecois and the Irish has fallen off a cliff. It is as if the once grand edifice of vigorous Catholic life, which produced a great abundance of religious and priestly vocations and sent thousands of missionaries to the antipodes, simply disappeared, like a house of sugar under a cascade of boiling water. One professor at a recent conference on economic development summed up these two cases in the following triumphant rule: "As a former altar boy, I say: *If you want to develop, stop going to church.*"

It is probably true that the great competitive advantage of the Catholic Church in "incarnating" itself in a particular culture—becoming flesh of its flesh, as it were, or "acculturating itself," in the new jargon—can be turned swiftly into a deficit when the local church is not ready to adapt its images, its thinking, its sensibility, and its modes of discourse into the idiom of a new phase in that nation's history. In the switch from an agrarian culture to a commercial one, from a relatively unchanging economy to a rapidly expanding, entrepreneurial society, unadapted Catholic preaching and teaching are too easily thrown off the carriage when it rounds a sudden turn.

The next problem to worry about in that case, I propose, is what will happen in two or three generations when the sound family habits, strict educational discipline, and cheerful attitudes inculcated by the old-time religion begin to melt as rapidly as the old-time religion itself did. There may well be a delay of two or three generations, for habits perdure some generations longer than their original inspirations. But such habits themselves cannot stand forever against "the silent artillery of time," as Abraham Lincoln soberly warned young America. The habits of the heart perish when they are no longer nourished at their source. Worse still, secularization has not yet shown that it has any brake that can halt cultural decline and moral decadence.

But that perhaps is to get too far ahead of the story. Certainly John Paul II has been worried that too many local churches, in too many nations, have not been readying themselves for the new transition to democracy and capitalism (which he prefers to call the "free market economy"). He has done his best to stir them to do so and to point out the intellectual path. If the Church is to prosper as each nation's economy and polity do, it will have to incarnate itself successfully, like yeast in dough, in the living stuff of the new commercial republics of the 21st century.

Intellectually, Pope John Paul II has articulated attitudes that favor the development of democracy and a dynamic capitalist economy. He has encouraged the poor "to acquire expertise, to enter the circle of exchange, and to develop their skills in order to make the best use of their capacities and resources."[28] The Pope recognizes that the Catholic spirit and the capitalist spirit properly require each other. Better than the Protestant spirit, with its theoretical emphasis on the individual (even though in practice it is communal and richly associative), the Catholic spirit brings to light the social dimensions of the free economy. Again, the Catholic spirit, rather more attuned to creation and to the goodness that the Creator Himself saw in the world, expresses better than the Protestant spirit the creative, healing, humanly beneficial aspects of liberal societies. There is a tendency in Protestant thought to stress crisis, sin, brokenness; in a certain way the dark side of vulgar Darwinism seems more attuned to a Protestant sense of the lostness of this world without Christ. In several dimensions the Catholic sensibility leads to useful insights into the lived realities of capitalist societies, as well as to useful statements of the positive ideals by which their practice ought constantly to be measured. And there are now a great many Catholic thinkers, writers, and political leaders in many nations marshaling the arguments behind these attitudes and undermining the arguments of "the cultural despisers of capitalism."[29]

The ardent search in Poland and the rest of Eastern Europe for an alternative to socialist thinking was motivated in great part by the long, dark experience of communism in those countries. The buoyancy of the Anglo-American economies during the 1980s and 1990s and the positive examples of the "Four Little Tigers," the "Irish Tiger," and others added powerful empirical arguments to the democratic and capitalist project. I do not think that the long-term issue is in doubt, but it is clear enough that the intellectual struggle will be fierce for at least two or three more decades.

Meanwhile, as I will elaborate in a later chapter, it would be highly useful to prepare a "catechism" of democracy and economic development for Catholic peoples in the developing countries, and even in the developed ones. We need a usable inventory of the habits (virtues) that a people must develop if they wish to experience economic and political progress.

From the four "cardinal" virtues of social well-being given in chapter 2—*humility*, respect for the regulative ideal of *truth*, the *dignity of the individual person*, and human *solidarity*—flow others that are necessary for political, economic, and cultural liberty but too numerous to cite exhaustively here. A free polity, for example, requires dispositions of character that build a high degree of *social trust*.[30] Economic success depends upon *initiative* and *creativity*, habits of *enterprise* and *invention, innovation, risk-taking, creative imagination*, and *practical skill* in turning mere ideas into realities.[31]

The habit of *enterprise* is the inclination to notice, the habit of discerning, the tendency to discover what other people don't yet see, so as to bring into reality things not before seen. It is the ability to foresee both the needs of others and the combinations of productive factors most adapted to satisfying those needs. The virtue of *building community* is the capacity to maintain in oneself and to inspire in others a certain level of creativity, teamwork, and morale. The virtue of *practical realism* develops goals, strategies, and tactics to carry out the activities of business in light of circumstance and contingency.[32]

In the political realm, citizens require the inner virtues that enable them to exhibit self-control and self-government, in lawlike behavior. Each citizen needs an internalized "inner policeman" (called "conscience") that guides him or her to act in lawlike fashion even when no one is looking. People exercise the virtue of *social justice* when they join with others to improve the institutions of society.[33] The principle of "*self-interest* rightly understood" attaches natural instincts of self-interest to worthy and socially beneficial projects, teaching people that their own self-development depends upon their becoming social beings.[34]

In addition, peoples new to democracy and capitalism have much to learn about the practical nature of such themes as these: a forward-looking spirit of *compromise*, a *loyal opposition*, the building of *associations* in the practice of self-government, skills in *coalition-building*, the ability to keep *profit-loss accounts*, the *voluntary cooperation* of free persons in common projects, and many other skills indispensable for capitalist and democratic progress.[35]

A Concrete Proposal

What else should the Church do in order to help all Catholic people move into "the circle of development," at least on the economic front?

When those who are not Catholic speak of "the Church," they tend to mean "popes," "the Vatican," or perhaps "the bishops." Catholics mean by "the Church" both the laity and the clergy, not simply the clergy, and certainly not only the hierarchy. The primary vocation of the clergy is not to lead the Catholic people into worldly prosperity and political liberty. Preeminently, that task belongs to the laity. A large number of the leaders of major public institutions around the world (including presidents, prime ministers, justices, and other high officers of the state) are lay Catholics. There are hundreds of Catholic university presidents and thousands of Catholic heads of companies, labor union leaders, newspaper editors, television executives, movie stars, scientists, generals, poets, heads of think tanks, brokers, financiers, and leaders of every secular description.

For the first time in history, lay Catholics are in a position to lead the church in several modest but important worldly areas. One thing they could do is to establish an "Initiative for the Poor," a major organized effort to stimulate economic development among the world's most needy ones. One obstacle is that many existing Catholic organizations appear to believe more in "redistribution," "caretaking," and what might be called "remedial welfare" than in stimulating economic enterprise, activism, and economic growth in the small-business sector so as to transform economic conditions from the bottom up. While this appearance may be deceiving, public mailings from Catholic Relief Services, Caritas, the Catholic Campaign for Human Development, and various religious orders seem to emphasize charity and handouts, not capitalist transformation.

Consider, however, the following proposition: *The best route to liberate the poor is grassroots capitalist development.* Perhaps only a minority of today's Catholic leaders, clerical or lay, have confidence in that proposition. But their numbers do seem to be growing, both because other methods have consistently failed and because of the examples of the poor nations that have made rapid progress out of poverty in this way. The greatest of all acts of charity is to teach the poor *a system* for escaping from the prison of poverty. (Like unto it is to teach those who have suffered from tyranny how to build limited governments on the basis of the consent of the governed, the rule of law, respect for the rights of individuals, and checks and balances.)

In our time, alas, there seem to be more failed economic experiments than successful ones. The societies that *do* succeed in raising up the poor follow a set of sound economic principles and nurture the required habits and practices. Economic reform begins with knowledge. That is why communicating this knowledge is an important act of charity.

Of course, it would be very helpful if the Vatican (and regional councils of bishops) put the weight of their own office behind the work of an "Initiative for the Poor" and would sponsor the most rapid possible dissemination of the ideas and practices that lead to the rapid creation of wealth at the bottom of society. Failing that, we need leaders of business—men or women like the late William E. Simon and W. H. Brady—to call such an organization into existence, to raise the money for it, and to direct it.[36] Perhaps, indeed, this might be a task for the Knights of Malta, an organization of hospitallers (and once upon a time, warriors) that goes back to its founding in Jerusalem in the year A.D. 1099; today it numbers some 10,500 eminent Catholics from every walk of life worldwide.[37] The Knights and Dames of Malta have as their main mission today to supply medical aid in circumstances of disaster and sudden need, but also food and other forms of assistance. Yet the talents of this organization and its worldwide scope would suit it for the more dynamic, fundamental role of reducing poverty represented by the "Initiative for the Poor."

This initiative need not create a new bureaucracy; it would be far better if it did not. But it could raise funds to prepare teaching guides and field advisers to demonstrate how the creation of wealth gets under way. Seminars could be organized in particular countries, targeting local elites and poor people alike to show how institutions and habits must be changed and offering technical support to ensure that local projects succeed in stimulating new small businesses.

Let me cite two examples from Bangladesh. Rose received a $100 miniloan from an American missionary to purchase seedlings, fertilizer, and a few small tools so that she might begin to grow flowers.[38] Bangladesh is a nation of much sun and water, so Rose has flowers growing nearly year-round. Every two days she has her daughter take her flowers into Dhaka, the nearest city, where they are quickly sold. With the money raised, Rose has paid back her loan and has been expanding her production. Her example has inspired other village women to imitate her with complementary production. Together, they have nearly doubled the annual income of the village.

In another village, Tahmina purchased a cell phone with an even smaller loan.[39] Her ability to telephone various markets for the going price of rice has greatly assisted her husband in making top dollar on each shipment. Neighbors also pay her small sums for the use of the cell phone for their own purposes. She has become a telephone exchange for the entire village.

The effort to precipitate economic growth from the bottom up has by now been successful in many regions of the world. One crucial case to study is Germany after 1945. Another is that of the "Four Little Tigers" of Southeast Asia. A third is Ireland during the 1980s. A fourth is Chile in Latin America. Others such as Poland, Slovakia, the Czech Republic, and, before them, Spain and Portugal have reinforced the same lessons.[40]

If Catholics are serious about liberating the poor from poverty, they must become serious about ground-level capitalist developments. Small business is the key to job creation. The encouragement of tens of millions of small entrepreneurs in the poorest regions of the globe is the number-one priority of social justice in our time. For social justice means concerted, cooperative efforts (one of the "social" dimensions of "social justice") to improve the condition of the earthly city (another "social" dimension) by liberating the poor from the ancient chains of poverty (the "justice" part). Poverty painfully cuts down the range of human flourishing. That is why unlocking the irons imposed by poverty on the legs of the poor is a crucial step toward helping them to become all that God made them to become.

In practical terms, the poor need knowledge and assistance. Those who teach them in the field need a simple handbook that explains to peoples in diverse cultures (and at diverse levels of development) the ideas, practices, and institutions necessary to make democracy and capitalism work. Many of these are not intuitively obvious; they are, rather, the product of long and painful experimentation. Mothers need some concrete examples of attitudes, skills, and virtues to teach their young. Fathers of families want to know what to do, how to do it, and how to solve the array of practical difficulties that thwart them. Moreover, the powerful interests, prejudices, and arguments thrown up in resistance to them need to be unmasked and patiently punctured, one by one. A handy set of short "catechisms" of frequently asked questions on each of these main subjects would be of invaluable assistance, especially to people who are genuinely confused, genuinely inquiring, and eager to find the best path for the human development of their families and their country.

More detailed work of that sort remains a book to be written, by someone with firsthand knowledge in the field to give it the bite of reality. I have heard from priests in Africa and laymen in Central Europe poignant pleas for books of practical advice of this type so that they will not waste their efforts. "What shall I tell my priests and catechumens to teach the people?" one priest from Nigeria implored me. He begged me to set down at least some criteria for what counts as practical progress and what should be avoided as mere illusion, sure to vanish with the autumn winds.

Economics is a humbling teacher of realism; it forces you to deal with the world as it is, to work by "the sweat of your brow," as the Bible says. It is also a teacher of important secondary virtues—not the primary things like love and faith, but preparatory disciplines such as hard work, attentive care, punctuality, and the like. The butcher puts up with the blood of his bench for the sake of his love for his family; the baker takes the heat of his stoves so that his wife and children will have income to live on. A whole society learns teamwork, checks and balances, market expectations, a taste for invention and opportunity, respect for others, and adaptability to challenges. These are a good preparation for learning the skills of a democratic republic.

Before turning to the political system of liberty, however, we need to face the questions raised several times earlier in this inquiry—questions about the realism with which a capitalist system deals with threats to our physical environment. This consideration, since it has a political component, serves as a good bridge between the economic and the political portions of our investigation.

Chapter Six

BLUE ENVIRONMENTALISM

TWO-THIRDS OF THE EARTH'S SURFACE (71 percent, to be exact) is covered with water. So if we care about the ecology of this planet, the party of realism and liberty already has blue as its color, not green. Even to take care of the green things of this planet (and we should), we must first take care of the great expanses of blue—the waters of the Earth, wherever they are found. For this reason, the great UN meeting at Johannesburg in August 2002 shrewdly focused on two central environmental problems: water and poverty. Water, since almost one billion of our fellow humans still lack access to a simple necessity of life, clean drinking water. Poverty, for another environmental reason: *where people are poor, environmental conditions tend to be both at a low level and impossible to attend to, for want of sufficient wealth.* The poorest regions of the Earth are environmentally the most devastated.

The 20th century proved that the best way to lift the poor out of poverty wasn't red, through the socialist state, but blue, the color of liberty, personal initiative, and enterprise. Even in the formerly Communist nations, like China, shrewd observers have discovered (at great cost) that the economic system that works best to eliminate poverty is private property, personal initiative, and markets. Blue environmentalism therefore builds upon the stunning success of the greens who preceded them, the environmental movement of the past 30 years.

The great social scientist Robert Nisbet once wrote, not long before his death, that the single most original social movement of the 20th century was environmentalism, which seemed to arise out of nowhere and immediately captured a huge consensus of almost unprecedented size within free societies.[1] Yet the amazing success of that movement lay not only in invoking a huge and instant consensus but also in getting new legislation passed; at least in the United States, the movement could within 30 years take satisfaction in measurable (and quite astonishing) gains in air quality, water purification, and land reclamation.

During the same period, of course, some mistakes were made by early enthusiasts and a few extremists. These mistakes were of three types:

- First, a few personalities were inclined to make environmentalism something of a *new religion*, a quasi-worship of nature. They showed little or no willingness to measure the many phenomena of nature that work *against* the well-being of humans and *against* "sustainable development." Through volcanic eruptions and many other natural activities, for example, nature spews far more carbon dioxide into the atmosphere each year than human beings do.[2] And variations in nature's emissions may be far greater than earlier thought.[3]

- Second, some of the early enthusiasts did not bracket their economic predilections when they analyzed the environment but brought their Marxist and/or socialist economic prejudices with them. In a word, they contaminated environmentalism with *eco-socialism*. Faced with any environmental problem, they immediately applied a socialist analysis and a statist solution, in the style of primitive economic socialism. Thus, the quip arose, "The greens are like tomatoes: they begin the season green, but by the end of the summer they are red."

- Third, some of the early environmentalists adopted the rhetorical style and outlook of *hell-and-brimstone preachers*, warning of the end of the world and demanding punishment, mortification, poverty, sackcloth, and conversion. In the words of U.S. senator and nearly successful presidential candidate Al Gore, "We must all become partners in a bold effort to change the very foundation of civilization."[4] The language of pessimism, apocalypse, penance, and salvation dominated the style in which environmental issues were discussed. Dissenting judgments were treated as sins, and sinners were expelled from the congregation of the elect.

Residues of these early faults persist. Yet to a remarkable degree, so many serious minds have now become engaged in the scientific analysis of environmental problems that the general tone of discourse has slowly but steadily become more quizzical, curious, and skeptical about rival claims. Environmental science is undoubtedly complex, and even small mistakes at the beginning of an analysis can have immense effects upon stages of inquiry down the line. Most practitioners have been burned once or twice and learned by experience to keep looking again at their starting points and methods.

In any case, the dramatic successes of the first 30 years of "green" environmentalism—from, say, 1970 to 2000—have led to signs of a new beginning, which for simplicity's sake I call "blue environmentalism." That term "blue" connotes, of course, the primacy of water in our natural environment. But it also connotes the proven requirements for the authentic development of human nature—liberty, personal initiative, and creativity—the economic right to personal property, and the economic instincts to truck and barter and to better one's condition. *Blue is the color of liberty*, as the sky is the symbol of our upward aspirations.

Blue environmentalism expressed three important turns at Johannesburg: toward the associations of *civil society*, including churches, businesses, and civic committees; toward *partnerships* among nongovernmental institutions, corporations, and governments; and toward *the link between environmental concerns and poverty*.[5] These turns signified a new realism.

Thus, the distinctive marks of blue environmentalism are three: realism, liberty, and recognition of the link between poverty and the environment. In other words, blue environmentalism is marked by a passion for making a real difference in the *real world*; a conviction that free, responsible, and inventive *individuals, working in association with others*, are the dynamic key to both environmental reform and sustainable development; and a conviction that *poverty* impedes the demand for environmental reform, while depriving the needy of the means to attain it.

Blue environmentalism takes seriously the obligation to help the poor escape from the prison of poverty. Accordingly, it works to reform economic systems so as to include every woman and man on Earth within the circle of plenty in ways that enhance the ecology of this small blue-green planet, which to the eyes of the first astronauts seemed to float alone in silent space.

We need now to review some of the conspicuous successes of environmental reform; to look briefly at the urgent task of providing access to clean drinking water to the nearly 800 million persons, mostly in Asia, who are today deprived of it; and to set forth a brief conspectus of a sound theology and philosophy of the natural environment. We will close with a brief look at the blue environmentalist strategy for the next 15 years (the approximate life span of a political generation).

A Stunning Record of Success

The rhetorical outlook of some enthusiasts of green environmentalism, like blinders on a drayhorse, forbid them from looking anywhere but straight ahead, with the effect that the public is seldom encouraged to look back to see how much progress in improving the environment has been made during the 20th century, especially after the first Earth Day, April 22, 1970. Yet it is actually more enlightening to go back to see the still earlier improvements in the human environment, rural and urban, by inventions not often enough considered from an environmental point of view. There are many such, among them: the lessons in human hygiene learned from 1880 to 1930 that led to the sanitation movement for the removal of human wastes; the replacement of the horse by the automobile (1900 to 1930), which removed the excrement and urine of thousands of horses from urban streets; and the advent of natural gas and electric ovens, heating, and lighting. These new sources of energy replaced age-old methods of burning wood and fossil fuels in thousands of stoves and open fireplaces in crowded urban dwellings. The growth of the cities, from about 1600 on, had brought pollution of a type and to a degree almost inconceivable after the maturing of these new improvements.

Consider, for example, the saga of the American horse. In the year 1900 there were 20.4 million horses in the United States, 17 million of them used for pulling plows and wagons in rural areas and 3.4 million for urban transport in cities. The transport capacity of all these horses was vast: three-quarters of the carrying capacity of all U.S. railroads. But there were three problems with horses: the average horse required about 39 pounds of food per day, or five tons per year; to grow that feed removed some 25 percent of all U.S. farmland, or 93 million acres, from all other agricultural use; and each horse produced about 12,000 pounds of manure and 400 gallons of urine per year. If you understand that the 3.4 million horses in city streets were particularly toxic for public health and offensive to public cleanliness, and that the long skirts women wore in those days were embarrassingly hard to manage in the horse-polluted streets, then you will not be amazed that the change in technology from horse to automobile was greeted as a great blessing for healthfulness and cleanliness.[6] More than that, it returned more than 90 million acres of good land to more productive uses.

In the United States, for example, the still further reduction of land under cultivation has returned about 500 million acres to woodlands, with the result that more people in New England "live in closer proximity to more wild animals in the Eastern U.S. today than at any time in history anywhere on the planet."[7] From an airplane, New England from Albany to Boston seems blanketed by forests from one downtown to another and has returned almost to its wooded aspect in 1600. One New York State wildlife biologist was quoted as saying: "Most Easterners don't realize it, but they live in a huge forest." Wildlife is multiplying, and species once thought endangered have been prospering. In earlier times, beavers were rendered nearly extinct by hunters and trappers but have now multiplied to more than 15 million. Fur-bearers, including raccoons, muskrats, coyote, and fox, are approaching or surpassing colonial-era levels. Deer now have increased to 20 million, more than in George Washington's day, black bears number 150,000, and elk over 700,000. The current wild duck population in North America is at least 35 million.[8] In a word, natural wildlife is flourishing as seldom before, even in the parts of America usually thought to be the most urban and densely populated.

As London, England, grew from rambling town to crowded urban center from 1580 to the present, its city air grew ever more foul (until about 1970) with smoke from wood-burning and coal-burning stoves and with unhealthful sulfur dioxide gases. These two forms of pollution peaked about 1900, when new forms of energy and heat (natural gas, electricity, and so on) came into use, and then rapidly declined. With the new push given to driving out pollution after 1970, this steady downward turn accelerated, and by the year 2000 London's air was as free of these two pollutants as it had been in the time of Shakespeare.[9] In addition, the River Thames was returned to a degree of cleanliness it had not enjoyed since Shakespeare boated on it.[10]

But historical perspective should not cause us to ignore the immense effects the environmental movement has had in improving our lives since 1970. In the United States the Clean Air Act went into effect in 1955 and was amended several times, including in 1970—there were no politicians who were willing to be in favor of *dirty* air—and from 1976 until 1999, a period of only 23 years, levels of the six types of air pollution proscribed and closely monitored by the Environmental Protection Agency (EPA) were brought down quite sharply. Lead pollution, for example, was brought down by 97 percent, sulfur dioxides by 65 percent, carbon monoxide by 68 percent, nitrogen dioxide by 38 percent, ozone by almost 30 percent, and particulates (PM10) by almost 25.8 percent, according to the EPA itself.[11]

The Pacific Research Institute has collected other data from the EPA regarding air quality and toxic chemicals that exemplify similar progress.[12] When first encountered, all this progress seems startling, because the press seldom reports it. Moreover, environmental activists of the apocalyptic type also never report it, and they even get angry if one does report it. But of course it is against their self-interest to report it, since such activists raise hundreds of millions of dollars in contributions to their organizations by their quasi-religious, apocalyptic calls for a transformation of systems and a conversion of life. They have found that they do best by scaring people with bad news.

Whatever the fund-raising needs of old-time environmentalists, however, each item in their litany of woes, scares, and tribulations deserves to be examined for its empirical accuracy and to be set in the context of the progress already made. The rest of us are heartened by successes and led to imagine fresh new efforts, to go the whole way toward making this a more healthful and self-renewing planet.

The pessimistic, apocalyptic litany of the green liturgy—recited almost daily in the media—deserves quotation here so that we may remind ourselves that all of it has been proven false. In one famous formulation, that litany of woes runs as follows:

Our resources are running out. The population is ever growing, leaving less and less to eat. The air and water are becoming ever more polluted. The planet's species are becoming extinct in vast numbers—we kill off more than 40,000 each year. The forests are disappearing, fish stocks are collapsing and the coral reefs are dying. We are defiling our Earth, the fertile topsoil is disappearing; we are paving over nature, destroying the wilderness, decimating the biosphere, and will end up killing ourselves in the process. The world's ecosystem is breaking down. We are fast approaching the absolute limit of viability, and the limits of growth are becoming apparent.[13]

All of these items in the litany have been proven to be false. They are false, in some good measure, because of the successes of the greens, and in part through the spur to better and better ecological practices that the greens helped to awaken.

It was only 20 years ago, for example, that the most dangerous pollution on the planet was thought to be the population explosion, or as British economist Barbara Ward pleasantly mocked it, "those thundering herds of pattering feet." I remember as a fresh new professor at Stanford hearing Professor Paul Ehrlich predict the end of the world through overpopulation, on the one hand, and the exhaustion of finite resources, on the other. By 2002 it was an obvious fact that much of the developed world was beginning to suffer, not from over- but from underpopulation, having fallen even below replacement levels. Further, there is a universal consensus that as the poorer nations become wealthier, population rates will rapidly decline there too, and estimates of future worldwide population have accordingly been falling steadily.

As for the famously mistaken "limits of growth" haplessly publicized by the Club of Rome, it turns out that, whatever vital resource the doomsayers wish to choose, its prices continue to fall as supplies grow and/or demand declines. The most famous case was the ten-year bet between the economist Julian Simon and the biologist Paul Ehrlich, one that Ehrlich lost, big time.[14] In 1980, Simon challenged Ehrlich to pick any five metals worth $1,000, and compare the price then with the price in 1990, adjusted for inflation. Ehrlich would win if the price of the metals in 1990 had increased, indicating more scarcity; Simon would win if the price had decreased, indicating less scarcity. Whoever lost would owe the winner the change in price. Ehrlich bet on copper, chrome, nickel, tin, and tungsten and ended up paying Simon $576.07.

Bringing Water to the Poorest

One of the characteristics of developed nations is that more and more aspects of life are brought under the domain of *mind*: these nations become well ordered by smoothly adapting to natural processes or else by patiently discovering better ways of doing things. It is natural for humans to order things; that is what the *sapiens* in *homo sapiens* means.[15] Developed countries are better able to order the economic elements of life to the good of human prosperity. In this way, they reduce scarcities, raise the average age of mortality, eradicate diseases, diminish illiteracy, and so forth. To be well ordered for the achievement of such goals is what it means to be *developed*.

In North America, for instance, according to the World Health Organization and the United Nations Children's Fund, 100 percent of the population (some 310 million) had a clean water supply as of 2000, as did 96 percent (729 million) in Europe. In Africa, by contrast, only 62 percent of the population enjoyed clean running water. (It is worth noting that Africa's population—at 784 million—is only a little larger than that of Europe.) For the somewhat smaller population of Latin America (519 million in the year 2000), the supply of clean drinking water was better organized than in Africa, with the result that 85 percent enjoyed access to water. In Asia, the largest population of all—more than half the world's population, or 3.683 billion persons—81 percent enjoyed clean drinking water.[16]

There is another way of looking at the present situation: As of the year 2000, 1.1 billion persons on this planet lacked access to clean drinking water. Of these, most by far (just short of 700 million) were in Asia. Another 300 million were in Africa, and 78 million in Latin America.[17]

Important progress was made during the ten years between 1990 and 2000. Even though world population increased by nearly 800 million during that decade, in both Asia and Africa the percentage of the population that had access to clean water jumped by *five* percentage points, from 57 to 62 percent in Africa and from 76 to 81 percent in Asia. Actually, 816 million people worldwide gained new access to water during that brief ten years (about 224,000 *per day* for ten years). That is a great achievement and should be duly noted. Such steady, dramatic progress in only ten years makes it reasonable to plan for even better gains in this decade and the next.

If we first single out Africa for a major effort in water management, we must grasp the full dimensions of the problem. In the vast northern Saharan region, rainfall can be as sparse as 20 millimeters per year, whereas in the humid tropical belt of Central Africa rainfall can run higher than 1,000 millimeters per year. Thus, drought in many countries and flooding in others can be occurring at the same time. Africa, with just over 10 percent of the world's population, possesses about 9 percent of the world's freshwater resources. Lake Tanganyika alone has the capacity to supply water for more than half the population of Africa each year (it could supply 400 million persons), while siphoning off less than 1 percent of its volume.[18]

Given its unusually acute internal variations in water supply, Africa's continental, regional, and local organization of water supplies needs to be among the best designed in the world; instead, its water supplies are the least attended to in the world. A constant cycle of civil wars, maladministration by fragile governments and kleptocracies, and poorly managed financial resources has penalized Africa's peoples severely. Africa's *political* deficits prevent it from enjoying the economic progress of most of the rest of the world, notably that of Asia, which not long ago was even poorer than Africa and has now leapt ahead of it.

Still, if Johannesburg means anything, it means that the other nations of the world are determined to go ahead and do all that can be done to develop an infrastructure in Africa that would permit steady progress in bringing freshwater to the needy millions. Three quite different technical problems must be faced: *drought* in the desert regions; pollution and *lack of treatment plants* for the purification of effluents, especially in urban areas; and a plague of *invasive aquatic plants* that destroy or restrict water supplies, especially in rural areas. None of these are challenges that have not been conquered on other continents. In some areas, it is true, the degree of difficulty is high. But the toughest problem in Africa may be the lack of capital for needed investments and the lack of knowledge about how to carry out massive organizational projects.

Beyond the problem of insufficient capital and technical know-how, however, there lurk other economic drawbacks that might be described as almost cultural, or at least habitual. By and large, Africans have become accustomed to receiving subsidized or noncost water, on the one hand, and on the other hand, not being obligated to pay for polluting existing streams of water. From the farmers whose agricultural runoff damages water use downstream to industrial polluters and the cities, villages, and ordinary citizens who pour their personal wastes and untreated effluents back into the water supply, none have any incentive to save and protect clean water. Water is too often, though not always, treated irresponsibly, and that irresponsibility is permitted to go unchallenged by policies that would impose both costs and incentives to encourage more responsible usage.

For instance, if citizens in certain regions were given water coupons that entitled them to an adequate personal share of water per year and obliged them to pay modest sums for any additional use, they would for the first time face incentives to use water responsibly—or else pay for it. (An alternative would be an adequate return of metered water provided free, with charges imposed only for higher usage.) In a similar spirit, costs should be imposed on polluters, whether industrial or governmental or familial, in proportion to their spillage of untreated water into sources of supply for others. Better still, financial or other rewards should be offered to any entities that build and maintain treatment facilities.

Drinking water companies should be encouraged by governments to set up new businesses to purify existing water sources, conserve waters, find new sources, and supply water to the entire public universally, under the regulation of public-private corporations such as those that regulate utilities in parts of the developed world. Since these would be for-profit companies, governmental subsidies would normally not be offered. However, guarantees of quick and certain governmental procedures expediting operations are certainly *sine qua non*.

The success of such companies in supplying and universally distributing clean water at low cost would be in the interest of peoples and governments. From the point of view of governments, such companies would not draw upon public financial resources but would supply their own. From the point of view of the companies, their owners would calculate such costs against the hope of recouping their investments in a patient, incremental, but steady profit stream made possible by their own efficiency. The regulatory regime under which they would work would be a public safeguard over the prices they could charge. The threat of driving such companies out of business would be a brake upon that regulatory regime. The record of such companies in serving the public weal would earn them public support.

It is obvious that the water problems of Africa will have to be solved on the ground, in Africa. But it is also obvious that help is needed from the rest of the world. Center-right parties in the developed world committed to blue environmentalism need to develop a specific action plan for those countries in Africa that would be willing to cooperate with them. A task force of practical leaders should be commissioned to manage this task. Along with experts in the international community well versed in problems of development, especially in connection with water resources, this task force should also seek out the advice and counsel of creative people active in water companies in the developed world, especially in the United States, where we also experience great regional variations in climate and ecological conditions.

Turning our attention to Asia, the huge problems with water faced by China deserve concentrated attention. Much of the land surface of China is arid and inhospitable, and great rivers are few and do not serve all water-needy regions equally. For this reason, China is contemplating huge canal projects to divert some of the waters of the great Yangtze River in order to carry water into Beijing and other cities.[19] For as China's cities become more industrialized, water quality deteriorates as industry places greater demands on water and more and more people gather in the cities looking for higher-paying work. Demand for drinking and bathing water by China's growing population, the intensive use of water for the cultivation of rice, spiraling industrial needs for water, and the growing demand for hydropower—all these are putting great pressure on China's limited supplies of freshwater. Water shortages are becoming acute, with worse to come. Traditional governmental structures in China—regional and sectoral—are inadequate to the vast national scope of the problem.

China is a great country, rapidly growing in wealth, and with a great profusion of learned scholars and technicians. Its military machine is one of the largest and most sophisticated in the world. For this reason, we can count on the Chinese to solve their own fundamental water problems, while we stand ready to offer such advice and help as they may request. The reduction in the number of Chinese who at present have too little access to clean water will go a long way toward meeting the goal of bringing water to all the needy in Asia. In much of the rest of Asia, water supplies are abundant.

Bringing water to all the world's people requires imagination and enterprise, capital, and high organizational skills. The human institutions best equipped to bring these requisites to the table are in the corporate business sector. Here is where the Johannesburg emphasis on public-private partnerships is both wise and practical. In some places, public utilities may be best for supplying water, if they can be both maintained free of corruption and efficiently run; in other places, well-regulated private companies will get the job done, and in still others, public-private partnerships will be the way to go. In all cases, blue environmentalism stands for practicality, enterprise, and a highest priority on clean water.

A Critical Philosophy—and Theology— of the Environment

Half the world—Jews, Christians, and Muslims—imagine the metaphysical narrative of the world in this way: this universe was brought forth in time by a Creator Who is separate from the world and far greater than the world. Five principles can be derived from that vision. All of them meet the tests of sound common sense.

First Principle: Nature Is Not God and Is Not Divine

Nature ought not to be worshiped; neither should it be idealized or regarded as a sacred icon.

The distinction between Creator and creation is one of the rock-solid foundations of blue environmentalism. Too many greens have divinized nature, reverencing environmentalism as a religion. For obvious reasons, no devout Christian (or Jew or Muslim) can accept this apotheosis of nature. In practice, the worship of nature renders realism about nature improbable. If we intend to preserve and protect the environment, we must be able to ask critical questions about it. We must, in short, exercise Augustinian realism, a pragmatism that does not allow the perfect to become the enemy of the good.

Second Principle: Nature Is Meant for Man, Not Man for Nature

It is humans, male and female, and not brute nature, that are made by their unique endowment of liberty to be provident over their own destiny; they are made in the image of God.

This principle is taken for granted by environmentalists but almost never made explicit—for instance, in the expression "sustainable development." Surely if that phrase means anything at all, it means "able to sustain human life." We worry about the environment for the sake of *humans*, not for the sake of dinosaurs or cockroaches. Humans are by no means necessary for the survival of this planet. If humans disappeared during the next thousand years, the planet might well go on spinning through silent space for millions of years, in a lively and ever-changing fashion, species appearing and species disappearing. The Earth would then become again, as it were, unconscious, that is, without conscious life upon it, trod upon only by brute creatures that can neither talk nor think nor laugh nor argue nor debate. A silent and un-thinking planet, like all the others so far encountered. And like them, en-during for ages and ages and ages.

When we speak of "the environment," then, we do not mean inanimate nature in and of itself, but nature *only insofar as it is the human being's temporary home*. According to contemporary science, there were millions of years in which there were no humans on this planet, and then over time they appeared (at time t_1), slowly multiplied, and "possessed" the Earth. At some future time (t_2), this planet may be empty of us again. The concept of "sustainable development" has meaning only between those two times, t_1, and t_2. In other words, the environmental movement has as its premise that humans are interested in nature insofar as nature is hospitable to humans.

Third Principle: Nature Is Man's Hostile Foe as Well as His Friendly Home

Since prehistoric times, nature has come at humans—as the poet says—"red in tooth and claw." From the beginning, nature's elements warred against our primitive human ancestors. Wild beasts and predatory birds devoured some of them. Swamps and quicksand sucked others to their deaths. Humans have been pummeled by storms, floods, avalanches, earthquakes, falling comets, hurricanes, and typhoons. Snows and ices, showing no mercy, took away life from hundreds of thousands. Bacteria, viruses, and all manner of diseases and plagues preyed upon them, killing in one season two-thirds of the in-habitants of Siena and many another town, keeping the total human popu-lation low and at an average life span of under 20 years. For thousands of centuries the life of humans on Earth was threatened by total extinction.

Even in recorded history (a brief section in the life of humans on this planet), as late as the year 1776, the human population numbered only 750 million, and most lived in desperate poverty (as Victor Hugo described them in *Les Misérables*) and under cruel and despotic rulers.[20] This fairly pitiable species was spread out thinly across Europe, Africa, and Asia, and even more thinly across the two Americas.

Fourth Principle: To Keep Nature Hospitable to Human Life, Humans Must Take Care Not to Foul Their Own Habitat

The capacity of nature to be hospitable to human life is given over only *in part* to the responsibility of humans; nature follows its own laws, which were in operation before humans came to be, and which may well endure long after humankind has vanished from this Earth. Nonetheless, humans must take care regarding their own impact upon nature. They must be provident over their own welfare and that of their children for ages to come.

Only in very recent times—since about the year 1800—has the human race begun acquiring sufficient knowledge to hold at bay the diseases that choked off its mortality. Only then could their numbers jump from almost 750 million in 1776 to 6 billion in the year 2000. During this same brief time span, human science, ingenuity, and enterprise have shown historically unprecedented capacities for industrial production. At first, this industry spewed smoke, ash, and gases into the circumambient air and water. Only within the last two generations (when electronics replaced mechanics as the main organizing principle of machines) have greater knowledge and new inventions allowed industry to become cleaner and more compatible with nature. The sciences of sanitation, hygiene, and medical care advanced within a single century by such leaps that the average life expectancy suddenly shot up from about 47 (as it had been throughout most of human history) to 64 worldwide.[21]

In a word, increasing longevity led to rapidly expanding populations. Increasing invention and production led to rapidly expanding economic and commercial activity, much of it beneficial to the environment (in making deserts hospitable and bringing lifesaving medicines to common people) and some of it harmful in the form of water and air pollution. Green environmentalists deserve a great deal of credit for awakening the people of the world to our responsibility not to foul our own habitat. They launched a revolution in attitudes toward nature—from taking nature for granted to recognizing its vulnerability.

Fifth Principle: If Progress, Science, and Technology Represent the Masculine Impulse in Human Nature, the Nurturing of Nature Represents the Feminine Impulse

The masculine impulse is symbolized in the image of the Dynamo by the great American historian Henry Adams, for whom the feminine impulse in human nature is symbolized by the image of the Virgin.[22] And the color associated with the Virgin is blue. For Adams, the Virgin (as he explains in his great book *Mont Saint Michel and Chartres*) symbolizes beauty, sex, nurturing, goodness, a religious "yes," wholeness, organic power:

> At the Louvre and at Chartres. . . was the highest energy ever known to man, the creator of four-fifths of the noblest art, exercising vastly more attraction over the human mind than all the steam-engines and dynamos ever dreamed of.[23]

Adams feared that the great Protestant thrust of modernity and its secularist cousins had rushed blithely past the feminine, the nurturing, to create unwittingly a coldly analytic masculine desert. He called the human heart toward balance once again.

In America, and perhaps in Europe too, the pristine mountains, waterfalls, lakes, forests, streams, and rivers of the West have become surrogates of the Virgin. Virginal nature was envisioned as a sublime, purer order that rebukes the order man has made.[24] Once human knowledge gained some victories over disease and other causes of early death, the fact that nature has through most of history exerted cruel and killing dominion over man has been repressed. Nowadays nature has suddenly been imagined to be innocent, not cruel.

In other words, a great psychic drama is also being played out in the environmental movement of modern times. Mythic elements of great power are involved. Those who choose to proceed with critical intellect intact must pay due respect to realities of that kind. The underlying arguments are not about policy only but about quasi-religious visions of the pure, the good, and the nurturing. At stake is a pagan idealization of nature, become if not a goddess then a surrogate vision of the Virgin.

A Blue Environmentalist Strategy

What, then, is the blue environmentalist strategy for the next 15 years?

The guiding principles are three: realism, liberty, and raising up the poor.

Realism

Two of the great founding books of the environmental movement may be commended for the alarms they sounded. Yet both have been shown by real events to have been wildly incorrect in their science and their presuppositions. The same fate has met other books of the early canon.[25] Paul Ehrlich's *The Population Bomb* (1968) predicted that hundreds of millions of people would die from famine during the 1970s, but such famines never occurred, and the nation in which one of the worst famines was to occur, India, became a net exporter of food late in that decade. The Club of Rome's *Limits of Growth* (1972) predicted a huge shortage of many basic substances with concomitant astronomical prices; instead, world prices fell substantially for nearly all basic commodities as new resources and new technologies were discovered or substitutes developed. The history of most other dire predictions by environmentalists over the years has followed much the same track: enormous notoriety, hugely broadcast publicity, and a remarkably speedy refutation by actual events.[26]

Partly as a result of the fierce politicization of reporting on the state of the environment, the federal government under the Clinton administration asked the Heinz Foundation to develop procedures for developing a full set of environmental measurements, so that over time an accurate, independent, and nonpoliticized reading of environmental trends would be available. After seven years of work, the Heinz Foundation released its first report in 2002.[27] That report listed nearly 103 different items for measurement and noted that 56 of them were not yet susceptible of accurate measurements (14 required more development), while only 33 could be reported in a tentative fashion, pending the discovery of better techniques of measurement. The foundation expressed the hope that public criticism would lead to a year-by-year refinement of measurement techniques, until a truly accurate picture would be available to the public.[28]

One finding was particularly illuminating, for it introduced a new technique of measurement. For the first time, the foundation was able to study satellite photos of the entire United States to determine precisely what proportion of the land is occupied by urban and suburban development. Most earlier forms of measurement had resulted in estimates in the range of 4 to 5 percent. Systematic counting by the Heinz researchers came to 1.7 percent.[29] This number fits well with the vision an air traveler gains in flying across the United States in clear weather. The land is vast and still sparsely settled at its most dense. The surrounding forests, deserts, and cultivated fields spread out as far as the eye can see.

The *preparatory* concern of blue environmentalism is to gain the most accurate, nonpoliticized, and independent view of the hard reality of environmental trends that is possible and to promote the development of expert techniques to achieve it. Its *main* concern is to propose courses of action that promote the well-being of the environment in measurable ways, within defined limits of time. Since 18 percent of the world's population still lacks access to clean drinking water, for instance, the goal of reducing that amount by one-third (6 percent) or even half (9 percent) in the next ten years should be realistic. During the preceding decade that number was lifted by 5 percent, unimpeded by a continuing population growth of about the same percentage.[30]

Liberty

While some environmentalists of the past have preferred to *castigate* and *punish*, blue environmentalists choose to work through methods of greater proven effectiveness—creating *markets* in which both positive and negative *incentives* function well. When people pay nothing for water, for example, they have no incentive to save it, but when after a certain basic free allotment they have to pay a modest amount for further use, they become far more careful in their behavior. In addition, with steady fees as an incentive, suppliers are more likely to enter that market and provide water to purchasers efficiently and cheaply. This policy of incentives is compatible with imposing penalties on those who befoul existing streams of water. When costs and benefits are carefully aligned so as to maximize the universal availability of clean water and minimize wastage and befoulment, the probability of bringing water to all rises substantially.

The principle here is that humans make free choices and normally calculate the costs and benefits of their own actions fairly carefully, in order not to suffer the consequences of not doing so. Therefore, these costs and benefits should be aligned so as to promote the common good while respecting free choice; they should serve both the common good and individual liberty at the same time. That way, by assisting in the achievement of the common good, citizens themselves also benefit directly. A rising level of the common good enhances the well-being of individuals who enjoy the blessings of a well-run system.

As much as possible, environmental policies should enhance personal liberty while clearly instructing citizens through well-chosen incentives and penalties to behave in ways favorable both to their own individual good and to the common good. For example, incentives paid to homeowners to improve energy efficiency at home lowers the whole community's energy use and simultaneously lowers annual costs for individual homeowners. In this way, the ideal outcome occurs when the personal good overlaps with the common good. As much as possible, policy ought to aim at that outcome.

Raising Up the Poor

Whatever may have been said of earlier times, it is true today that some of the worst pollution in the world occurs in very poor countries. This new environmental damage arises from primitive methods of heating and cooling, inadequate (or nonexistent) sanitation systems for the removal of human wastes, and other causes rooted in poverty. Some of the worst environmental sites are in formerly Communist nations, now impoverished, near now-idle nuclear and chemical facilities of various kinds. In August 2002, a huge brown cloud gathered over Asia, the result, experts said, of an air inversion fed by fumes from burning peat, firewood, and other primitive materials in millions of homes and kitchens.[31] Deforestation and desertification are other consequences of reliance on traditional methods.

The deepest motivation for trying to help the poor gain a more becoming affluence is for their own liberation and basic dignity—so that they might become all that God has given them the potential to become. But it is also true that the relief of poverty gives much promise of helping to preserve a more healthful environment.

It is a Jewish and Christian belief that God gave to every woman and man the right to personal economic initiative,[32] as well as the capacity to invent, discover, and create. Blue environmentalists hold that the best way to help the poor of the distressed continents to rise out of poverty is the way that has been working spectacularly in India and China for the past 20 years. It is to recognize the strict relation of the right to private property to the right to personal economic initiative and to take the necessary political and institutional steps to give these basic rights realistic support in practice. As Hernando de Soto has shown, the use of mortgages makes private property fecund, more than doubling its wealth-making potential.[33]

Whereas it is fundamental, for example, that the right to enterprise not be criminalized, most entrepreneurs in Peru and many other Latin lands are forced to work as *informales* or *illegales*.[34] The right to incorporate a small business follows from the right of association. The state has a right to regulate such registration and may charge a small sum to cover its expenses. But such registration must be cheap (not more, say, than 30 Euros), quick (within two weeks), and easy (by mail if possible). Incorporation brings three crucial goods to poor people: legal protection, limited liability in case of lawsuits, and legal standing to borrow start-up funds from lending institutions.

In addition, it is crucial that a large supply of microloans be made available for poor persons who have a promising business plan. New institutions that specialize in making such loans, as well as in providing technical support to help borrowers succeed, will need to be founded, since most existing banks in Third World nations lend little or nothing to the poor. Borrowing is the mother's milk of infant businesses, since poor people have no preexisting capital with which to launch or expand their businesses. All they have are their ideas, their sweat, and their good habits; since these are the main cause of the wealth of nations, that is quite enough to justify establishing such institutions.[35]

These three reforms—clear title to private property, open and easy incorporation of small businesses, and new institutions to make microloans to poor entrepreneurs—require major changes in the philosophy, legal structure, and practice of most Third World countries. But these reforms are essential if the creativity of the people and their capacities for invention and creating new goods and services are to come to flower. The hundreds of millions of poor persons in the world who today are *un*employed or *under*employed can rise out of poverty only through private-sector jobs. Most of these jobs, necessarily, will have to come from small businesses. Most of these small businesses will, of necessity, be indigenous.

Every nation's most important resource is its own people. Every effort must be bent to match this precious resource with institutions that allow the multiple talents of people to come to flower. It is a great crime when a nation represses the creativity of its own people.

Blue environmentalism therefore stands for the spreading of those institutions of empowerment that make the ownership of property universal; that give concrete support to the genius of creativity endowed in every woman and man; and that generate a groundswell of new wealth from the bottom of society upward. This is the task of the system of natural liberty written by the Creator into the human heart.

It is not the natural endowment God gave the poor that is currently at fault, but the inadequacy of the political systems and social institutions that fail to nurture and support a people's attempt to use that endowment. Freedom too has its own ecology. Blue environmentalism cherishes the ecology of liberty.

In liberty lies coiled the spring of creativity. Liberty releases the eminently realizable hope of bringing every woman, man, and child into the circle of universal affluence that this planet has been fashioned to support. For the goods of the Earth have been given a universal destination, and that destination is the freeing of every woman and every man on Earth from the prison of poverty, so that their gifts and talents might flower for the mutual benefit of all.[36] As Don Luigi Sturzo taught us, universal destination is reached by one path only, the path of liberty.

But human liberty is achieved through three sets of institutions: cultural, economic, and political. The goal of the institutions of cultural liberty is to discover and inculcate those ideas and habits that lead to the flourishing of our minds, hearts, and souls in the full enjoyment of liberty. The goal of the economic institutions is to liberate the human race from poverty and open up manifold opportunities for the development of the full panoply of human talents. The goal of the political institutions of the free society is to free human beings from tyranny, bondage, and oppression and open up to them the paths of self-government and personal responsibility.

We turn now to the complexities of the free polity.

PART THREE

THE POLITICS
OF LIBERTY

Democracy and Human Rights in
Christianity and in Islam

Chapter Seven

RELIGION

The First Institution of Democracy

The Discoveries of Alexis de Tocqueville

Better than any other great social thinker of modern times, Tocqueville perceived in a sophisticated way the importance of *religion* to the modern democratic republic, and he meant by "religion" the Jewish and Christian religion. Since most secular scholars understandably lay little stress upon this motif in Tocqueville's thought, some of what I write here may seem new, though it really isn't. First, however, let me recall some of Tocqueville's most important discoveries and then turn to his arresting views on the crucial importance of religion to democracy.

Alexis de Tocqueville was born in the wake of the bloody French Revolution of 1789 into a family of the minor nobility that had given their share of victims to what the bloodthirsty were pleased to call "Reason." The circumstances of his birth assured him of certain sinecures and preferments, which by chance came to include an assignment to voyage abroad to study the prison system of the new American republic. This faraway republic had already survived some 45 years since the writing of its Constitution, with rather more stability than France had experienced after 1789, and it interested the young liberal thinker very much. Tocqueville intellectually reveled in his long voyage back and forth to America and his many months of quizzing hundreds of people throughout various states of the Union during the years 1831 and 1832.

Returning to France, Tocqueville discovered that what he had learned about American prisons was the least interesting part of what he had observed. He wrote that Providence had raised up in America a new model of self-governance—of liberty and equality—that was bound to sweep Europe and, indeed, the rest of the world.[1] He felt an obligation to try to understand what was coming and to prepare his fellow Europeans for it—the French of course most of all. What constituted this new model? What were its principles and its preconditions? What were its weaknesses and its likely fate?

Around the world, Tocqueville is regarded as a genius who wrote more intelligently about the American experiment than anyone before or since. No fewer than four English translations of *Democracy in America* have appeared in the United States over the years, the latest having arrived quite recently from the hands of the eminent political philosopher from Harvard, Harvey Mansfield, and his wife and fellow scholar, Debra Winthrop.[2]

No one has ever traced in more elegant detail the subtle differences of imagination, sensibility, habits, and expectations engendered by life in an aristocratic order compared with those engendered by a democratic order. No one paid more attention to the strong and weak points of each than Tocqueville.[3] No one saw more clearly the concrete, lived meaning of "equality" in the new order.[4] No one before him saw the precise lineaments of that new phenomenon in human history, the democratic "individual," which had no exact counterpart in European cultures.[5]

Tocqueville also grasped the extraordinary power of *voluntary associations* in the daily texture of American life, as a social force far more potent and extensive than the state. What the French turn to *l'état* to do, he wrote, and the English turn to the aristocracy to do, the Americans do by turning to one another and forming an association.[6] It is through associations that Americans practice self-government, he said. They do not depend on government— they organize themselves to accomplish their own ends. He concluded that the law of association is the first law of democracy.[7] He did not think that there were ten men in all of France in 1835 who had the habit of forming associations as the Americans did every day.[8]

Tocqueville feared that, in the end, the experiment in democracy would end in tyranny. That would happen when the lust of democrats for equality led them to demand such an extensive governmental network of services to remove the insecurities, edges, and hardships from life that they would fall into the honeyed grip of a new "soft despotism."[9]

Americans of all persuasions have found sobering Tocqueville's prediction of the inevitable contradiction between liberty and equality. Even the partisans of ever greater equality are careful to couch their appeals in terms of "choice," thinking in that way to avoid the inevitable collision. Those of us who are known as neoconservatives[10] (or, as I prefer, Whigs[11]) believe that Tocqueville presciently foresaw precisely that state of willing servility into which the welfare state of social democracy has been inexorably leading us.

Tocqueville was also uncommonly astute in his analysis of the totally different meanings of "self-interest" in Europe, where the term was rooted in an aristocratic moral vision, and in America.[12] The European aristocratic vision of life is at root Catholic, feudal, Aristotelian, and Greek. In this line of thought, a sharp distinction is drawn between those things that are mere means, vulgar and servile, and those that are ends in themselves and noble. The liberal arts (whose object is the true, the good, the beautiful, the best that has been put into words or wrought in marble, oils, or other materials) are distinguished from the servile, manual, and mechanical arts (whose object is to be useful). A related distinction is drawn between *deeds* that are merely useful (what servants do) and those that are beautiful (what nobles do, or should do). As much as possible, people of noble rank devote themselves to the cultivation of the beautiful, the good, and ends in themselves (whence comes the affectation "Never let them see you sweat!"). *Noblesse oblige.* The ways and means to these beautiful ends are supplied by their inferiors, to whom belongs the grubby servile work.

On such matters, as recently as the 1930s *Baedeker's Guide* warned German visitors to the United States not to be surprised if even the most upper-class Americans showed a want of aristocratic manners. The manual reported that a military attaché at the German embassy in Washington, invited to visit an American admiral in his home, was amazed to interrupt the latter late that autumn afternoon taking down his own screens and putting up storm windows all by himself.

All these traditional distinctions have their proper validity, and all make an important point about self-interest, which Tocqueville did not mean to deny. Nonetheless, his own eyes and ears revealed to him that Americans have an altogether different way of speaking about self-interest.[13] Practically every American, being a descendant of immigrants, knows that the same quantum of work performed in America as elsewhere reaps him here a more ample reward. Clearly, it is not personal effort alone that leads to the increase. The system is more beneficent than those their families had experienced elsewhere, and for this discernible difference in the system's blessings he or she gives thanks.

Thus, virtually every American, by the same measure, is sensible of an obligation to contribute to the common good, in order to ensure the continuance of this same beneficent system into the future. Americans imagine that it is in their own interest to make contributions to the common welfare and the public good, Tocqueville observed. It is more than a duty, since it inures to their own future benefit and that of their children. Americans consider the public good to be their own personal good, and they link their own self-interest to the public good.

Every day, Tocqueville noted, Americans perform generous deeds for the common good, but they do not describe these as deeds performed for the common good; they describe them as deeds performed in their own self-interest, broadly understood. They do not speak, Tocqueville said, of beauty but of utility.[14] They never speak of solidarity, but of self-interest. Clearly, this is a novel type of self-interest, Tocqueville deduced, and he called it by a novel name, "self-interest rightly understood." Europeans formed to aristocratic manners, he noted, disdain the merely useful and the motive of self-interest.

> Americans, on the contrary, are pleased to explain almost all the actions of their life with the aid of self-interest well understood; they complacently show how the enlightened love of themselves constantly brings them to aid each other and disposes them willingly to sacrifice a part of their time and their wealth to the good of the state.[15]

In fact, he noted, Americans are likely to insist that they are acting from self-interest even when by European standards they are not.

In short, Tocqueville discerned with great delicacy and uncanny perspicacity the many subtle and powerful ways by which the inner life of Americans differed from that of Europeans in his time—and still do today, I believe, despite the many convergences of the intervening generations.

Nonetheless, Tocqueville wrote as a Catholic. Indeed, it is highly unlikely that any mind unformed by the Catholic tradition would have so readily discerned, and been able to articulate, the subtle differences between the new democratic way of life and the Catholic aristocratic roots of European thought and sensibilities. Precisely because America is Protestant in sensibility and Tocqueville was Catholic, his sensitivity and fine intelligence took note of minute differences in the slightest vibrations of the soul. He was an outsider in America not only because he was French and aristocratic but also because he was Catholic. In his book, in fact, he described himself as a practicing Catholic who, on this account, came into frequent contact with Catholic priests wherever he went in America and had many long and intelligent conversations with them.[16] He learned to see America from their vantage point too and thus drew on a perspective that he and they partly shared in common (since the Catholic theology studied by the priests of the time—often in Europe—was by its own history steeped in European intellectual culture).

Along with Tocqueville, in fact, virtually all other Catholic visitors to America discovered here a fresh way of thinking about Catholicism that seemed to reveal new possibilities in their faith, as if in America it might achieve a more fundamental self-expression than it had ever achieved in Europe. For at least two ideas at the heart of the American experiment are also at the heart of the Catholic faith: the twin ideas of the common *equality* of all men and women (whatever their rank) before the face of God and the high *dignity* of the individual, who has been given by the Creator the awesome liberty to say yes or no, to choose his or her own destiny. In the Catholic faith, humans are in this way the only creatures in this world who, as images of God, are ends in themselves, not means.[17]

In hearing in America mystic chords familiar to his soul, Tocqueville was like the Marquis de Lafayette, Thaddeus Kosciuscko, Casimir Pulaski, Philip Mazzei, and others who cast their lot with the revolutionary generation of Americans. And like many European visitors before and since who have written on the meaning of America, from Michel de Crèvecoeur to Jacques Maritain, Raymond-Léopold Bruckberger, Raimundo Pezzamenti, Rocco Buttiglione, Michael Zoeller, and others, Tocqueville saw in America lessons for the whole world.[18] We are confronted, therefore, with the high importance for democracy that Tocqueville ascribed to religion.

The First Political Institution

Tocqueville claimed that the first *political* institution of American democracy is religion. This claim seems odd to those writers who accept "the secularization thesis," namely, that the main trend of the modern era is the decline of religion vis-à-vis an ascendant secular philosophy. In the main, secular writers have explained Tocqueville's claim by interpreting it as a comment on an earlier historical stage in which, admittedly, religion was highly visible and vocal; now, they say, things are different—more secular.

Unfortunately for this thesis, empirical evidence does not show that religion has lost public salience in recent times. On the contrary, in region after region religion seems more dynamic, and the secular tendency seems weaker and less self-assured, than at any time in the last two hundred years.[19] A higher proportion of Americans go to church and engage in daily or weekly religious activities today than in 1776. Over any given weekend in the autumn, more Americans attend church, synagogue, or mosque than attend all the football games (professional, college, and secondary school) in the nation; there are even more attending church *in person* than watching football *on television* both Saturday and Sunday together. Five times more Americans go to church each week than go to the movies.[20] The religious factor is highly potent in American electoral politics; some would even say it is the single most important factor.[21] The pro-life movement, for instance, is the largest and best-organized such movement in the world. (This movement of course includes some atheists.)

A second shocking claim of Tocqueville's—admittedly more an implicit suggestion than an outright proposition—is that one day Catholics might be in the best intellectual position to explain and defend the presuppositions of democracy. As we have seen, Pierre Manent of France, a Tocqueville scholar himself, noted that the Church has been better able over the last century to adapt itself to democracy than secular democracy has adapted to religion. In addition, the Church, regarding the future, may be in a more assertive, creative, optimistic mode than the secular democracies. I would add that the premises of Catholic faith include the premises of democracy, while the premises of secular thought, left to itself, not only do not suffice for the defense of the premises of democracy but actually undermine them. On what generally agreed grounds today, for example, do secular philosophers defend human rights? On what ground do they discern a dignity distinctive of human beings among all other creatures?

Even if we were to concede that secular philosophy is perfectly adequate to the defense of democracy, many today are no longer persuaded that a merely secular philosophy offers a credible philosophy of human destiny. Among such people, the suggestion of Tocqueville that over time the Catholic faith would prove to be an important ally of democracy has been too little discussed. "America," he wrote,

> is the most democratic country in the world, and at the same time, ac-
> cording to reliable reports, it is the country in which the Roman Catholic
> religion is making the most progress. . . . If Catholicism could ultimately
> escape from the political animosities to which it has given rise [in Europe,
> carried over into America], I am almost certain that that same spirit of the
> age which now seems so contrary to it would turn into a powerful ally, and
> that it would suddenly make great conquests.[22]

What is it about the Jewish and Christian religions, in particular Catholicism, that led Tocqueville to see them as the primary political institution of democracy? The first reason is their powerful conviction about *the centrality of human liberty* to the entire purpose of the universe. The axis of creation is human liberty and destiny; every story in the Bible illustrates this axis. The primacy of liberty is the very ground not only of the biblical view but also of the Whig view of the world. The Bible understands liberty in a way that lends human persons distinctive dignity. In addition, it understands liberty as the opposite of license—as the triumph of practical reason (*phronesis*) over animal instinct, as self-government and self-mastery over libertinism. It is not an accident that descendants of Tocqueville and Rochambeau were among those Frenchmen who designed the Statue of Liberty, so that it might stand as a precise tribute to the *American* idea of liberty: a sober woman with the torch of *reason* raised aloft in one arm and the book of the *law* clasped in the other—*reason* over passion, bigotry, and ignorance; and liberty *under law*.[23]

The dignity of the free person—free under law—is one underpinning that Catholicism gives democracy. The Catholic metaphysic also underpins the idea of *equality*. For equality is not (in an empirical sense) an idea reached by natural reason. When the Athenians bade the citizens of Melos to treat with them in a spirit of equality, they received the following scornful reply: "You know as well as we do that right, as the world goes, is only in question between equals in power, while the strong do what they can and the weak suffer what they must."[24] By contrast, the Hebrew tradition introduced to the whole world by Christians taught a different lesson: that in the eyes of our Creator, all men and women, of whatever station or rank, are equal. This Judge is impressed by neither power nor wealth nor position. In nature some are strong and some are weak, some handsome and some plain, some richly talented and others not. No matter. The Creator calls everyone, equally, to be His friend. If humans are equal, therefore, it is solely in His eyes.

The Catholic faith, Tocqueville observed, over many centuries had firmly established the idea of equality in the consciousness of the world:

> Among the various Christian doctrines Catholicism seems one of those most favorable to equality of conditions. . . .
>
> In matters of dogma the Catholic faith places all intellects on the same level; the learned man and the ignorant, the genius and the common herd, must all subscribe to the same details of beliefs; rich and poor must follow the same observances, and it imposes the same austerities upon the strong and the weak; it makes no compromise with any mortal, but applying the same standard to every human being, it mingles all classes of society at the foot of the same altar, just as they are mingled in the sight of God.

Catholicism may dispose the faithful to obedience, but it does not prepare them for inequality. However, I would say that Protestantism in general orients men much less toward equality than toward independence.[25]

In addition, the Catholic faith emphasizes the incommensurable value of the human person through its teaching on the immortality of body and soul. This teaching bathes human rights in a brilliant light. Human rights arise not just from nature but from the higher destiny with which God gifted humans. As Alexander Hamilton wrote:

> Moral obligation, according to [Hobbes], is derived from the introduction of civil society; and there is no virtue but what is purely artificial, the mere contrivance of politicians, for the maintenance of social intercourse. But

the reason he ran into this absurd and impious doctrine, was, that he disbelieved the existence of an intelligent superintending principle, who is the governor, and will be the final judge of the universe. . . .

To grant, that there is a supreme intelligence, who rules the world, and has established laws to regulate the actions of his creatures; and still to assert that man, in a state of nature, may be considered as perfectly free from all restraints of *law* and *government*, appears to a common understanding altogether irreconcilable.

Good and wise men, in all ages, have embraced a very dissimilar theory. They have supposed that the deity, from the relations we stand in to himself and to each other, has constituted an eternal and immutable law, which is indispensably obligatory upon all mankind, prior to any human institution whatever. This is what is called the law of nature. . . . Upon this law depend the natural rights of mankind.[26]

Take away the immortality of the soul, and it is difficult to establish the dignity of man any higher than that of any other animal. Even if such a difficult philosophical task is successful, its result is not likely to have the radiance that it would gain from the added luminosity of Jewish and Christian faith.

Note where Tocqueville has brought us then: the foundations of democracy lie in the three principles of the dignity of the free person, the equality of all in the eyes of God, and the immortal value of every person before God. For these, democracy owes an enormous debt to Jewish and Christian faith. This point may not be obvious to those to whom President Washington referred in his "Farewell Address" as "minds of a peculiar character,"[27] but for large majorities, including many of the most brilliant and learned, faith adds powerful arguments to the weaker arguments presented by philosophy on the three great questions of human dignity, equality, and the immortal value of the human person.

What Does Faith Add to Reason?

Beyond noting the fundamental principles that religion makes available to democracy, Tocqueville also noted that Jewish and Christian faith adds other indispensable benefits.

First, *faith corrects morals and manners*. As an ill-fated bill in the Virginia Assembly put it in 1784, "The general diffusion of Christian knowledge hath a tendency to correct the morals of men, restraining their vices, and preserve the peace of society."[28] Although Americans are bold and enterprising in making their fortunes, Tocqueville wrote:

> American revolutionaries are obliged ostensibly to profess a certain respect for Christian morality and equity, and that does not allow them easily to break the laws when those are opposed to the executions of their designs; nor would they find it easy to surmount the scruples of their partisans even if they were able to get over their own. Up till now no one in the United States has dared to profess the maxim that everything is allowed in the interests of society, an impious maxim apparently invented . . . to legitimatize every future tyrant.[29]

Thus, while in a free society "the law allows the American people to do everything, there are things which religion prevents them from imagining and forbids them to dare"—such as breaking the law.[30] When consciences are active, policemen needn't be numerous. Citizens are law-abiding willingly. Colonial Americans had already experienced periods of declines in religion, accompanied by a steady moral decline. They had also seen religious awakenings lead to tangible improvements in social peace. That was why they all believed that religion "is necessary for the maintenance of republican institutions. That is not the view of one class or party among the citizens, but of the whole nation; it is found in all ranks."[31]

Second, Tocqueville noted: "*Fixed ideas about God and human nature are indispensable* to men for the conduct of daily life, and it is daily life that prevents them from acquiring them."[32] Since daily life keeps most people so busy, these "fixed ideas" are difficult for most to reach. Even great philosophers stumble in trying to come to them. But biblical faith provides to reason practical fixed ideas that only a very few philosophers—and they only uncertainly—can reach for themselves. Thus, sound religion, tested in long experience, gives a culture an immense advantage. For men cannot act without living out general ideas. Clarity of soul prevents enervation and the dissipation of energies. Some ideas, Tocqueville wrote, are a particular boon to free men: ideas rooted in the unity of humankind, duties to neighbor, truth, honesty, and love for the law of reason. Regarding these essential ideas, the answers that biblical religion gives are "clear, precise, intelligible to the crowd, and very durable."[33]

Third, religion adds to reason indispensable support for the view that *every human being is not simply a bundle of pleasures and pains,* a higher kind of cow or kitten or other contented domestic animal. "Democracy favors the taste for physical pleasures," Tocqueville wrote. "This taste, if it becomes excessive, soon disposes men to believe that nothing but matter exists. Materialism, in its turn, spurs them on to such delights with mad impetuosity. Such is the vicious circle into which democratic nations are driven. It is good that they see the danger and draw back."[34] The principle of equality that animates democracies, pulling men downward, will slowly destroy what is most human in them—their souls. It is religion that checks and reverses this process and, more than that, spurs greatness, Tocqueville thought. Faith sows its good effects in art and manners as well as in the arena of practical action. Belief in immortality prods humans to aspire upward and in this way grounds their awareness of their own special dignity and natural rights.

Fourth, faith adds to a morality of mere reason an acute sense of *acting in the presence of a personal and undeceivable Judge* Who sees and knows even actions performed in secret, even willful acts committed solely in one's heart. Thus, faith adds motives for maintaining high standards and for seeking to do things perfectly *even when no one is looking.* Faith gives us reasons to paint the bottom of the chair and clean the unseen corners of a room: godliness entails attention to details that no one but God sees. Whereas morality construed within the bounds of reason alone is, at best, a matter of utilitarian calculation or deontological rules, faith sees moral behavior in terms of relations between two persons—ourselves and the God to Whom we owe much. In this vein, Benjamin Franklin chastised his colleagues at the Constitutional Convention for their ingratitude to their beneficent Friend Who had assisted them when they were in need.

In this situation of this Assembly, groping as it were in the dark to find political truth, and scarce able to distinguish it when presented to us, how has it happened, Sir, that we have not hitherto once thought of humbly applying to the Father of lights to illuminate our understandings? In the beginning of the contest with G. Britain, when we were sensible of danger we had daily prayer in this room for the divine protection.—Our prayers, Sir, were heard, and they were graciously answered. All of us who were engaged in the struggle must have observed frequent instances of superintending providence in our favor. To that kind providence we owe this happy opportunity of consulting in peace on the means of establishing our future national felicity. And have we now forgotten that powerful friend? Or do we imagine that we no longer need his assistance? I have lived, Sir, a long time, and the longer I live, the more convincing proofs I see of this truth—*that God governs in the affairs of men.*[35]

Fifth, in America, Tocqueville wrote, religion *"reigns supreme in the souls of women, and it is women who shape mores."* Faith in America has had a dramatic effect on mores, especially in the home. "Certainly, of all the countries in the world, America is the one in which the marriage tie is most respected and where the highest and truest conception of conjugal happiness has been conceived." Tocqueville had no doubt that the "great severity of mores which one notices in the United States has its primary origin in beliefs." The comparative laxity of morals in Europe bred mistrust even in the home, and broader ripples of mistrust in the public sphere beyond the home.

In Europe almost all the disorders of society are born around the domestic hearth and not far from the nuptial bed. It is there that men come to feel scorn for natural ties and legitimate pleasures and develop a taste for disorder, restlessness of spirit, and instability of desires. Shaken by the tumultuous passions which have often troubled his own house, the European finds it hard to submit to the authority of the state's legislators.[36]

When there is no trust in the home, trust in public life is highly improbable. Where there is a lack of self-government at home, self-government in the public sphere has little probability of success. If one cannot say "that in the United States religion influences the laws or political opinions in detail," Tocqueville continued, "it does direct mores, and by regulating domestic life it helps to regulate the state."[37]

In sum, to say nothing of otherworldly benefits, Tocqueville argued that faith adds to reason five worldly strengths: restraint of vice and gains in social peace; fixed, stable, and general ideas about the dynamics of life; a check on the downward bias of the principle of equality and the materialism toward which it gravitates; a new conception of morality as a personal relation with our Creator, and thus a motive for acting well even when no one is looking; and through the high honor paid to the marriage bond, the quiet regulation of mores in marriage and in the home.

Based on the experience of our own time, religion (specifically, Judaism and Christianity) may be especially necessary in a period of radical individualism—that very radical individualism spelled out in principle by Justice Anthony Kennedy in *Planned Parenthood v. Casey* and repeated with emphasis in *Rust v. Sullivan.* "At the heart of liberty is the right to define one's own concept of existence, of meaning, of the universe, and of the mystery of human life."[38] At such times, reason has no moorings in natural law, only in personal desire. A more anarchic principle would be hard to identify. The Kennedy principle is the opposite to law. It throws every person into a region of lawlessness and personal arbitrariness. Its commandment is: do as you please.

Precisely here Kennedy has left reason without social guidance and social support. Reason so untethered is powerless against brute force in a tyranny, and also, for the vast majority of people, against the mass of popular opinion in a democracy. In any society there are not many who can stand against the crowd. Even those who can need to be able to fall back on reason as their defense against the mob, and in particular on a form of reason that argues from the general law and universal principle. After all, it is only such principles that have a chance to hold the mob at bay, by a glint from whatever dim light of reason still moves some among them. Yet it is precisely these principles of which Justice Kennedy's principle has deprived them. All Kennedy can offer them is this: each man for himself. Woe, then, to any who would defy a mob. Such persons have no longer any principle of law to stand on. If the principle to which they hold is hated by the mob, the mob will accuse them of hate speech, discrimination, or whatever charge they need to invent. The Kennedy principle is the death of the law.

As Tocqueville noted, religion supplies fixed principles—call them the moral laws—that philosophers reach unsteadily and in cacophony. If we depended on modern philosophers for moral living, we would be thrown—because they disagree so much—between their *boo!* and their *hurray!* We need philosophers to work out the reasons and to criticize bad arguments, but reason-supporting religion does better and shorter work in formulating the necessary fixed principles, and the North Star, of the moral life. Given those points on the compass, critical philosophy can show their reasonableness, their coherence, their implications, and the misinterpretations to which they are vulnerable. In this way, for instance, each of the Mosaic Ten Commandments has been shown by philosophers down the ages to be susceptible of formulation in philosophical principles based upon broad human experience. Once given the Commandments, one does not need faith to accept them. In fact, philosophical reason itself, when it is steady enough, can (and often has) come to them on its own. Examining how philosophers down the centuries had in fact done this, Thomas Aquinas supplied an argument as to why, nonetheless, it is a mercy for God to have given most men, through Moses, a highly useful shortcut to necessary practical guidance for the good life.[39] For most people, Moses is a lot more reliable than having to go through university courses in ethics.

Yet as Tocqueville ended by showing, religion is especially necessary in matters of sex, procreation, and marriage. The fidelity of parents to the marriage bond is one of the greatest foundations of republican government under the rule of law, he noted, for it teaches children in their most tender and teachable years that men and women can be trusted with the most important and intimate responsibilities of parenthood, even when they live in privacy and in secret. Here is where children learn to trust the law and to trust the individual citizen, in the person of their parents and the parents of their friends. In France, by contrast, where the cultivation of romantic love, liaisons, mistresses, and adultery was a major pastime of "civilized" society, Tocqueville points out, social mistrust and cynicism were inevitable by-products. On this foundation, republican government was necessarily insecure, and far more dependent on the visibility of naked force. Better than any other thinker, Tocqueville saw the tie between a strong marriage bond and the chances of success of republican government. He identified the source of that dependence: the network of trust inspired by fidelity, nourished within the walls of the family home and suffusing the happy lives of children. It is from that trust that trust in fellow citizens and in the government of the republic is rooted. Moreover, Tocqueville saw that marital fidelity is preached, nurtured, and supported by firm Christian and Jewish faith. Here too faith adds strength where reason is weak, and this strength is well in accord with the inclinations of reason. Republican reason is strengthened by faith.

In contemporary terms, persons reduced to reason alone claim that a gay or lesbian couple have the same "right" to marriage that a man and a woman have. In that case, marriage needs to be redefined in terms of an intimate, long-lasting, legally binding friendship, with all the responsibilities and entanglements of assets thereof. There can be no question of a Catholic sacrament here (persons of other faiths will speak for themselves), and no question of the classic commitment to openness to the generation of children in the context of a father-mother family. Given the traditional religious definition of marriage, the tissue of the common law on marriage down the ages makes great sense, and not only for the continuation of the human race and its prosperity but also for its civic trust and its liberties. The cultural, political, and economic fruitfulness of the monogamous husband-wife marriage bond has been abundantly proved. Indeed, it is one of the glories of the human race. That is why Tocqueville took admiring note of it and commended it to the world.

Reason left to itself, without Judaism or Christianity, empties marriage of these "extra" roles. It sees only the attractiveness of intimacy, affection, and (temporary) mutuality. It will be obliged to answer further questions that are bound to arise. What, really, is the stake of the state in privately contracted friendships? If the answer is state pensions, welfare benefits, medical benefits, and so on, wouldn't a better answer be the devolution of such responsibilities on the part of the state, by vesting the funds for these benefits in each person, who might then do with them what he likes? Why should the state be brought in to meddle in private friendships?

Further, if the criteria for marriage are intimacy, friendship, affection, and a long-term bond, what is the principle by which one distinguishes who may enter into it? If the criteria are no longer based on procreative potential and the future family bond formed by a mother and a father, what are the criteria? Must a friendship be limited to two people? On the above definition of marriage, reason has no conclusive ground for objecting to polygamy. There does not seem to be any special sanctity to the number two stemming from reason or human custom. That may be why polygamy has been so common in human history.

Further, if any man may marry any man, and any woman any woman, may an uncle in a family marry a favorite nephew, or an older brother a younger brother? If affection, intimacy, and friendship are the criteria, is there a limitation by species? May one marry a favorite pet? In France in 2004 a woman married her fiancé after he had been dead for several days. "He would have wanted it."

Reason, left to itself, can be a pretty poor thing. Indeed, if Jewish and Christian faith did not rank it so high in the order of creation, as the jewel in the Creator's crown, it is doubtful whether reason would enjoy the prestige it has long had in our civilization. The question is not whether Jewish and Christian faith may be reconciled with reason. The beauty is that Jewish and Christian faith tout reason as the human vocation *par excellence* and have greatly facilitated its work by nourishing such virtues as honest inquiry, careful deliberation, sound judgment, and social responsibility, which are the preconditions of reason's good functioning. Without the libraries, museums, schools, universities, and schools of dialectic nourished by the synagogue and the church down the ages—without the long, patient work of monks and rabbis, manuscript copiers, inventors, librarians, logicians and dialecticians—reason in the West today would be only a shadow of itself. And without the vision of radical freedom at the heart of the human project and the powerful claim that the human project is in some way at the heart of the mysteries of the universe, modern science would have lacked the confidence it has had that it can be a progressive, liberating, and ultimately illuminating venture. The human mind has reasons for pride, and Judaism and Christianity have supplied them. Daily practice also teaches the human mind humility.

Most scientists today seldom think about how much they owe to the religious devotees who cleared the way for them and imbued our culture with confidence in reason—far beyond what it had then earned on its own merits. Even most ordinary decent people, with good solid moral views, too seldom recognize how deeply those fixed principles by which they live and breathe were implanted in our culture by faith. Since our generation is in the process of uprooting and destroying as many of those fixed principles as possible, we (or our children) may yet have reason to learn whether a republic without faith, reduced to internally conflicted reason alone, can long remain free.

George Washington warned in his "Farewell Address" that religion is an *indispensable* support of this republic. I used to think that a bit extreme.

The Spirit of Religion and the Spirit of Liberty

One of Tocqueville's most penetrating passages has touched me deeply ever since I was a young man. This is his passage on the historically novel combination of *the spirit of religion and the spirit of freedom*. The passage deserves to be read in its entirety, but I here content myself with an excerpt:

> I have already said enough to put Anglo-American civilization in its true light. It is the product of two perfectly distinct elements which elsewhere have often been at war with one another but which in America it was somehow possible to incorporate into each other, forming a marvelous combination. I mean the *spirit of religion* and the *spirit of freedom*. . . . Far from harming each other, these two apparently opposed tendencies work in harmony and seem to lend mutual support.
>
> Religion regards civil liberty as a noble exercise of men's faculties, the world of politics being a sphere intended by the Creator for the free play of intelligence. Religion, being free and powerful within its own sphere and content with the position reserved for it, realized that its sway is all the better established because it relies only on its own powers and rules men's hearts without external support.
>
> Freedom sees religion as the companion of its struggles and triumphs, the cradle of its infancy, and the divine source of its rights. Religion is considered as the guardian of mores, and mores are regarded as the guarantee of the laws and pledge for the maintenance of freedom itself.[40]

What are the implications of these Tocquevillian insights today? Granted, Jewish and Christian faiths put in place three crucial preconditions of democracy: truth, freedom, and dignity. It is not at all certain that, for most people, secular philosophy supports these other than pragmatically; nor is it clear that other world religions support these preconditions with equivalent intellectual clarity. Enunciated in a little more detail, these three ideas are: a strong idea of *truth*, in the sense of a regulative ideal of our minds driving our inquiries to weed out all that is bogus, false, and unworthy of reasoned assent; a moral conception of human *freedom*; and a profound sense of the *dignity* and nobility of the human being, body and soul. These are the three background beliefs that make intelligible the conception of human rights and the spiritual primacy of liberty.

Without the regulative ideal of truth, the practice of liberty lapses into license, and self-government decays into self-indulgence. No criterion—no social check-and-balance outside the self—stops the self from asserting: "What the heart desires, the heart desires." The Supreme Court of the United States in *Casey* and again in *Lawrence v. Texas* comes very close to endorsing such lawlessness as a fundamental axiom.[41] That proposition unleashes a logic of vast potential destructiveness. Its logic is that right and wrong are whatever we desire them to be.

From Tocqueville's point of view, the spirit of religion is indispensable to the successful incarnation of the spirit of liberty. That was also, he noted, the view of the early Americans without exception.

But are these ideas only American? What about peoples whose religion (or lack of it) does not assist them in grasping the reasons for affirming the dignity and liberty of every person and the equality of all before the Creator of all? In the next two chapters, we must examine the prospects of democracy in those many countries outside the United States that are Catholic or Islamic. More than 50 nations are predominantly Catholic, while many others have sizable Catholic populations.[42] There are at least 18 officially Islamic nations, several other predominantly Muslim nations (such as Turkey), and another two dozen with large Muslim populations.[43] In such nations, Catholic and Islamic alike, how is it possible for religion to be the first political institution of democracy?

This is a weighty question, since of the world's six billion people, one billion are Roman Catholic, and one billion Islamic. In addition, these two religions are the fastest growing in the world.

Chapter Eight

HOW THE CATHOLIC
CHURCH CAME TO TERMS
WITH DEMOCRACY

FROM 1789 UNTIL 1918, "DEMOCRACY" in Continental Europe showed the Catholic Church two faces: sentimental words and an iron fist. "Liberal" regimes in Continental Europe aimed to wipe out the Church ("Écrasez l'infâme!"). In France the attempt pretty well succeeded. France established a record of bloodshed, destruction, and despoliation that deeply scarred the Catholic Church. Under Napoleon, two separate popes had been seized and dragged away into captivity in Paris, jostled about on rough wagons. From about 1790 until 1880, occupying armies made their successors fear for life and limb,[1] while many philosophers cheered the assault on the popes as a radical overturning of the past.[2] Scores of thousands of monks and nuns were driven from their religious homes. Seminaries, universities, and libraries were closed. Churches were used as barracks and stables. Tens of thousands of the devout were cruelly slain.

For about a hundred years after 1820, the popes put up their backs against democracy.[3] Then, in the 20th century, bitter experience taught the Church that, in their disdain for human rights, totalitarian regimes are even more ruthless. Models of democracy better attuned to respecting religious liberty and other basic rights swept at last through European consciousness. Pius

XII made the first strong papal appeal for democracy in his "Christmas Message" of 1944.[4] Yet even though later popes expanded Catholic teaching in this area, the Vatican has not even to this day articulated a systematic vision of democracy.[5] Nor has it developed easy-to-use teaching materials to instruct Catholic peoples around the world in the virtues that make democracy work. Catholic social teaching regarding democracy has not yet been brought to definitive decisions on some important issues.[6]

For seven years, the Pontifical Academy of Social Sciences (PASS), under the instigation of Pope John Paul II, launched a major set of studies to prepare the way for such work. Three separate collections were published by the PASS: *Proceedings of the Workshop on Democracy* (1996); *Democracy: Some Acute Questions* (1998); and *Democracy: Reality and Responsibility* (2000).[7] These studies set forth a number of definitions, distinctions, and rules for action that might be of use to Catholics and other peoples in many different regions of the world. To go quickly over the highlights of these studies is to get an unusual, close-to-the-ground look at how hard it is to make democracy work, given the diversity of cultures in which it has been transplanted.

Why Should Christians Support Democracy?

A powerful answer was given to this question by John Paul II in *Centesimus Annus*:

> The Church values the democratic system inasmuch as it ensures the participation of citizens in making political choices, guarantees to the governed the possibility both of electing and holding accountable those who govern them, and of replacing them through peaceful means when appropriate. Thus she cannot encourage the formation of narrow ruling groups which usurp the power of the State for individual interests or for ideological ends.[8]

During the long night of the Church under the bloody "democracies" of Europe in the 19th century, the fairly benign democratic experiment in the United States, although praised by Leo XIII in 1888, seemed remote.[9] Only after the rise of the totalitarian governments of the 20th century did Pius XII, Pope John XXIII, and the Second Vatican Council discern powerful comparative advantages in democratic institutions.[10] Only after decades of hesitation did the Magisterium then ratify the groundbreaking democratic efforts of lay thinkers such as Jacques Maritain and Yves Simon, as well as Catholic statesmen such as Konrad Adenauer, Robert Schuman, and the remarkable priest-philosopher and founder of Italy's Partito Populare, Don Luigi Sturzo.[11] As Mary Ann Glendon's history of the Universal Declaration of Human Rights demonstrates, a number of Catholic laymen played catalytic roles in its formal articulation, including the Thomistically educated Greek Orthodox layman and Arab statesman Charles Malik of Lebanon.[12] Thus, although Catholic intellect joined late in the modern articulation of democratic institutions, Catholic efforts to strengthen democracy just before, during, and after World War II have been formidable.

The main mission of the Church is not politics; its "kingdom" is not of this world. It has no political ideology of its own to present in advance. Like the rest of the human race, it must learn by studying events. That is how the Church came by experience to see that in establishing the rule of law, limited government, and an orderly process of transferring power, democracy (at least in some forms), better than other regimes, protects individuals and minorities from torture, tyranny, and the abuse of their rights. Vatican II's great decree, *Gaudium et Spes* (1965), described this historic achievement in these terms:

> The present keener sense of human dignity has given rise in many parts of the world to attempts to bring about a politico-juridical order which will give better protection to the rights of the person in public life. These include the right freely to meet and form associations, the right to express one's own opinion and to profess one's religion both publicly and privately. The protection of the rights of a person is indeed a necessary condition so that citizens, individually or collectively, can take an active part in the life and government of the state.[13]

By keeping intact the sphere of human obligations to the Transcendent, a well-ordered democracy also protects religious liberty, the rights of conscience, and the free exercise of religion in the public forum.[14]

During the next three decades, phenomenological reflection on the classical concept of the "person" led Karol Wojtyla, then a philosopher, later Archbishop of Krakow, and finally Pope John Paul II, to make a specifically Catholic contribution to the theory of human rights. The classical secular conception, formulated by Thomas Hobbes and John Locke, derives from a new conception of a "state of nature" in which every human possesses a natural equality and from which "civil society" emerges when, out of fear of violence from others, a social contract is arrived at among contracting individuals that cedes all legitimate use of force to the state.[15] By contrast, John Paul II's theory grounds human rights in a richer and more internal ("subjective") concept of the person rather than in the "thin" individual of Hobbes and Locke.

In classical and medieval thought, the human person enjoys a dual personal and social nature. A person is an agent of his or her own destiny, independently capable of deliberation and choice. But he or she is also bound to other persons by consciousness of family and culture and by communion with one same Creator.[16] John Paul II stresses the experienced "subjectivity" of the person and the exercise of due care in the inalienable act of choice—the act that throws part of oneself into one's actions, whether in matters of daily work or in matters of religious faith.[17] By opening up the frequent exercise of such freedoms, democracy seems to be better attuned to the natural moral order (attentive intelligence, free will, responsible choice) than earlier monarchical regimes and better protected against abuses of power. Unlike Hobbes and Locke, who focus rather more on freedom from external control, Wojtyla focuses more on inner conscious acts of making choices and their internal conditions.

The natural love for liberty is coming to universal consciousness in our times.[18] This universal hunger for liberty is leading many new peoples to build democratic societies. Democratic states at various stages of maturation now make up a near-majority of world states, and these democratic states more steadily attain high levels of economic development than nondemocratic states.[19] Nonetheless, "the 19th century Church did not equip itself early enough with analytical tools that would have allowed it to analyze and understand better the emergence of the phenomenon of democracy and its novelty."[20]

By keeping government limited, the Church eventually learned—later than it should have—democracy encourages citizens to pursue a wide range of ends on their own. Whether as individuals or in associations, citizens of democratic nations shape their own societies. This ability of the baptized to participate fully in the direction of their own societies gives the Church a method for fulfilling her duty quite superior to what was possible under earlier regimes. Instead of commanding societies from the top, the Church teaches indirectly, through teaching her members, who in turn use their own well-formed judgments to make decisions that shape the world. But this mission depends upon the education of Catholic citizens, and that fact raises a whole new set of questions.

Against Majority Rule

What Is Democracy?

On this subject, the scholars summoned by the Pontifical Academy of Social Sciences were divided. A few, mistakenly, linked democracy merely to majority rule. Most more properly insisted that the protection of the rights of minorities (and dread of the tyranny of a majority) is crucial to the essence of democracy.[21] Then, since many more nations *attempt* to build democracy than *succeed in doing so*, experience makes it obvious that mastery of the institutions through which democracy is actually exercised is a necessary precondition for success.[22] A further precondition is the widespread personal appropriation of democratic *beliefs*, *habits*, and *values*, since in moments of conflict or crisis, merely mechanical skills avail little without underlying moral commitments.[23]

Taketoshi Nojiri, for example, stressed attention to both the institutional and the subjective dimensions of democracy. First, "democracy means an *institution* for political or social administration, above all a way to determine the will of the whole, as is usually the case when a state is called a democratic nation."[24] But democracy also "denotes a *way of thinking* where everyone is equally a person, precisely because they are human beings. Democracy in this sense is good in its own right, i.e., as an end in itself, beyond being merely an instrumental value."[25] Michel Schooyans adds that democratic *rights* "have the value of *rules* which constrain citizens and institutions, governed and governors. A democratic state is based on the *rule of law*."[26] John Paul II calls the attention of the less developed world to some of these basic institutional principles in *Centesimus Annus*, underlining the importance of separated powers, checks and balances, and the rule of law:

Pope Leo XIII was aware of the need for a sound theory of the State in order to ensure the normal development of man's spiritual and temporal activities, both of which are indispensable. For this reason, in one passage of *Rerum Novarum* he presents the organization of society according to the three powers—legislative, executive and judicial—something which at the time represented a novelty in Church teaching. Such an ordering reflects a realistic vision of man's social nature, which calls for legislation capable of protecting the freedom of all. To that end, it is preferable that each power be balanced by other powers and by other spheres of responsibility which keep it within proper bounds. This is the principle of the "rule of law," in which the law is sovereign, and not the arbitrary will of individuals.[27]

There are three parts to the free society: political liberty, economic liberty, and cultural/religious liberty, involving a set of institutions for each of these spheres. Since democracy presents itself as limited government, its political system must not by definition suffocate the *other* two social systems, which help articulate the full nature of human beings. Along with the political system, there is also the *moral-cultural system*, through which humans seek the beautiful, the true, the good, the holy, and the just, and the *economic* system, through which humans express such other natural desires as the drive to create, to improve their economic condition, and to trade with one another. These other two social systems do not lie under the direct control of the democratic state but enjoy their own proper autonomy.[28] The democratic state has some proper regulatory and coordinating responsibilities, but it must also respect the autonomy of the other two systems.[29]

The History, Spiritual Lineage, and Geography of Democracy

When we recall that the democracies of the ancient world could hardly be considered democracies today, we better appreciate the modern practice of democracy. As recently as the year 1850, barely four democracies were to be found anywhere in the world, and during the early 20th century a passionate ideology of dictatorship washed over the world.[30] Nonetheless, democracy's roots are very ancient, reaching back both into Jerusalem and into the ancient republics of Greece and Rome. Indeed, several ideas crucial to modern conceptions of democracy owe their origin to the Jewish Testament: for example, the equality of the children of the Creator, the imperative of concern for "widows and orphans" (i.e., the poor and the vulnerable), and the dignity of each individual, each of whose names has been known to the Creator ("before Time was").[31] Most scholars also hold that the West derived the idea of progress from the Hebrews and their eschatology, which was quite contrary to the myth of eternal return prominent in the pagan world of antiquity.[32] Part of the authentic lineage of modern democracy therefore hails from Jerusalem.

In addition, the rights of conscience and religious liberty have some precedent in the pagan classics (for example, the defense of obligations arising from piety toward ancestors in *Antigone*) but mostly owe their modern realization to a Jewish and Christian conception of God as Spirit and Truth. From this conception arises the obligation to worship Him, not solely by rote observance but also "in spirit and truth." This conception created a sacred space between the inner conscience of each individual and his Creator, into which no one else, neither mother nor father nor brother nor sister, can intrude. Only when such a conception had become a commonplace to multitudes of ordinary citizens could the *political order* of religious liberty become institutionalized on the basis of broad consent.[33] Whether an analogous conception may be derived from Islamic understandings of God and conscience will be our concern in the next chapter. It is highly unlikely that religious liberty is a principle accessible *only* to Jews and Christians.

The political philosophies of Plato and Aristotle also contributed to our modern thinking about republics, as did the reflections of Cicero, Seneca, and other Roman masters. To Greece and Rome we owe conceptions of virtue, character, the natural moral law, and even a model of administrative order that recognizes both unity and diversity, maintaining a scope that is more universal than is encompassed by any single people or ethnic group alone. The Greek love for universals, like the Roman love for practical law and practical virtues, was so powerful in the West that it not only fed the way of thinking of the Catholic Church in its ascendancy during the First Millennium but sparked a series of renaissances just before and during the Second Millennium, beginning with that of Charlemagne in the year 800 A.D. The humanism and universalism of these early centuries, matched with a transcendent faith whose vision was to build "a city on a hill," was in many dimensions a powerful preparation for modern conceptions of democracy.[34]

Today, however, democracy does not take one form only, not even in the West. Franz-Xavier Kaufmann warns that, in later centuries, "political theory starts from different assumptions in the Continental European and in the Anglo-Saxon traditions."[35] Democracies in Continental Europe emerged from a history of centralization shaped by absolute monarchies. Thus, even the democratic tradition there retains a concept of "the state" that still centralizes its political, administrative, and legal systems. In the Anglo-Saxon world, by contrast, democracy emerged within societies that were far less subject to a centralized, professionalized civil service. In Britain the power of the king had been circumscribed since 1215, first by the barons, then by the Parliament. Thus, the Anglo-Saxon democratic tradition cherishes a concept of "government" that stresses the minimal state and the separation of powers—most notably the separation of the judiciary branch from the administrative bureaucracy. On the Continent, by contrast, democratic states grew from "the principles of legality and constitutionality" that had for centuries flowed from the top down, not from the experience of ordinary peoples upward. For this reason, the growth of voluntary associations and civil society experienced in Europe "a slower process than in the case of the United States, whose very foundation was a democratic process."[36] Before there came to be a United States, Americans had learned for more than 150 years to govern themselves, first in their own voluntary associations, then in villages and towns, later in counties, eventually in separate states, and only at last in one nation. In Europe the process was wholly different.

Despite other significant differences among democracies in different regions, however, the dream of building democracy inspires a very broad range of nations today, of every race and religion, in every part of the world. The harmony of the idea of democracy with human nature is coupled with a universal striving for liberty and individual dignity. The stage for democracy today is planetary. The mission of the Catholic Church is planetary as well, as is made obvious by the range of nations and regimes covered in the studies by the PASS.[37]

Key Ideas, Institutions, and Habits

Central Ideas About Democracy

Although democracy may be said to be "natural" in the sense that it harmonizes well with the nature of human beings as they are, the institutions through which it is articulated are so complex, and so dependent on generations of trial and error, that the modern idea of democracy cannot be said to be simply intuitive. On the contrary, democracy's key conceptions need to be arrived at and refined through a kind of "experimental science" of politics. Some of democracy's central ideas—for example, that human rights are safer in a larger orbit than they are within a small city-state, and that the division of powers and the careful invention of checks and balances work better than concentrations of power—were discovered the hard way, after costly mistakes.

In other words, though democracy is highly dependent for its successful realization on certain basic ideas, these ideas are neither utopian nor a priori but reached through trial and error by way of actual experimentation. They are the fruit more of practical than of speculative reason. The intellectual habit appropriate to them is practical wisdom, what the ancients called *phronesis* or prudence. This wisdom is not "Reason" (with a capital "R") of the sort employed in geometry, logic, mathematics, or deductive metaphysics, nor is it utopian thinking or constructivism.

An inventory of all the ideas crucial to a full science of democracy would run to thirty or so items. The PASS primarily focused on five, both because of their importance and because of widespread contemporary confusion about them.

A Regulative Ideal of Truth.   Of these, the first is a regulative ideal of truth to undergird practices of courteous argument and the mutual examination of evidence. Without such an ideal of truth, there is no appeal except to power, which turns away from civil argument and civil consent to force.[38] Many people who today call themselves "relativists" are not really serious. They do not doubt the superiority of their own truth claims to those of their intellectual adversaries. The functional utility of their appeal to "relativism" is to cast suspicion on those who believe in God or simply in a knowable moral order.[39] The functional utility of the so-called critical thinking that thrives in some law schools, which analyzes all propositions into their relation to power and interest rather than their relation to truth, is to clear the way for a regime that exercises naked power. For who can question such a regime by a standard of truth or justice once the very existence or applicability of such criteria has been ruled out? In a parallel way, the rise of "theories of the absurd" during the 1920s was a necessary precondition for the Fascist exaltation of power.

A Loyal Opposition.   The idea of a loyal opposition commands rivals for power to cooperate in making steady forward progress, no matter which party is in power. Related to this idea is the idea of *compromise*, which entails fidelity to principle but recognizes that not everything can be demanded at once and that the perfect is often the enemy of the good.[40] In every negotiation, in order to accommodate the possibility of at least a little progress for all, those on all sides must both gain a little and also give up a little. Related to these ideas is skill in *building coalitions*, that is, a talent for forming majorities out of constantly shifting smaller groups. Some coalitions are formed ad hoc, case by case, but others are formed for long-term strategic purposes.[41]

Tyranny by a Democratic Majority.   One of the prevailing dangers of incompletely formed democratic systems is tyranny by a democratic majority. It is prevented by multiplying the number of lively interests in society, particularly economic interests, so that these too may be set in check and balance against one another. Since the interests of one industry are different from those of another, and since the interests of different firms within the same industry are different from one another, the multiplication of interests contributes to the fragmenting of potential majorities.[42] This fragmenting, in turn, creates an incentive for learning skills in how to form coalitions, which may form around one axis with regard to one issue and around another with regard to a different issue. In this way, even peoples with quite diverse interests become accustomed to cooperating with one another when some of their interests coincide. Further, it is in the interests of all to keep the entire cooperative system working and therefore not to insist upon getting their own way at the expense of bringing all progress to a stop (at which point the others would turn against them). Instead of insisting upon "all or nothing," they are counseled to relent and to seek a point of compromise. Thus, individual interests are made, despite themselves, to serve a common good, and even the competitive appetite is made to serve cooperation.

The Difference Between License and Liberty.   The third key idea is the difference between license and liberty. *License* is the freedom to follow one's instincts and do as one desires, as naturally as cats and dogs do. *Liberty* is the duty to do what, after reflection and deliberation, one knows that one *ought* to do.[43] Cats and dogs cannot help following the law of their own nature; they are not free to do otherwise. Our own children are confronted with more than one set of instincts and laws, flowing from their complex natures, and they must learn to reflect, discern, and deliberate as to which of these inclinations to follow, and in what way.[44] To do justice to the fullness of their complex natures, they must reflect, deliberate, and take responsibility for their choices. Acting as a free woman or a free man is therefore neither a reflex nor a given, but a rather high achievement.[45] This *moral concept of liberty* was overlooked even by so influential a thinker as Isaiah Berlin, who stopped short of this indispensable "third concept" in his essay "Two Concepts of Liberty."[46]

Human Fallibility.   The fourth idea is the role of human fallibility or sin. If I may paraphrase the great American Protestant theologian Reinhold Niebuhr: because humans are sometimes capable of acting justly, generously, and well, democracy is possible. Because humans do not always act justly, generously, and well, democracy is necessary.[47] Democracy cannot and does not eliminate evil from the human heart, nor does it banish evil from human practice. On the contrary, the ineradicable human tendency toward self-aggrandizement makes limited government, the separation of powers, and a profusion of checks and balances necessary. Such devices have had to be carefully set in place in order for democracy to avoid the worst evils and mitigate the lesser evils.[48] As Professor Kaufmann notes, Winston Churchill (and Reinhold Niebuhr) used to say that democracy is the worst system of government known to man, except for all the others.[49]

The Democratic Republic.   The fifth idea is the classic argument against democracy and in favor of the democratic republic. The *democratic principle* is majority rule; the *republican principle* is a self-limiting check on popular consent through the election of a small body of representatives, disciplined in turn by frequent recurrence to electoral approval or ejection. To the extent that democracy is understood solely as majority rule, democracy is vulnerable to being turned into the tyranny of a majority. Such a tyranny is even more irrational and incorrigible than tyranny by a single individual.[50] That is why James Madison commended investing much energy in devising checks and balances against potential majorities. It is also the reason he commended mixing republican and democratic principles, as sentinels upon each other.[51]

The Institutions That Undergird the Practice of Democracy

The first institutional requirement of democracy is *a limited political system.* There must be a division of systems so that the political system does not suppress the spheres of culture (conscience, religious exercise, information, ideas, the arts, the sciences), on the one hand, or the spontaneous and vital economic energies of the economic system, on the other.[52]

Second, the political system *must not suppress the manifold and essential energies of civil society*, which spring from the right of association and which enable associations of individuals and communities to further their own proper ends in full freedom and vigor, with due respect for the common good of all.[53] In all these areas, the democratic political system retains certain regulative powers that it exercises to secure the common good, but it must be exceedingly careful in employing these powers not to suffocate the vital civil energies of the larger society.[54]

Within the political system properly so called, the first key institution is *the separation of powers*, so that these central powers are safely located in the hands of different persons with different interests. Especially important is the institutional separation of executive powers, legislative powers, and judicial powers into three mutually related but independent spheres. Officeholders in each of these spheres are given a certain responsibility for overseeing and checking the other two, in the hope that all of them will be kept within their proper and lawful limits and working in due service to the common good. It is not wise to trust any one person or group with too much power; it is necessary to make certain that every power is checked by an equal power.[55]

Moreover, the principle of the separation of powers needs to be carried downward throughout the *whole* political system in such a way that at every point power is balanced against power and every interest is checked by a rival interest.[56] In this way, "the rule of law" is protected by blocking the merely egotistic, individualistic abuse of power in any one office.

But collectives can also abuse power, as the 20th century taught us at unforgettable cost. Even democratic majorities may do great evils.[57] To prevent the abuse of power by majorities—and block the passions that may sweep through a people at a given moment—all powers in a democracy are vested in an elective, representative assembly: *a legislature.* It is not the people who rule directly, but the people through their representatives. Moreover, the powers of the legislature are limited by the Constitution, formal and informal, so that limited government is protected.

The most indispensable feature of democratic governance is *an independent judiciary*, for without an honest, courageous, and forthright judiciary, the rule of law can never be discerned and properly observed.[58] Arbitrary and individual judgment must not be allowed to have the final word. The rule of law must prevail, and this rule can be upheld only by judges with both the moral integrity and the material independence to be faithful to the law, even in the face of the most powerful interests.[59] There must also be a sufficient love for the law among the general population to provide the social strength on which an independent judiciary relies. The people as a whole must be very jealous of the independence of their judges, even in those cases when the judges rule against the popular will.

It is important to have an executive officer who, although checked and balanced by the other two great powers of government, retains *a sufficient degree of executive power* to be able to show energy and concentrate national purpose in cases of war, natural disaster, and other emergencies.[60]

Many administrative institutions, always under democratic supervision, are also necessary for the functioning of democracy.[61] A comprehensive system of *electoral institutions* is needed on a regular basis for the election or rejection of candidates for public office.[62] A well-articulated *justice system* providing for trial by jury in the relevant range of cases and for the trial of cases both in civil and in criminal law must also be articulated. A *police power and a military power* must be constituted and duly placed within the framework of the laws, under civilian control.

Outside the administrative structures of the government itself, democracy depends upon a panoply of other institutions of great political effect. As we saw in chapter 7, in America *religion* is the first of the political institutions.[63] For it is in religion, specifically Judaism and Christianity, that Americans discovered the ideas of rights of conscience, equality, and liberty itself. Since democracy depends on certain general ideas of this sort, the source of these ideas is foundational.

Next in importance to religion is *a free press*, for to the extent that democracy depends upon the will of the people, it also depends upon the quality of their information and their ability to hear contrasting arguments, well and thoroughly presented.[64] For this purpose, only a free and open public square and public media of communication alive with reasoned discourse from many points of view can refresh the public argument on which democratic consent depends.

In a democracy, citizens are the sovereigns, and political officeholders are in an important sense their employees for a defined and limited period of time. Although societies may differ in how they decide who is entitled to be a citizen and who is not, it is more in keeping with what might be called "the democratic spirit" to make the criteria of citizenship as inclusive as possible.[65]

The Habits Necessary to Making Democracy Work

The Pontifical Academy's scholars made frequent reference to the habits and virtues necessary among a people if they are to make democracy work. Among the virtues sometimes cited were respect for the rule of law,[66] solidarity and justice,[67] equality,[68] tolerance,[69] trust,[70] cooperation,[71] the capacity to reflect and to deliberate,[72] reasonableness,[73] civility,[74] and the like. At least partly with these virtues in mind, some authors also stressed the importance of the system of education for the inculcation of certain virtues.[75]

Some authors preferred the use of the more modern term "values" to the older and traditional "virtues."[76] In the task of maintaining a democracy over a long period of time, it is the more permanent dispositions of a people (their "virtues") that matter—that is to say, the actions they take by second nature and the actions characterizing them when they are caught by surprise or under great pressure from a critical emergency or in the teeth of a powerful temptation.[77]

Civil Society: Religion, Education, Public Opinion, and Media

The Concept of "Civil Society" and the Dependence of Democracy on Culture

Since the year 1900, scores of nations new and old have attempted to replace authoritarian or dictatorial regimes with democratic government but after a time have failed. Many social scientists concur that the problem lies less with the mechanics of political institutions than with much-neglected cultural factors, namely, the ideas, attitudes, and habits that make a people ready for democratic responsibilities. As long ago as 1836, Alexis de Tocqueville discussed three factors that determine the success or failure of new democracies: laws, geography, and above all cultural factors.

> Europeans exaggerate the influence of geography on the lasting powers of democratic institutions. Too much importance is attributed to laws, too little to mores. . . . *The contribution of physical causes is less than that of the laws, and that of laws less than mores.* If in the course of this book I have not succeeded in making the reader feel the importance I attach to the practical experience of the Americans, to their *habits, opinions, and, in a word, their mores*, in maintaining their laws, I have failed in the main object of my work.[78]

At the heart of democracy lies the practice of self-government, by which citizens through their own associations attain their own ends without always turning to the state to take care of all things. Thus, civil society is another form of "government of the people, by the people, for the people," especially in spheres beyond the competence of politics and government officials. For by civil society is meant the active associational life of free citizens pursuing together both the common good and their own particular ends within it. Democracy depends so much on the free activities of *civil society*, both within and outside of politics, as almost to be a synonym for it.[79] Wherever you find a successful democracy, you find a vital civil society.

For most of the activities of a democratic society, though always under the umbrella of the rule of law, take place outside the immediate reach of government agencies through the vast array of associations, organizations, and civic institutions that citizens generate on their own by exercising their right of association. This is the vast panoply of actions carried out by civil society. The Catholic Church has long defended the right of association and singled out associations as not only the heart of civil society but also the preferred dynamic of the social order, as Leo XIII ("the Pope of Associations") did in *Rerum Novarum*.[80] The free society is alive with the energy and initiative of its individual citizens, engaged in multiple activities through their own free associations. It is one of the main purposes of the democratic state to protect, empower, and nurture these vitalities. The state is the servant of civil society, not civil society the servant of the state.[81]

Some of the experts of the PASS, in the Continental tradition, link "civil society" to quasi-official, semi-statal functions.[82] Emperors and kings handed out certain civic tasks to some favored citizens, by way of sinecures or privileges. It was by means of one such grant that Tocqueville was financed for his study of prisons in America, for instance. The political philosophy of the European Enlightenment tended to concentrate on two new modern realities, the individual and the state, while disregarding a more crucial third reality: the many associations and intermediate societies that nurture and undergird both individuals and states.[83] In this spirit, Tocqueville noted that in America the most striking feature of the social order was that wherever one looked, one found associations. He concluded that "the law of association is the first law of democracy."[84]

It comes as no surprise, then, that two of the Pontifical Academy's American experts provided especially rich and positive descriptions of civil society. Glendon wrote:

> Civil Society, in its broadest sense, encompasses all the institutions and social systems that lie between individuals and the state. But I suggest that an important distinction needs to be made between the megastructures of civil society (large corporations, foundations, special interest organizations) and smaller communities of memory and mutual aid.[85]

For Glendon, these institutions and social systems include church, families, guilds, workplace associations, neighborhoods, schools, small businesses, and the like. Jean Bethke Elshtain added:

> For contemporary advocates of civil society, civil society signifies a sphere of associational life that is "more" than families, yes, but it is also other than government. Civil society encompasses labor organizations, professional associations, and social service networks. Political parties are also part of this picture. This network lies outside the formal structure of state power. One aim of maintaining a robust civil society is to forestall concentrations of power at the top or at the core. A second lies in the recog-

nition that only many small-scale civic bodies enable citizens to cultivate democratic civic virtues and to play an active role in civil life.[86]

The relations between civil society, associations, individuals, and states are not always so clear. The traditional ideas, habits, practices, or institutions of people in some cultures pose obstacles to democratic ways of thinking and acting. For instance, Taketoshi Nojiri pointed to obstacles to certain ideas of universal truth.[87] Moreover, Nicholas McNally objected to Western models of free speech, which in his view have destructive results in Africa.[88]

In addition to an active civil society, certain important general ideas must also be widespread if democracy is going to work. For instance, a large number of individual citizens must become aware of their (God-given) power to become agents of their own destiny, to take initiative, and to imagine (and to begin to realize) a new future for themselves and their families.[89] A sufficient number must be willing to see that what has been need not necessarily continue forever. Whole peoples need to learn that fresh thinking and new initiatives are wholesome human characteristics.

Not only does culture differ from culture; the culture of any one nation may very well change over time. Such change is particularly likely when that culture allows a great deal of room for liberty, "heresy," and experiment. One can only imagine the differences in culture between the America that formulated the democratic principles of 1776 and the America that has since passed through such wrenching cultural changes as industrialization, secularization, and the sexual revolution, to mention but a few. In their essays for the PASS about the United States, Professors Elshtain and Glendon discerned in the United States worrisome cultural trends that are potentially corrosive of democracy.[90] A general conclusion from the studies by the PASS may be drawn: *it is particularly in the realm of culture that democracy today, whether in the less developed or in the developed nations, seems most vulnerable—even in crisis.*

Some Individual Fields of "Civil Society"

Since the term "civil society" shelters under its leafy boughs all those smaller societies and associations that operate in the large field between the individual and the state, it is natural to want to inspect some of the more important mediating institutions more closely.

Religion.   In a penetrating paper, Pierpaolo Donati showed how classical views of religion, civil society, and democracy such as Tocqueville's have been eclipsed by new social developments. From religion, the American founders got their understanding of the source of human rights ("endowed in them by their Creator"). By contrast, in Europe the Enlightenment saw "transcendental religion as an obstacle to democracy." It forced religions, in order to be heard in the public square, to adapt themselves to the linguistic codes of secular democracy. The result has been that "(political) democracy has lost its conceptual bases, and (established) religion has lost its identity."[91] Nowadays, however, secular activists ignore religion as if it no longer has relevance.

Donati offers a robust view of the indispensable contributions made by Catholicism, Judaism, and even Islam from the 13th to the 14th centuries in producing "currents of thought and social actors which worked in favor of various models of modernity and in particular, of different models of relations between religion and democracy." He cites the work of Randall Collins, who shows that political democracy in the West does *not* have secular roots, but rather that "Western democracy is only conceivable on the basis of its Christian religious presuppositions." Gradually, however, the hostile Enlightenment view of religion drove out historical memory. "The nation state came to take the place of the church." Religion has now been confined to the private sphere where, always held under public suspicion, it is "restricted to the sound upbringing of the person." Modern society insists upon principles of ethical neutrality, driving the language of religion "to the rubbish heap."[92] A new possibility is emerging, however, Donati argues, since the democratic state, in becoming increasingly secular, has lost all sense of soul, interior vitality, and humanizing energy.

Just at this time, Catholic social doctrine has become "the most *articulated and complex*" vision of actual political reality—namely, that religion is "a prerequisite of democracy [but] is at the same time distinct from, and supra-functional in relation to, democracy." The Catholic position avoids both secularization and fundamentalism, avoids the rocks on the one side and the whirlpools on the other, "avoids both the privatization and the radicalization" of religion. The Church has developed a theory of democracy and human rights, a concern for the common service that religion and democracy must render to the human person, and a proof that religion can infuse a materialistic democracy with a new soul.[93]

In Donati's new semantics, "democracy is not merely procedural and religion is not a mere private affair. Religion becomes the sphere of a vivification of a civil society which gives substance and motivation to democratic procedures."[94] Religion provides a narrative framework for both an entire culture and each person within it and holds even the simplest of citizens, as well as the most intellectual, to a supra-human standard of human excellence.

Education.   As Paulus Zulu puts it, "A sound education broadens the cognitive frames of reference, develops the capacities to think critically, and facilitates the range of options."[95] Another point of his is also valuable: "In political terms, an education for democracy will educate students in the analysis of how power works in producing and shaping knowledge, and how ideological barriers to democracy such as class, race, age, gender and birthplace lead to one form of domination or another."[96] It is quite true that whatever the power position of any citizen or group of citizens, or whatever their ideology, and certainly whatever their class, race, age, gender, and birthplace, all persons must be subject to checks and balances, and none must be allowed to gather concentrated and unchecked power. The successful functioning of democracy depends crucially on the Jewish and Christian notion of original sin, or on some secular equivalent, such as, "Since everyone sometimes sins, no one may be trusted with unchecked power."

Since democracy is a difficult political order to establish, and even more difficult to maintain in all its rigor, education must supply young citizens with stories, narratives, and models that fire their imaginations and inspire them to accept self-discipline and face hardship and sacrifice. Since democracy depends on the faithful transmission of a certain number of practical insights, education must also include the careful and self-critical appropriation of its fundamental practical ideas by every succeeding generation. As the Virginia Declaration of Rights insisted in 1776, "frequent recurrence to fundamental principles" is a necessary condition for the survival of human rights.[97]

Finally, of course, education in a democratic society must equip citizens with both the analytic habits and the information necessary for sound deliberation. For in giving their consent to particular public actions at critical moments in the history of their nation, citizens must make well-informed judgments.

Public Opinion.   As Janusz Ziolkowski points out, one must distinguish between two different conceptions of "public opinion."[98] One is merely the opinions held by a majority, which "can be manufactured as well by minority pressure groups"[99] and can also be used by a majority to stifle minority views. Most political opinions "ultimately rest upon instincts; that is to say, upon moral sentiments of approval or reprobation, and upon emotional proclivities of like or dislike. This kind of public opinion should be seen as biased."[100]

By contrast, public opinion in the sense on which the genuine practice of democracy depends is formed by extended and protracted *argument* in which many persons in the public listen carefully to reasons for and against, raise objections, study how these objections are met, and thus slowly put together a reasoned view of the matter, and perhaps not the view with which they began the discussion. Ziolkowski puts this succinctly: "The formation of public opinion [rightly understood] in a given grouping of people occurs through the give and take of discussion."[101] And again:

> In a nutshell, public opinion to be truly worthy of the name, to be the proper motive force in a democracy, must be really public; and popular government is based upon the reception of a public opinion of that kind. In order to be public, a majority is not enough, and unanimity is not required, but the opinion must be such that while the minority may not share it, they are bound by conviction, not by fear, to accept it; and if democracy is complete, this submission must be given ungrudgingly.[102]

It will be clear that if democracy is to work, public opinion in this sense must be widely diffused throughout the society, persistent and lasting, intense enough to provoke argument, and forged in the give-and-take through which reasonableness is shown.[103]

The Media.   In analyzing the media, the PASS experts paid special attention to such very recent media as fax, the Internet, and the telephone. All these very recent media played important roles in the short-lived revolution in China in 1989, in the collapse of the Iron Curtain, and in many other struggles for human rights and democracy in our time. Predominantly, however, PASS experts seemed to be thinking of newspapers, radio, cinema, and television—the major mass media for the discussion of political and social questions. "Such media are not seen as commercial companies like others of that kind, because they ought to contribute to long-term social benefits, mainly in the cultural and political area." In other words, the public holds such media to the standard that they "should serve the common good (the social interest)." The media themselves put forward this standard "when they proclaim their public mission, expecting legal and economic privileges in return."[104]

But what does it mean for the media "to serve the common good"? Ziolkowski put forth three main criteria: the media should "express all that is best in the cultural achievement of the nation" and, in that and related ways, "perform an educational role," lifting the minds of citizens toward still higher cultural achievements. They should also "reflect the culture and language of the people they serve according to the latter's life experience"; this role requires good and sympathetic contact between the media elites and the ordinary people they serve. Finally, the media should also support originality and cultural creativity. Otherwise, cultural decline will set in, and democracy will suffer with it.[105]

Culture and Economics

The Challenge to "Values" in a Pluralistic Context

Under the conditions of pluralism common to most democracies today, the question of "values" is a vexed subject. Curiously enough, our pluralistic situation makes the concept of "values" extremely useful to social science.[106] For the term is by itself noncommittal as regards truth. Values are quite vulnerable to mere subjectivism. There are *your* values, *his* values, *her* values, all sorts of values. The term suggests by its most common usage that the individual human subject puts into reality whatever importance or significance he chooses. Value is conferred not by an objective moral world, which commands the respect of all and separates out (from among proposed values) the sheep from the goats, but by the individual human subject, who merely chooses what he chooses. As some philosophers have noted, the more common coin of ethical discourse before Nietzsche was "virtue," but after Nietzsche "values" became the new currency. Thus, unless scholars are careful, several of our experts warned, even the use of the term "values" may prejudice an argument in favor of moral relativism or (more exactly) sheer subjectivism.

Taketoshi Nojiri explained why many today fear the principle "that there is an absolute and universal truth and that it can be accepted without reservation by anyone."[107] Such a position stifles dialogue. What does a man who possesses universal truth have to learn from others? Historically, Christian, Muslim, and other theocracies have used appeals to truth to justify the use of force against the consciences of others. This history has discredited any abrupt appeal to absolute truth, a Scylla where shipwrecks abound. The common opposite reaction, an abrupt appeal to relativism, throws one into the whirlpools of Charybdis.[108] If all values, including the true and the good, are purely subjective, then dialogue is pointless, for no criterion exists to distinguish what is closer to the truth from what is more remote.

To meet this problem, Nojiri proposed, against the absolutists, that although there are certain universal criteria whose existence incites an effort to discover them more exactly, no one is in complete possession of them. To grasp that one's own perception of them is imperfect is to concede that some degree of truth may be grasped even while there are further degrees yet to be grasped—and which may perhaps already be seen by others. In this light, dialogue is a positive advantage to oneself: it offers a chance to advance in the truth. "To be imperfect is not to be false. And it often happens that a truth only vaguely known in the beginning eventually comes to be clarified."[109] This proposal offers a powerful new motive for democracy and gives democracy an important epistemic function. It affirms that the consent of a majority may be formed around an imperfect but real grasp of the truth. Thus, real progress in coming to grips with the truth about humankind might be attained, and an attitude of personal humility and respect for others can be nurtured.[110]

Since modern democracy *is* an experiment testing whether governments can be formed through reflection and choice or must forever be formed through force or chance, it is a necessary condition of democracy that reasoned dialogue be possible and in fact occur.[111] By its very nature, then, democracy relies upon a notion of truth sufficient to distinguish wise deliberation from foolish, truth from falsehood, the common good from common misfortune, and the public interest from the public woe.[112]

An example may make this clear. At the beginning of the American republic (1787), the union of all the states was necessary for survival, yet although nearly all recognized that the institution of slavery was evil, not all states were ready to eliminate abruptly their long reliance on slavery. The temporary toleration of slavery was understood as a necessary evil. The moral distinction between freedom and slavery was one of those "truths" held to be self-evident to common sense, even though the political time was not ripe to follow through on its full implications.[113] By 1865 the new nation was tested in a great civil war, experiencing in unprecedented bloodshed "the grapes of wrath," until emancipation was at last put into practice. Under great pressure, something like Nojiri's "imperfect recognition" advancing toward greater clarity had slowly occurred. Such emergences of moral truth under historical pressure offer a refutation of absolute relativism. Under absolute relativism, there can be no measure of "progress." One man's "progress" is another man's "decline." Everything becomes a matter of power. The step from relativism to fascism is short, and dull-witted thugs will again jump that distance quickly, as they did in the third decade of the 20th century.

Nonetheless, the compatibility of democracy with truth is, as underlined by Habib Malik of Lebanon, uneasy. Malik was poignantly aware, living under threat within a Muslim nation, that a majority can too easily render a minority helpless against a pervasive injury steadily inflicted upon it. He emphasized by many different arguments the need for a concept of democracy that goes well beyond majority rule in order to place equal weight on the principle of "the protection of the equal rights of minorities." Minorities need full institutional protection against the tyranny of majorities. Malik was particularly concerned about notions that define truth in terms of the views of a majority:

> Truth is sacred and absolute, meaning it has divine origins and is ontologically grounded in the Creator Himself. Truth can therefore reside in a numerically small group—even in a minority of one. The imperium of truth is not and cannot be democratic. There is no escape from the inherent

opposition that pits political notions of democracy and what they assume about truth against the unchanging and universal concept of truth offered by religion.[114]

Nojiri adds another point. No majority possesses the whole truth. Minorities may have hold of an important part of the truth that needs to be heard both for the sake of the whole truth and also to prevent blind autocracy.[115]

Kaufmann also provided an important warning. Many critics of the West complain of a decline of values, a decay of moral habits. But in fact options have multiplied before our eyes, and many possible values that now shine before us are in conflict. Moral tentativeness results because we are overpowered by an *excess* of moral possibilities, not by an unwillingness to do the right thing.[116]

Is democracy itself a value? Some of the Pontifical Academy's experts thought so.[117] They linked democracy to such *ideals* as equal dignity, participation in governance, and solidarity. In a very European way, Schooyans distinguished between "political" democracy and "social" democracy.[118] He means by the latter efforts to raise up the economic level of the poor, to advance "social justice," and the like. Other writers resist limiting the term "democracy" to matters of procedures and mechanics and want at least to connote by the word the ideals, beliefs, and values associated with it. Hans Zacher, however, argued against too loose a meaning for the term: "Democracy represents a chance for those values that are alive in society, but it cannot in the long run create greater respect for values than they already enjoy in society. *Democracy* does not in itself introduce values, nor does *democracy* itself produce values. It mediates between values."[119]

Indeed, there does seem to be a great gain for clarity of thought if we differentiate among the functions of each of the three systems necessary for a free society—the political system, the economic system, and the cultural system (as suggested by the threefold subdivision of *Gaudium et Spes* and the explicit differentiation in *Centesimus Annus*.)[120] Like Zacher, I would say then that the political functions belong to *democracy* and its proper institutions, and the formation of ideas, values, and virtues belong to the *moral-cultural system* and its institutions. The political system depends on the moral-cultural system (and on the economic system, as we will shortly see).

In a word, the very large task of thinking through the virtues and "values" necessary for democracy in today's intellectual climate has not yet been completed, but several overly simple solutions have been pointed out and surmounted.

The Relation of Democracy to Economics

It has become widely accepted that a certain degree of oppressive poverty keeps populations so close to the sheer struggle for survival that the prospects of democracy among them are slim.

> When people are preoccupied with basic issues of nutrition, shelter, health and education, when they are unable to read and understand the most basic items of news on matters occurring within their own countries, let alone those on the international plane, it is unrealistic to expect that they will be particularly exercised by the activities of government officials or the operations of big business or organized labor.[121]

Another way of putting this point is to say that a dynamic economy is a necessary but not sufficient condition for democracy. For if all democracy affords people is the chance to vote every two or four years, without bringing about improvement in their economic conditions, especially among the many poor, people will not love democracy—they will reject it. Thus, the state of the economic system is crucial. National elections, indeed, often turn on economic questions.

To be a good match for democracy, a nation's economic system needs to operate under the rule of law and respect the rights of personal economic initiative, private property, and association (among both business corporations or partnerships and labor unions). It needs also to encourage invention and discovery, recognizing that the cause of wealth is primarily the human mind.[122] And it needs to practice the art of subsidiarity so that excessive regulation and taxation do not prevent the formation of new small businesses, which are the chief creators of new employment. A society is not likely to have new employees without encouraging new employers: no employers, no employees.

The Welfare State.   Since most of the essays on economic problems were presented by experts from Europe, they inclined in the social democratic direction and kept the public policy needs of the European welfare democracies in fullest view. Even critics will happily note that the condition of democracy in Europe is far better today than it was 100, or even 50, years ago, and that much of the credit for popular contentment is due to the European welfare states. Schmidt listed several impressive achievements of the European welfare state.[123]

Still, Americans are likely to see matters differently. In particular, those Americans critical of the center-left are likely to judge that the social democracies of Western Europe are heading into a major crisis. There are many sources of this looming crisis: excessive promises of future benefits, a shrinking birthrate, extended longevity, and increasingly expensive medical technologies. This crisis is likely to be more severe for not being sufficiently feared.

In *Centesimus Annus*, Pope John Paul II recognizes the benefits brought by the welfare state in the decades after World War II but also notes certain problems that have occurred since then. The Pope points to some especially damaging unintended consequences of the modern "Social Assistance State," as he calls it. It has become insupportably expensive. Rather than ameliorating important social problems, it has made several of them worse. And it has imposed a certain impersonality, distance, and coldness on relations that were once marked by the warmth of personal attention.[124]

Labor.   Since the great mistake of the 19th century had been the loss of the laboring classes from the Church (Leo XIII), the Church made huge efforts to stay close to labor during the 20th century and to plead labor's cause before the powers that be. The research of Colin Crouch has shown that, as the 21st century begins, changes are occurring within the class of labor itself; that economic globalization is affecting the conditions of labor (probably) unfavorably within the developed democracies and (perhaps) favorably within the poorest nations, which are only just beginning to attract or develop industry. Important factual questions have arisen, such as whether "outside the old cores" of "male, manual manufacturing work" other recently growing occupations, especially in the private service sector, will find some form of institutional expression and protection. Crouch also has asked whether "the marginal and the insecure" will remain outside existing labor organizations, relatively powerless and silent.[125]

Dr. Therborn pointed out that "the labor movement produced both the major revolutions of the century—directly in the Russian case, more indirectly by molding the revolutionary cadre in the Chinese case—and the most important program of comprehensive social reform in the form of Scandinavian Social Democracy."[126] He neglected to point out that journalists and other intellectuals were often in the vanguard of the working class, and often more reliably both socialist and internationalist. Therborn also neglected to point out that the labor movement of Poland, Solidarnosc, led the way in bringing down communism in Eastern Europe and eventually the Soviet Union itself. By contrast, Ziolkowski noted that "patriotism and religion, in combination, are more important influences than class conflict."[127] He expressly praised the liberating energies of "the Christian vision of man" inside the labor movement.[128]

Unemployment.   One of the great problems for many social democracies in Western Europe has been the persistence of unemployment. The burdens placed by law on employers discourages the hiring of new employees. The barriers that need to be surmounted by new entrepreneurs prevent the rapid and frequent creation of new enterprises, which in dynamic economies are the most abundant sources of employment. In some nations with low unemployment, more than 80 percent of all new jobs created during the last 40 years have been in the small-business sector, mostly among new businesses. In some countries the political class regards a given level of employment as more or less fixed, and thus its favorite remedy for unemployment is to further divide the existing sum of work hours by shortening the workday for all workers, hoping to encourage some openings for the unemployed. In other countries the political class has become convinced that openness and ease in forming new small businesses is the most successful avenue for creating new jobs and constantly expanding the circle of existing jobs. This last strategy is, of course, the one I support.

The Decline of Democracy

Global Pressures upon Democracy

As Russell Hittinger has written, "In 1500 there were about five hundred independent political units in Europe; when Leo wrote *Rerum Novarum* [1891], there were twenty-five."[129] In that movement, the modern nation-state took shape from its smaller constituent parts. Then, in a different historical turn, the Austro-Hungarian Empire (and others) broke up in 1918 and a number of new nation-states were created; that was followed by an even more worldwide breakup of empires after World War II and a tremendous expansion of independent nation-states. In this way, the great political reality of the last 200 years has been the invention and growing importance of the nation-state. But as the 21st century begins, the nation-state is losing its salience—or is it?

One of the preconditions of the invention and maturing of the social democratic state in the decades following 1945 in Europe was the relative isolation of each nation-state and the ability of its government to administer it in considerable independence from other states. The stated aim of the European welfare state is to provide a basic security and decent living to all classes of citizens. In this way, the welfare state overcame the millennial poverty that had weighed heavily on Europe's lower classes for centuries. But the necessary precondition for the social democratic experiment was tight control by the nation-state over its own monetary, fiscal, and other economic policies. The social democratic state had two further preconditions: it depended on a strong preference in the population for social security rather than for opportunity and risk and on an equally strong popular tolerance for high levels of taxation, both on income and on purchases. In an increasingly interactive global order, all these premises have now suddenly been put in question. That is why the powerful international movement called "globalization" has awakened considerable resistance in many of the social democracies.

The term "globalization" has many meanings. Scholars who stress the *economic* dimension are focused on phenomena such as: the diffusion of the products of one country to many other countries (Toyotas, McDonald's hamburgers, Volkswagens); the immense increase in the volume of global trade from one country to another; instantaneous movements of capital from one country to another; intensified competitive pressure upon local producers by producers from other countries; the quickened tendency of large national corporations to move some of their activities into distant locations with lower costs; and the pressure on nations to lower their tax rates to levels competitive with other nations, lest citizens and businesses move abroad. This is a significant list of economic worries for political elites trying to maintain tight control over the resulting turbulence within their own national borders.

Other scholars emphasize the *cultural* dimension of globalization. Louis Sabourin wrote:

> We are seeking to understand how national communities can preserve their identities while accepting new social values, how they can maintain a collective memory while integrating themselves into the contemporary global society, how the necessity for profit can exist alongside the importance of sharing, how competition can go hand in hand with cooperation.[130]

Thierry de Montbrial criticized American and French pretensions to define the "universal values" that other civilizations must adopt.[131]

Other scholars call attention to the *political* dimension of globalization—a nearly universal awakening of individual men and women to their proper dignity and rights and a new vision of at least a minimal decent prosperity for those who now suffer terribly. Thomas A. Mensah described the effect in Africa:

> With the improvement in the global communications system, large proportions of the populations of Africa have come to know much more than their governments would have wished them to know. In this way they have learned much more about the achievements and failures of different forms of governments and economic systems in other parts of the world, and the standard of life in countries with different political and constitutional systems. They have also become aware of the growing interest of the international community in democratic governance and sound economic management, and the international support for democracy and human rights in the continent of Africa and elsewhere. This development has not only undermined the previously successful propaganda of governments, but has also given very potent incentives and encouragements to those who fight for democracy in these countries. In the past these persons were often discouraged by the fact that there was not much support at home for their efforts or much interest in their struggle internationally.[132]

Globalization, then, has economic, cultural, and political dimensions—some favorable, some stressful.

The Entropy of Democracy

Hot water cools, mountains erode, and all nature is vulnerable to entropy, as Newton taught us; the clock of nature ticks down. In an even more perishable state, democracy is also subject to entropy. Exercising the free consent of the governed, the governed themselves may at any time freely yield up their liberty to a dictator. Furthermore, over time there are tendencies within even the best-run democracies that result in the gradual slipping away of liberties. Tocqueville himself predicted that democracy would end in a "new soft despotism" brought about by the triumph of the idea of equality over the idea of liberty. Finally, the loss of civic virtues—accompanied by personal moral decadence—also threatens the texture of daily democratic life. Democracy requires citizens who can practice self-government in their private lives if they wish to maintain self-government in their public lives.[133] Progress is not automatic; on the contrary, decline is automatic, unless vigilant renewal prevails against it.

The sustained existence of democratic regimes is relatively rare in history, especially in the modern sense that democracy is "the responsible participation of the human person in elaborating the collective destiny."[134] As Hans Zacher observed, such a form of government is "always under attack."[135]

Our experts found, for instance, that democracy deteriorates when:

- People under a democratic regime do not promote the virtues necessary for maintaining authentic human freedom.[136]
- Majority rule suppresses the rights and interests of minority groups.[137]
- Lack of dialogue silences significant social groups, and disenfranchisement denies them the power of the vote.[138]
- Poor economic conditions make survival so difficult that people have no space in which to reflect upon their political situation.[139]
- The culture does not encourage responsible social activity on the part of its people, as when an excess of materialism, individualism, corruption, or social apathy suffocates political activity.[140]
- Government becomes so powerful as to severely compromise the responsible social activity of its people.[141]

Glendon lists several peculiarly contemporary threats to democratic experiments: the atrophy of the democratic elements in modern republics; the decline of mediating structures; the specter of new forms of oligarchy; materialism and extreme individualism; and finally, a spreading lack of confidence that there are any common truths to which men and women of different backgrounds and cultures can repair.[142]

Recommendations for the Future

The 37 papers produced by the PASS on various aspects of democracy are rich, complex, and at many points in argument with one another. It is not an unfriendly observation to note that they sometimes clarify disputes of theory better than they illuminate practical paths for ordinary Christians to follow in day-to-day living. In any case, the development of Catholic social thought requires in its next stage that social scientists bring these theoretical principles down two or three steps closer to practical action.

The formulation of "practical-practical propositions" would be a significant service to the pastors and lay activists of the Church, not only in the developing nations but also in the most developed nations. By "practical-practical propositions," following up on a suggestion of Jacques Maritain's, I mean propositions of a certain generality and yet of sufficient immediacy that they could be put into practice by hardworking and serious Christians already deeply involved in the practical complexities of daily life. Maritain favored relatively short-term, achievable goals for social action designed to meet existing (i.e., changeable) historical realities.[143] For example, the various definitions of Christian democracy and its concrete methods, as developed in the 1930s and 1940s, provided one set of useful maxims for laypeople in Europe and Latin America and elsewhere for the next two generations. New problems lie before us now.

In the ministry of Pope John Paul II, the Church is fully on the side of democracy and human rights. In free societies, individual Catholics can implant the yeast of the Gospels into the texture of daily life, both in their businesses and in the exercise of their political responsibilities. Yet still there is far too little instruction for ordinary Catholics in the pews concerning what they ought to do to infuse the democratic order with an inspiring vision of the human person. A free society allows them the free exercise of their consciences in the economic and the political order. This freedom opens up to the Church a new method for making itself present in history—to incarnate itself, so to speak, in the very tissue of its times. Instead of trying to make its presence felt from the top down, in the institutional apparatus of church and state, it is now free to make its presence known from the bottom up, from deep roots among ordinary and humble people. The Church could vivify the institutions of democracy from within, along the lines spelled out with scientific clarity by Donati.

Imagine a young priest in Nigeria, for instance, called upon to provide leadership in the field of Catholic social thought for the priests and leading laypersons throughout his nation. This priest sees the need to prepare his people for democracy, as well as for economic initiative and cooperative work in the workplaces of modern business. What sort of practical instruction can he give them in forming associations, organizations, and political and social movements of their own? Which virtues should he encourage mothers to foster in their children? Which specific modern vices should mothers encourage their children to avoid? His people have had no experience of modern institutions; they have been taught neither the inner principles nor the moral hazards of such institutions. They do not know precisely how the middle classes of the West reached such levels of wealth as they have. Did they do so by stealing from the state, as his parishioners see so many in their own midst—often the champions of modernization—doing? His people do not know what responsibilities public servants have in a modern society. In their immediate surroundings, they have few role-models to follow. How to behave democratically involves behavioral codes to which no one has given them the key. "Economic progress," "small-business formation," and even "democracy" are terms that conjure up something mythical and distant; they have no immediate or familiar referents in their own experience.

Democracy and modern business practices, in sum, have had a specific historical genesis in nations far away. Moreover, the practices of both democracy and a modern economy embody specific virtues that are not connatural to all cultures equally, even though the vision of human dignity and the ideal of freedom from torture and tyranny belong to all humans (if often subconsciously felt rather than consciously articulated). As Tocqueville pointed out, democracy takes on different forms in different cultures—its development would be different in France, he predicted, from its development in America.[144]

Using the 12 questions that frame the subsections of this chapter, I recommend that Catholic leaders—and others who wish to follow suit—develop three or four practical-practical propositions under each heading. Such a teaching guide would offer to our young priest in Nigeria a useful course of instruction to hand out to his priests and leading laypersons; they in turn might use it in teaching others. The aim of such a program would be that the Catholic faith be realized more perfectly in a new democratic and modern economic setting, in such a way as to command the respect of all who observe it. In secular terms, this would contribute substantially to the health of democracy in many significant nations around the world, not least in Eastern Europe, Latin America, and parts of Asia.

Next, we might imagine a similar priest in Aachen, or LeMans, or Chicago. We need a different set of practical-practical propositions suitable for Catholics living under a more mature, perhaps even tired, form of democracy. The problems of mature democracies are not at all the same as those of cultures in which democracy is still in its infancy. The temptations and fresh possibilities of Europe and North America may be quite different from those of the Mideast, Africa, Asia, or Latin America. Nonetheless, the 12-point outline developed for use in Nigeria could serve as an equally useful framework in both old and new democracies, even though the practical-practical propositions to be listed under each schema would be appropriately different.

Finally, the framework developed for the Nigerian priest might also have a quite different use. It is highly probable that other scholars and practitioners would see gaps in it and discern better ways in which to structure it. Merely placing it out where we could all examine it would provide a useful service by inviting significant correction.

In sum, Catholic social thought has not yet fully developed its practical guidance for the building up and vivifying of democracy and the institutions of human rights. This development can be hastened by the articulation of practical-practical propositions. Like it or not, the vast majority of Christians around the world are likely to live for this generation and the next striving to build or maintain democracies that protect them from torture and tyranny and protect their rights. Although no one democracy is exactly like another—each is tempered to the realities of its own culture and history—still, each draws nourishment from a common stock of hard-won institutional principles and an analogous list of necessary "humanizing" virtues. If the Church could state these practical principles clearly and describe these virtues (and opposite vices) informatively, it would provide the whole world with a quite useful teaching instrument.

Here then is my first proposal. Under the outline of the 12 questions listed in this chapter, two short teaching documents or practical guides could be prepared, offering practical maxims on infusing democratic societies with a Christian vision of human flourishing. The first document should be proposed for societies just considering or in the early stages of building democracy. The second document should be designed for mature democracies in danger of decline.

Does the Catholic Church promote democracy? Yes, but it could do so in much greater depth and practical detail, to the immense benefit of the rest of the world.

My second proposal is a detailed study of the mutual understandings and distinctive differences between Western Europe and the United States concerning both democracy and the welfare state. Many of the PASS experts alluded to these important differences between Europe and America, many on profound matters of principle, which are scarcely ever addressed (on either side of the ocean) in sufficient depth or extension. In the long struggle against Nazism and communism, our differences were happily overlooked and blurred. But left unexamined, these natural differences might give rise to resentments and suspicions that could grow over time to quite dangerous proportions. In the new century, the future of both democracy and Judaism/Christianity and the condition of the less developed world will be much affected by how well Europe and America understand each other and work together. Among the many nations throughout the world that are taking their first steps in democracy, a certain confusion reigns concerning some of the contrary ideas to be found in the two most significant strains of democracy, American and European. The whole world has a stake in coming to understand these differences clearly, as regards both democracy and the welfare state.

What better institution than the Church, unifying and healing force that it is, to sponsor this serious study of the important differences in the ideals, ideas, and habits of Europeans and Americans? I wish the Church would commission a special study group to spend at least one meeting annually for at least three years with the assigned task of specifying distinctive differences between European and American understandings of democracy and social welfare. In later years, this comparison could be extended to other world cultures. This would begin the transcultural conversation that the world of the 21st century very much needs. Such a study would be a first step in the shaping of Caritapolis.

Chapter Nine

⟨∞⟩

CAN ISLAM COME TO TERMS
WITH DEMOCRACY?

In EARLY SEPTEMBER 2002, I was asked to give five lectures to the senior field commanders of the Sudanese resistance fighting against the oppressive Islamist government of Sudan. From what I had read in the papers, I expected most of these commanders to be Christian. To my surprise, more than half were serious Muslims. All together, Christians and Muslims and representatives of ancient African religions of nature wanted me to lecture on the religious roots of human dignity, liberty, and human rights. They were willing to hear about secular justifications of these concepts (as in Hobbes and Locke), and they were attentive to a discussion of how Jews and Christians had their own religious imperatives to develop these concepts and to support experiments in institutionalizing them. But what they really wanted to hear was how Muslims could develop concepts of human liberty, dignity, and equality, including a Muslim doctrine of human rights. "We are serious Muslims," the majority said. "We try to live as devout Muslims. Please, help us to find a Muslim theory that embraces the best of the modern world, such as democracy and the Universal Declaration of Human Rights."

"Why," they asked, "when Bin Laden finally moved to adopt the methods of the 20th century, why did he choose as his models the worst of the century, Hitler and Stalin, rather than the best, the tradition of democracy and human rights?" "It cannot be," one said in plaintive tones, "that dignity, equality, liberty, and human rights are for Jews and Christians and secular humanists only, but not for Muslims!"[1]

This vivid experience in Asmara taught me that there is immense turmoil in the bosom of Islam these days. One of the commanders had been a professor at McGill in Canada, another a professor at the Sorbonne; both said they were serious Muslims, but not specialists in religion. The others too, most of them professional people, thought themselves to be both modern men and women and devoutly Muslim. Nonetheless, learned imams had accused them of abandoning Islam by their commitments to human rights and democracy. They could not comprehend how this could be so, but did not know how to argue against the imams. They begged me for help. Not being an expert in Islam, I could not do all they asked. I felt helpless.

Yet it did seem to me, I said to them, that Islamic belief in the Creator and in reward and punishment for our deeds on Earth must give grounds for a rich theory of human dignity and liberty, whether or not any group of Muslim theologians had yet drawn out all the relevant implications of these doctrines. And I agreed with them that it cannot be that economic development and the blessings of democracy have been intended by Allah only for Christians, Jews, and secular humanists but not for Muslims. What I learned from these resistance fighters was that, at the beginning of the 21st century, one of the most dramatic struggles on Earth now rages inwardly in the souls of devout Muslims.

Another dramatic struggle rages out in public between a minority of Islamic terrorists (such as the world saw in the dramatic plane crashes of September 11, 2001) and a large majority of Muslims who love their religion but wish to live under governments that respect their rights and liberties. Why, my new friends asked me passionately, are the vast majority of Muslims living in poverty, with so little opportunity for advancement and personal growth, under the relentless eyes of secret police? Why can't Muslims be free like other people and find opportunity and prosperity like other normal people?

A Catholic's View of Islam

To introduce a note of concreteness into a discussion that, however rare until recently, has usually been airy with abstraction, I would like to describe my own awareness of Islam ever since I was in the eighth grade. In that year, my parents moved to McKeesport, Pennsylvania, the hometown (although we did not know it then) of Andy Warhol, championship high school football, and declining steel mills, where they enrolled me in Saint Pius V School. Pope Pius V (1566–1572) was famous for popularizing the rosary as a family tradition in Catholic life. That happened this way: While begging European princes to face up to the menace of gathering Muslim naval power in the Mediterranean, Pius V simultaneously encouraged Catholics everywhere to pray the rosary, not then in such wide use as today, to beseech the Mother of Jesus to extend her motherly protection over the menaced Catholic lands. The threat was altogether real. Muslim fleets were raiding Christian cities with ever more daring, carrying off huge numbers of men as prisoners for their galley slaves and boys and girls for their harems, burning churches, and looting treasuries. There was no unified Christian fleet to oppose them. All Italy was in danger of occupation.

I grew up learning about the Battle of Lepanto, whose anniversary was celebrated every October 7, in honor of Our Lady of the Most Holy Rosary, also now known as Our Lady of Victory. Lepanto was a great story of wit and courage and victory against all odds. That day's outcome brought an outpouring of relief to all Europe, the lifting of a great dread. Miguel de Cervantes, who fought in the battle, called it one of the greatest days in the history of the world. As a naval clash, it was of an order and magnitude that outranked any that had gone before. Needless to say, when in the spring of 1947 I suggested at Saint Pius V that our class publish a yearbook by which to remember our graduation, the natural name for us to choose was "the Crusader."

The "clash of civilizations" was not therefore a new theme to me when some 50 years later I heard Samuel Huntington deliver his first lecture by that name at the American Enterprise Institute. It was a clash that had already left its mark on my imagination. I had learned in my days at Harvard, and then as a young professor at Stanford, and of course in my reading in history, that outside the Catholic world of my youth the "Crusades" were commonly looked upon by secular and Protestant scholars as a disgraceful chapter in Western history. A warlike Christianity was presented as a contradiction in terms. The cruelty and looting rampages in which the crusader armies sometimes, alas, engaged received considerably more attention than the depredations that had stirred them to action and given them the moral energy to spend years away from home and in danger of death in order to free their fellow Christians to the East. Muslim writers sometimes suggest that "the West" has a common anti-Muslim view of the thousand-year clash between East and West from about 630 to 1690 A.D. That was not my experience. It seemed to me that many secular and Protestant writers rather took the side of the Muslims against the Catholics in assessing rights and wrongs.

However that may be, I think it useful to tell the story of Lepanto briefly, to give a flavor of the clash of civilizations when Islam was by far the superior power and still expanding westward and northward. In this light, Lepanto forms a useful background for a contemporary discussion of a new period of Islamic resurgence and for a side-by-side discussion of the struggles of both Catholicism and Islam to engraft modern democracy onto the living vine of their own traditions, as a fitting fruit of their respective religious visions. The Catholic tradition has a head start in the process of institutionalizing the theme of human liberty—certainly so on the theoretical level, as we saw in chapter 1—but it has had many practical problems to overcome. A dialogue with Islamic scholars and statesmen about analogous difficulties, objections, fears, and anticipations, one might imagine, ought to be of considerable fruitfulness. The explosion of vulgar secularism in the West during the past 50 years has presented convincing lessons as to why a purely secular, irreligious, and morally relativistic solution to the problem of society and state is not likely to be either workable or attractive. The religious half (probably more than half) of the world will find it unlivable.

I am far from suggesting that the Battle of Lepanto is immediately relevant. But recalling it with some vividness does serve the purpose of reminding ourselves of the days when Islamic power was the greatest in the world, especially on the seas, and very near its highwater point. That time was not so long ago. The discovery of America by Columbus was by 1571 already 80 years in the past. So it is worth swinging the mind backward for a moment, to bring to mind the long sweep of Muslim glory that led up to Lepanto.

Barely 100 years after Muhammad founded the rapidly expanding faith of Islam in what is today Saudi Arabia, his armies had conquered all of the Middle East, all of North Africa, all of Spain, and were soon marching into southern France, where, in 732 A.D., their astonishing advance was finally checked. In 1095 the Christians of Europe at last began the counterattack, the First Crusade. By 1099 they had regained the Holy Land and much of the eastern Mediterranean coast, and they held these for some generations. By 1200, however, Muslim armies began pushing the Christian forces back toward Europe, and generation by generation they gradually reclaimed the eastern Mediterranean as a Muslim sea.

By 1571, threatening Europe on its eastern flank and aiming first at Italy's Adriatic coast, an enormous Muslim fleet under the Ottomans gathered in major ports in Greece. In August a smaller Muslim fleet had taken Famagusta, the Venetian port on Cyprus, and brutally tortured its inhabitants. In October the Muslim commanders expected their new assault on all of Italy to be just as easy. They believed that it would open up for them a major base on their way to the total conquest of Europe.

Rather than heed the urgent calls of Pius V to take to arms to defend Europe from the gathering assault, the Christian monarchs of Europe, now divided by the Reformation and many other internal rivalries, dithered, dallied, and yakked. In G. K. Chesterton's well-known ballad:

> *The cold queen of England is looking in the glass;*
> *The shadow of the Valois is yawning at the Mass;*
> *From evening isles fantastical rings faint the Spanish gun. . .* [2]

In that vacuum, the young Prince Don Juan of Austria struggled virtually alone to put together a presentable European fleet, composed of squadrons from the Knights of Malta, from the Kingdom of Genoa and the Republic of Venice, and from Spain and the papal states, plus a few stray ships from France and Britain. By September of that year, he had managed to put this small armada to sea and made a swift preemptive strike on the Muslim fleet before it could come near to Italy.

By early October, Don Juan had lured the Muslim fleet out from its safe haven in the Greek Isles to sail into the Bay of Lepanto. So it was that on October 7 the Saracen fleet loomed into sight on the horizon in all its confident magnificence. So certain of victory was the Sultan that he had his treasure ships follow close up in the rear, for he intended to cut the smaller Christian fleet to shreds and then sail on for the unimpeded conquest of Italy. The two fleets sailed directly into one another on that fair October day.

Splendid new technology and tactics gave the European fleet a surprising advantage, and they were also powerfully assisted by a timely rebellion of

Christian slaves below the Muslim decks, who worked their chains free from their oars and emerged into the bright daylight, chains swinging, to engage the Muslim sailors from their rear. With these advantages, the Christian center, led by Don Juan's own flagship, split the Muslim line. The Venetian fleet on the Christian left, fighting with a fury ignited by the previous August's barbarities in Cyprus (a Venetian colony), made short work of the Muslim right. Altogether the Christians destroyed the backbone of the Caliph's navy for a generation.[3]

Of course, that defeat did not make the Muslims give up their dream—their God-given mission, as they saw it—of conquering Europe. Within a generation, they began a 60-year march overland from their bases in Greece and the Balkans and up through Budapest to assemble an enormous army on the plains of Vienna. Their aim this time was to cut off Italy from the north, to divide Europe, and to defeat it part by part. There on September 12, 1683, a Polish army led by Jan Sobieski's cavalry charged forward at full speed, to the eerie sound of its whistling feather headgear, and panicked the Muslim center. Sobieski's brave cavalry drove straight through the Muslim ranks to capture the headquarters and even the green harem tent of the esteemed Sultan himself. (One of the Sultan's tents, faded from its early glory, is now displayed with other booty from that day in Czartoryski Museum in Krakow.)

From that highwater mark, the Muslim world has receded for more than 300 years and fallen into sullen impotence. In recent generations, Muslims have borne the collapse of 20th-century secular versions of Islamic power such as Nasser's socialist pan-Arabism, the earlier, important secularism of the Shah of Iran, and cruel and unpopular Baathist repression in Iraq and Syria. The West looks to be alarmingly powerful and, hard as it is for some Muslims to say, even in some ways admirably so. Against this, Islamic nations and peoples, until very recently, seemed embarrassingly incompetent. After a thousand years of glory, this new impotence was hard to take.

Resurgent Islam: Democracy or Terror?

Why has Islam endured the humiliation of stagnation and impotence? To address this dilemma, alas, small disciplined bands since the Wahhabis of Saudi Arabia have had a potent diagnosis and disturbing remedy. They reply that

Allah is angry because Muslims have forgotten their religion in empty imitation of the secular and decadent West, a demeaning exercise. Arab emergence from humiliation depends, therefore, on returning to the original faith and discipline of early Islam. Too much questioning, dissent, and discussion is only an impediment; what is needed is action. For centuries, recurrent movements of renewal (*tajdid*) and reform (*islah*) have reawakened the old victorious, advancing spirit of Islam. Indeed, in a powerful collection of essays brought together in 1983 by John L. Esposito, this very theme is lifted up into the title—*Voices of Resurgent Islam.*[4]

The background of this recent resurgence, all agree, is widespread recognition of the cultural decline and relative political impotence of Arab civilization during the past 300 years. For a proud civilization, this decline has been humiliating. The ignominy has been deepened by the stunning success of little Israel, the one spot in the region that seems to have no native sources of oil but nevertheless has the most thriving democracy and a thriving program of constant modernization and advance. The inability of hugely populated Arab nations to crush Israel, or at the very least to push it back within (as they see it) its proper narrower limits, makes many in the Arab world burn with cold fury. They blame Israel's protector, the United States. As forces of modernization, both the United States and Israel are linked together in the imagery of the Great Evil.[5] Yet Israel is a neuralgic point for a much broader humiliation.

In particular, three relatively recent events have stirred the pride of the Arab world with a new sense of resurgence. The spectacular military success of Sadat's armies during the first weeks of the war of 1973 cheered Arab hearts mightily. Because many thought Israel ended up winning the war only because of the quick intervention of American technology and power, Arab spirits soared. Three years later, many took even greater satisfaction in the suddenly visible power of Arab oil made manifest by the great energy crisis—the long lines at gasoline pumps and soaring fuel costs brought on by the Arab oil embargo. Arabs seemed no longer quite so powerless. Thus, there grew in the Arab mind a recognition that Allah might not have abandoned his people as much as had been thought. Were not the Earth's greatest resources of oil hidden beneath the very crust of the land of Mecca and Medina? Had not one of Allah's greatest blessings been saved until last?[6]

The third factor was sweeping and much larger than the first two. That was the painful recognition that "secularization" did not work in the Arab world, did not satisfy, did not have moral power or religious content, and opened too many hearts to dissipation, corruption, and profligate morals. Story after story emerged about the rapacity, cruelty, luxury, and self-aggrandizement of the secularizing rulers of Arab nations. The moral ugliness of these tales was tied not so much to modernization as to Westernization. Arab peoples remained hungry to share in the good things brought by modernization; they were not hankering for a return to the rigors of primitive desert life. But many deeply resented the enforcement upon them of Western clothes, Western manners, and Western morals. Many hated being forced to abandon the veil for women, the formal hours of prayer, the public pilgrimages. They longed for greater public support for a more rigorous moral life. As Khurshid Ahmad wrote in 1983:

> The two classic examples of Westernization in Muslim countries are Turkey and Iran. Whether we judge on the basis of the material results these experiments have produced or the moral havoc, the social ills and the psychological shock that have come in their wake, it is the profound feeling of the Muslim people that the Westernization experiment has decisively failed. Both its variants, the capitalistic as well as the socialistic, have been tried and found wanting.

The Islamic resurgence, he continues, clearly differentiates between development and secularization. "It says 'yes' to modernization but 'no' to blind Westernization."[7] Secularization ended by causing widespread revulsion.

Looked at historically, Ahmad writes, there have been three stages of Muslim resistance to the West in recent centuries. The first was resistance to foreign invasion, which finally failed. The second was resistance to colonial powers, which eventually succeeded, but then undermined itself by turning away from Islamic spiritual sources in the attempt to build new societies upon Western secular foundations—especially Arab socialist societies but also, as in the Shah's Iran, Persian capitalist societies. Eventual revulsion against these pseudo-regimes, which married Arab inefficiency to Western secularism, led to the Islamic insurgence of the post-1978 period. This resurgence took visible political form after the fall of the Shah of Iran in the enthusiastic installation of the Islamic regime of the Ayatollah Khomeini.[8]

The early chapters of *Voices of Islamic Resurgence* introduce six pioneers of this resurgence: Sayyid Qutb of Egypt, the philosopher-ideologue of the resurgence; Abul Ala Mawdudi of Pakistan; Muamar Qaddafi of Libya; Mohammad Iqbal of India; and Imam Khomeini and Ali Shariati of Iran. These names do not include all the influential theoreticians and practical pioneers, nor all the powerful sources—some of them contrary to others and pulling in quite different directions—but they do give a hint of the geographical spread of the movement.

Special mention must be made too of the symbolic excitement in the Muslim world caused by the emergence of Pakistan as an independent Islamic country, its emergence as a nuclear power, its ability to hold off its more powerful neighbor, India, and even its turn to democracy.[9] In terms of population, Pakistan is the second-largest Islamic nation, behind only Indonesia. Its symbolic role in the Muslim world is large. Many Westerners do not recognize, further, that the Muslims of Asia are almost twice as numerous as the Muslims of the Middle East. Their growing wealth and high levels of education give them increasing salience in Muslim thinking worldwide.

A fourth stage in the Islamic resurgence began with strong popular dissatisfaction with heavy-handed, failed regimes, such as those of the Taliban in Afghanistan and the cruel government of Sudan, already responsible for the killing of some two million of its own citizens in the South. The desperate situation of the people of Iraq under the megalomaniacal Saddam Hussein, broad restlessness in Iran, and, more recently, stirrings of discontent in Syria and Saudi Arabia are further evidence. Thence, the turmoil in the Muslim soul I spoke of at the beginning of this chapter, torn between a longing to be truly Muslim and a longing for democratic dignity, liberty, and opportunity. Many are struggling for a way to put these two longings together.

Ironically, it was Hindu (not Muslim) rebels in Sri Lanka, the Tamil Tigers, who gave birth to "suicide bombers." One of them immolated himself by exploding a bomb as he approached the young Ravi Gandhi, killing both of them. Thus was born the cruel tactic of the homicide bomber, which was soon enough imitated by the Palestinians in the cities of Israel, to demoralizing effect.

Meanwhile, other strands of terrorism also began to intermesh. The long flirtation with Arab socialism taught many a political Islamist the way that Communists had long perfected, the arts of organization by highly disciplined and well-trained secret cells. Considerable exposure in much of the Mideast to Italian and German fascism in the 1930s and 1940s also reinforced forms of organizational discipline, training, and practice in the arts of terror.[10] But there were also indigenous traditions of clandestine warfare, terror, guerrilla tactics, and desert warfare to draw upon. The Muslim Brotherhood and other semi-underground organizations have roots that go back at least to 1750, in the founding of the Wahhabi movement in Saudi Arabia.[11]

A friend of resurgent Islam, John Voll concedes that the critical mood adopted by the Islamic resurgency does become, "in extreme cases, the nihilistic anarchism of some of the terrorist organizations of Europe."[12] One saw this, I believe, in the destruction of the ancient Buddhist monuments on the cliffs of Afghanistan by Taliban extremists. What real point was served by that act? Perhaps they were destroying something they thought idolatrous. Still, one might have thought they would respect the antiquity of the monuments. Similarly, there was more than a whiff of anarchic nihilism in the wanton destruction of life and civic buildings in the airplane crashes into the World Trade Center in 2001. What good is served the human rights or prosperity of the peoples of Islamic nations by such destruction? The motive smacks more of Nietzschean *ressentiment*—sheer vulgar resentment, an *in-your-eye-take-that!*—than of real benefit for any real people. Terrorism for the purpose of liberating one's own public is at least understandable, if plainly immoral. But terrorism for show seems far more terribly immoral.

In addition, one must recall the tangled roots of Islamic extremism. It stems in large part from festering resentment at the decline of Islamic power and glory, but this was expressed as long ago as 1750, by Muhammad ibn Abdul Wahhab (1699–1792), the founder of a militant sect united to the Saud family of Saudi Arabia.[13] As Voll notes: "The current 'fundamentalism' has its roots in the eighteenth century. Lines of conceptual similarity can be drawn, for example, between the eighteenth century Wahhabis and the twentieth century Muslim Brotherhood even though there are no direct organizational connections between the two movements."[14] In this way, renewal and reform (*tajdid* and *islah*) go on, recur, are neglected, and are picked up again across the centuries.

Yet a new element appears to have been added with the emergence of Osama bin Laden, a multimillionaire and highly trained guerrilla leader from Saudi Arabia. No one before him had created training camps like the ones he set up in remote areas of Afghanistan, northern Iraq, the Sudan, and perhaps elsewhere—camps capable of turning out each year hundreds of trained extremists willing to die for the cause of political Islam. No one before him had so clearly trained his sights on the greatest of the Western powers in his time, the United States. No one else had so clearly sketched out the strategies and tactics of asymmetric warfare, whereby the supposedly weaker party could turn the vast strength of his opponent into a weapon against that same opponent. Thus, the same power and wealth that allowed U.S. engineers to thrust the Twin Towers into the sky left those towers vulnerable to attack from U.S. domestic aircraft. Loaded with fuel for the long trip to California, and then seized by trained hijackers and flown into the Twin Towers, one after the other, to explode in a sight to strike terror into the hearts of New Yorkers—and all the world that watched.

Bin Laden had already seen other clever plans go awry. He had had a plan to welcome the millennium by planting a new type of small explosive in the seats of a dozen different airliners scheduled to fly from Asia to the United States. If all had gone right, one by one at prearranged times the aircraft would have disappeared without trace into the Pacific Ocean. By a sheer fluke—an accident in handling one of the bombs—police in Manila were summoned to a smoke-filled apartment, where they seized a computer on which they discovered all the information for the plot.[15]

In bin Laden, the world suddenly faced the menace of a secret army composed of an unknown number of terrorists, scattered in unknown locations, with plans for dramatic terrorist actions. Modern chemical, biological, or nuclear materials, even in small quantities, could cause enormous destruction if planted with expert care in sensitive public locations. Bridges, tunnels, train tracks underneath major cities, airline terminals, ships in city harbors, nuclear power plants, dams, factories, the lavatories of government buildings, letters or packages sent through the postal service—the targets of opportunity in an open and trusting society were endless. The very patterns of trust in one another built up by a law-abiding people could be turned against them.

Armed with small quantities of destructive materials, cadres composed of foot soldiers ready to immolate themselves were in themselves weapons of mass destruction. Through asymmetrical warfare, one could cause even a strong nation to lose faith in its ability to protect itself. One could extort respect.

Meanwhile, the rule of the ancient sharia law in fully Islamic nations could function as an instrument of total control over the host countries imposing it. Religious police could keep watch over even private behaviors. Criticism of official actions could be construed as blasphemy, punishable by death. In Afghanistan, prior to its liberation from the Taliban in 2001, prisoners of the regime were skinned alive, as a lesson to others.

Throughout the Muslim world, there was revulsion at the governance of the Taliban, not only because of its extreme cruelty but also because of its incompetence. The conditions of the people were sliding backward to levels not seen for centuries. The revelation of the crimes of Saddam against his people—the uncovering of so many mass graves—was another humiliation that stung Arab and other Muslim peoples. How had this been allowed to go on, in the name of some form of pan-Arabism?

The suddenly emerging possibility of some form of moderately free regimes such as those that began to take shape in Afghanistan and Iraq in 2003—not perfect democracies all at once, but civil societies with a free press and other expanding liberties—posed a new choice for young Muslims, especially the males.

To overcome the widespread discontent of Muslim peoples, there now appear to be two paths. Young men and women can *either* hear the siren call of the political extremists and terrorists, who promise almost nothing by way of economic opportunity or political liberty to their people but only humiliation of the secular enemy. *Or* they can join in the effort to build societies of open economic opportunity and prosperity, conjoined to a regime of liberty and individual dignity, under a form of democracy compatible with Islam.

Which will it be?

The Hopeful Majority

Arrayed somewhat uncertainly against the terrorist alternative, the Muslims who wish to live their lives in peace, freedom, and growing prosperity refuse to concede that Islam is incompatible with universal human rights, personal dignity, and opportunity. For them, the essence of Islam is amity, hospitality, welcome to the stranger, help for the needy, and respect for unforced conscience. They think modern war is a repugnant choice for Muslims—where has it benefited Islam? They want the conscience of every kind of Muslim respected, whether Sunni or Shiite, Kurd or Arab, Asian or African. They want to live at peace with their Christian, Hindu, Buddhist, and secular neighbors.

These Muslims pursue prosperity and personal dignity, while cherishing their religion as an especially pure and intense source of transcendence in their lives. Fortunately, then, the war in which the civilized world is now engaged, and will likely be engaged for 20 more years, is not a war against the religion of Islam nor even against the vast majority of Muslims. It is against a much smaller political sect within Islam, which has distorted the traditional religion to fit its own political doctrines. This political Islamism (to give the extremist groups a name) is often harshly secular, certainly far more political than religious, and quite willing to depart from theological and ethical Islam whenever political motives require it to do so. Its source is neither a deeper and more vigorous study of Islam's spiritual origins nor a deeper reappropriation of Islam's magnificent intellectual resources—from those early centuries when the lost manuscripts of Plato and Aristotle were known to the Muslim world but barely available in Christian Europe. The source of political Islamism is not so much deep study and profound inquiry as resentment; not so much transcendent religion (although religious intensity is intermixed in it) as an itch to inflict injury on others.

As we saw at the end of August 2003, the extremist movement did not hesitate to plant huge car bombs outside the holiest shrine of the Shiites, Najaf, to kill an important imam just after a solemn service and to blast to death more than 100 other Muslims worshiping with him. In September and October, they blasted the United Nations building, the Red Cross building, and a half-dozen Iraqi police stations. Their aim is destruction and disorder.

The sheer secular misuse of Islam by extreme political Islamists is so great that many devout Muslims around the world are prepared to give their lives rather than accept them as rulers. That is why so many in Afghanistan fought against the Taliban, and why so many Muslims in Sudan are warring shoulder to shoulder with Christians and others against the Islamist government. It is crucial, then, to distinguish the destructive political ideology of extreme political Islamism from Islam as a religion.

What is the relative strength of political extremism within the Islamic world? Back in 2001, some experts put the proportion of Muslims who cheer on the extremist politicalization of Islam at 10 to 15 percent, but by 2004 there were indications that the proportion of actual supporters is at the lower end of that range, or even lower.[16] The year before, Fareed Zakaria showed evidence that the terrorists had begun rather rapidly to lose the support of other Muslims.[17] Among these indications are the widespread rebellion of many in Afghanistan against the Taliban; public strikes and protests by millions of young people in Iran against the politicized Mullahs; and the lack of loyalty to Saddam Hussein in Iraq. Other indications are the ability of many Muslim leaders, such as President Musharaf in Pakistan, to run counter to the militant Islamists, whose ranks had previously been swelling for many years. The best evidence of all has been the calm leadership of Shiites in Iraq, despite repeated bombings by foreign terrorists that killed hundreds upon hundreds of them in early 2004.

Of course, even 1 percent of one billion Muslims in the world equals 10 million supporters and cheerleaders for political *jihad*. From this number, even 10,000 actual warriors could cause great international terror. But it is wise to look also at the other side: many more than nine of every ten Muslims prefer a world of personal dignity and prosperity in which their rights would be protected and their opportunities for growth and advancement would become abundant.

We have other reasons to esteem greatly Islam's extraordinary sense of God's greatness, vastness, and transcendence. With a little effort, it is easy to imagine God's affectionate hold upon the souls of hundreds of millions of Islam's adherents. Under the vast starry sky above the desert, Arab Muslims may have seen more starkly than others the enormity of God's power and mystery. Under the implacably hot, blistering daily sun, they have also witnessed the fragility of a single human life. Islam is one of the world's truly great religions. It justly commands the love of hundreds of millions and the respect of millions more who are not its adherents. The manifest devotion of Muslims to the greatness of Allah fills many Christians with awe. And it is sometimes said that Jews feel closer to Islam because of its severe monotheism than to Christianity, with its puzzling belief in the Trinity.

Let me state clearly my thesis: although extreme political Islamism is violently antidemocratic and has declared deadly war on the West (and the

United Nations),[18] other intellectual resources burning deeply in the bosom of Islam may yet lead to a Muslim defense of several ideas crucial to democracy. These include, among others, the dignity of the individual, consultative government attuned to the common good, religious liberty, and the fundamental equality of all human beings before God.

There are some other darkly pessimistic aspects of Islam to cope with, however, before we turn to these positives. It is not easy for Westerners, whether Jews, Christians, or secular humanists, to enter into either the Arab or Islamic way of thinking. Arabic is itself a far more metaphoric, passional, allusive, allegorical language than contemporary Western languages, and even more so than classical Greek or Latin. Moreover, the Muslim way of seeing the world is not the same as the modern Western way.

For example, we imagine many nations divided by different religions, but Muslims imagine one true religion shared by many nations, and beyond that peoples in darkness who need one day to submit to the will of Allah. Islam is structured neither like the Christian churches nor like the Jewish people, and the mosque is not structured like the synagogue or the church. We may try to see Judaism, Christianity, and Islam (in that historical order) as the three great monotheistic religions, worshiping in different modalities the same God, but Muslims do not exactly see it that way. They date their own founding back to Abraham and see Judaism as a deplorable turn into error, followed by the even less attractive errors of Christianity—which to some Muslim eyes is a form of polytheism and, in holding Christ to be one with God, a blasphemy of immense proportions.

Worries About Islamic Law

Critics of Islamic nations, even those who wish them well, point out that traditional Islamic law may be incompatible with modern democracy in at least three ways: first, regarding the inferior role it ordains for women; second, regarding the ultimate control it vests in religious, clerical "advisers," whose role is to secure the formulation and application of secular law within the traditional understandings of Islam; and third, with regard to the freedom of individual conscience and the free exercise of religions other than Islam—or perhaps even the free exercise of any other than the particular faction of Islam dominant within the nation (Sunni or Shiite). The people of Iraq have recently faced all three of these issues in their efforts to write a constitution. Released on March 8, 2004, the interim Iraqi Constitution offers a bright beacon of hope to the entire Muslim world. That remarkable document outlaws discrimination on the basis of "gender, nationality, religion, or origin" (article 12). It provides for the separation of governmental powers among a legislature, an executive, and an independent judiciary (article 4). And perhaps most importantly, while acknowledging that "Islam is the official religion of the State," the constitution nevertheless guarantees "the full religious rights of all individuals" (article 7).[19]

Is it possible for authentic Islam to value the creative adaptation of its tradition to a new future, in the same measure as it values strict fidelity to past formulations? It is easy enough to see the dangers of too lightly abandoning the hard-won lessons of the past. Yet for a tradition to live, it must continually be changing, growing, sending out new shoots. A living tradition is maintained through the formulation of principles for discerning which changes are authentic developments of the inherited tradition and which are fraudulent wanderings after the new and the exciting. As the decline of liberal Christianity powerfully demonstrates, an itch for novelty is no guarantor of fidelity to faith. Much of post–Vatican II Catholicism fell into "neodoxy," that love for the up-to-date, that rage for being with it, that desperate need to prove to one's secular progressive peers that whatever they believe, progressive Catholics can also believe. The fidelity most prized in that case was not fidelity to the long-held teachings of the Church but fidelity to the progressive wing of the Zeitgeist.

Has Islamic scholarship—or Islamic statesmanship—a theory of the development of doctrine for sorting out which new proposals represent true, integral, and organic freshness in expression and which are outright, if subtle, betrayals of the past? Which changes represent an enrichment of the tradition and add a luster to it and which are merely mechanical and rote and deadening to thought? Which are exciting but deceitful?

For instance, a fresh theory of personal liberty might add luster to the Islamic doctrine of reward and punishment for one's actions during life by showing in more detail how a free man chooses between good and evil. How does human freedom work? What is the role of the mind? What is the role of the will? What are the roles of the tacit and of background assumptions? Does human freedom make us more like God—that is, if any comparison with God, no matter of what kind, is not blasphemous?

Since millions of Islamic women have now had the experience of completing the best university educations and practicing distinguished careers in virtually every field open to men, is it not manifest that, whatever may have been the conditions of earlier periods of Islamic life, Islam will be much the poorer if the great talents of better than half its population are frustrated? Does such an amputation of reality really do honor to the Creator of these women and their talents, and how does it do so? Al-Faruqi does not think so:

> Our present circumstances demand that every woman be a career woman at least during some portion of her life. . . . She ought to have acquired the skills to awaken and teach other Muslims, and to mobilize them in service to the divine cause. . . . Practically every field of activity is open to and needs her. There are whole professions which she can monopolize; but Muslim society has far more need for the Islamic woman worker than any mobilization of women can bring in this generation.[20]

I ask these questions in a friendly spirit, for I know as a Catholic what it is like to receive questions from outsiders who have not made sufficient efforts yet to understand what it is they are asking. It is my aim simply to formulate questions that I cannot suppress and that I hope serious Muslims will find it useful to address, for their own purposes.

And recognizing the seriousness of the question, I must also ask: is Islamic faith really compatible with the democratic form of government (not necessarily in the form in which we know it in Europe and the United States)? I believe that it is, or well might be. But I must mention some examples from the practice of Islamic law today that make many inquirers into this question doubtful.

In August 2003, a dispatch from the *Gulf News Report* described a judgment by a criminal court in the United Arab Emirates (upheld by the country's Supreme Federal Court) decreeing that the punishment meted out by a sharia religious court for an adultery by a 15-year-old girl—90 lashes—had to be carried out, no matter her tender age, no matter if the punishment should kill her.[21] In Afghanistan the mere act of criticizing sharia law can lead to condemnation for blasphemy, which is punishable by death.[22] In a curious irony pointed out by some Muslim writers, it is the Islamic religious courts that tend to be the least likely to be self-critical and the most ruthlessly bloodthirsty, while the secular courts often seem more "religious" in their sense of justice and compassion, more true to Islamic ideals.

Islam: The Turn Toward Democracy

Let us turn our attention to the positive side. Muslim scholars today are finding more and more resources within Islam for moving existing Arab nations toward religious liberty, democracy, and international standards of human rights. One reason is that during the past century the Arab nations have suffered more than their share from autocracies and cruel dictatorships. In many Arab nations, succession in office has followed no rule of law; one ruler has simply removed another by assassination. In the oil nations, the abundance of revenues from oil has freed governments from the need to exact heavy taxation. No taxation has led to low representation, arbitrary government, and relatively inert and passive peoples.

Add to this the fact that many of these governments became militantly secular during the 20th century. Following the example of Ataturk, they judged religion to be the cause of Islamic backwardness, and in its place they pursued a vision of secularism on the French anticlerical model. Governments as diverse as Turkey, Iran, Iraq, Syria, and even Egypt have shown hostility to religion and all its sustaining networks of symbols. Some of these secular governments proscribed Arabic typography in preference for Roman and abolished the fez and the turban in favor of the Western hat. They stripped the burkas off women's faces by mandatory decrees. They tried feverishly to "Europeanize" the culture of the people by every means at their command.[23] A generation of Muslim scholars trained in the West supported them.

Meanwhile, a new generation of Muslim scholars educated in the West have come to find the secular prejudices of their earlier predecessors naive, even cruel, and certainly off the mark. The secular cry "There is no second civilization—civilization means European civilization, and it must be imported with all its roses and with all its thorns"[24] was demoralizing, demeaning, and disorienting to the Muslim peoples. The worst feature of Europeanization, moreover, was its coerciveness. It also generated a new class division between the "emancipated" and the "unwashed." These two features were bound to lead to revolution from below, and they did: a massive revolt against coercive secularism. Yet this new revolution, led by Khomeini and others like him (in Sudan, for example), has merely coerced and abused ordinary people from the opposite direction.

As a consequence, the experience of living through these two revolutions, the first secular and the second countersecular, has led many in the new generation of scholars to plead for greater humility and common sense on the part of both secular and religious leaders. Neither secular leaders nor the imams should practice coercion, have everything their own way, or attempt to dominate the whole of life.

The Sudanese storyteller Tayeb Salih, for instance, in his short story "The Doum Tree of Wad Hamid," tells of a new secular government in Khartoum deciding to build a loading dock on the Nile precisely at a place where a Muslim saint is buried. The new socialist government aims to relieve poverty, but instead the villagers break out in open anger and revolt. When the socialist official arrives to begin the destruction of the shrine and faces the villagers' hostility, an old man approaches to mediate:

> Look, there can be a place for your development project and there can be a place for the shrine. There can be no harm done if you will leave this shrine alone and take your shipping dock a little further down the stream.[25]

The Ayatollah Khomeini and Salman Rushdie do not exhaust the options open to modern Islam, Ahmad writes. Nor does blasphemy, on the one hand, and the systematic absence of religious liberty (and pluralism), on the other. There has to be a middle way between militant theocracy and militant secularism. Humility and common sense must be the order of the day.

As it happens, Islamic theology and tradition offer many resources for recovering that middle way, particularly when examined in the light of the modern scholarship in which so many Muslims are now quite learned and in the light of the sad experiences of the last 20 or more years. Ahmad is one such scholar, and he claims with some justice to represent a consensus of many others.

What most Western experts have the most difficulty understanding, some Muslims say, is the twofold cutting edge of the sheer religious faith at the roots of these political movements. On the one hand, these movements are propelled by revulsion at a world without faith, such as many Muslims perceive in the West. On the other, they are moved by a deep longing for inner order, a need for connectedness to the Divine Principle at the heart of all things, a deep sense of the homage the creature necessarily owes his Creator.

As Professor Ahmad comments, the real choice that Muslim activists face is between Islamic values and a flat materialism and nationalism. "Had western culture been based on Christianity, on morality, on faith," he observes, the Islamic resurgence's "language and *modus operandi*" would have been much different than they are. But the only real "choice is between the Divine Principle and a secular materialistic culture."

Nonetheless, Ahmad points out, this radical clash between civilizations will probably be mitigated by political necessities. If such different civilizations as those represented by China and the United States can have friendly relations, he writes, why not the Muslim resurgence and Western nations?[26] This indirect appeal to some minimal degree of "friendly relations" is evidence that what I have called Caritapolis (see chapter 2) makes its attractiveness felt among Muslim thinkers as well as others. Some initial, primal call of friendship pulls on peoples even of the most disparate backgrounds, as if foreshadowing at some later point more substantial forms of friendship. Friendship is the sort of relationship that can begin with the most casual forms of contact, lie fallow for a long time, and then deepen to an unexpected degree as new challenges are overcome together.

That said, there is a profound difference between the implicit cosmology of the secular liberal West and both Islamic and Christian views of reality. For the secular liberal, the fundamental unit of analysis is the individual human being and, more precisely, the individual's untrammeled freedom of choice. A grim example is the secular principle enunciated a little over a decade ago (and recently repeated) by the U.S. Supreme Court: "At the heart of liberty is the right to define one's own concept of existence, of meaning, of the universe, and of the mystery of human life."[27] In this odd concept, the secular individual answers to no one else in the cosmos. Society comes into existence solely by the individual's consent to a social contract, and so does the state. The little atoms whirling in space in the empty universe, therefore, are the conscious, willing, individual human beings "defining their own concepts." From these atoms are societies composed.

For Muslims (and for Christians) reality is very different. The greatest of all centers of attention is transcendent, and everything else flows from and must answer to this Wholly Other, the Creator, whose Name is utterly unlike other names, about Whom our faint knowledge is like darkness. "Great is Allah, and there is no other like Him." For his own purposes, this Creator made heaven and earth and all things within them. Far from the human individual being alone in his or her solitariness, the Creator made all of them together for union with Himself as one family. He brought individuals into being through society, through families first of all, and gave them by nature an instinct to form cities (states). Humans by nature are political animals, to quote Aristotle on behalf of Christians and Muslims. By contrast, Christians and Muslims cannot be surprised that secular societies generate a vast inner wasteland, spiritual emptiness, chilling disorientation. Without God, reason is not only cold and empty but unable to justify even itself. Why in a world without purpose, resulting from blind chance, should human beings follow reason? Of what avail is reason in a reasonless world? Avoid that question if you choose. Such avoidance will not persuade others that yours is a reasonable choice.

In this horizon, the poet-philosopher of India Mohammed Iqbal found liberal secularism to be a force for social disintegration. It also opens the door to racism, he wrote, because it has been divorced from the broad universal concerns in which religions of the Creator imbue the race. Iqbal is famous for the aphorism "Separate politics from religion and you are left with Genghis Khan." A secular ideology does not satisfy the human heart. In place of food for the spirit, it offers dust. "Humanity," he wrote, "needs three things today: a spiritual interpretation of the universe, spiritual emancipation of the individual, and basic principles of universal import directing the evolution of human society on a spiritual basis." These three needs expressly include the emancipation of the individual—but not on any basis at all, and not without universal context. "Believe me," he later added, "Europe today is the greatest hindrance in the way of man's ethical advancement."[28]

The movement of Islam toward democracy, according to Abdulaziz Sachedina of the University of Virginia, chairman of the board of the Center for the Study of Islam and Democracy, depends on the two key institutions of Muslim life: the seminaries and the universities.

Seminaries represent what Islam teaches about itself as interpreted by the ulama. Universities represent what the moderns teach about any and all subjects that human beings want or need to learn. Hence, both universities and seminaries as the repositories of human knowledge become the centers of power, in constant competition with each other and the state, to control the people's minds so as to make them agree with what they uphold to be of epistemic value. Although there is a difference in their approach to knowledge, they build upon one another, to provide solutions to the pressing problems of social ethics for the people today. As a result, they cannot afford to work in isolation.[29]

Sachedina argues that "the Muslim world is still searching for ways to make Islamic studies an academic discipline that can be studied critically." The key, he adds, "is to work toward an inclusive epistemology, without any claim to absolutism about the past heritage."[30] In other words, Islamic democracy must take flight on two wings: a humble, not overlording, faith, and a form of reason more akin to common sense than to European rationalism.[31] Faith must be humbled by bowing before the fact of deep religious differences and by taking with new seriousness the ancient declaration that genuine faith must be free and uncoerced. Reason must not be conceived of as abstract, totalistic, and conceited, but as humble, practical, and commonsensical.

Mumtaz Ahmad cites to this effect the strongest text supporting pluralism in the Koran:

If God had willed, He could surely have made you one people, professing one faith, but He did not do so. He wished to try and test you. So try to compete with one another in good deeds. Unto God shall you return, all together. And He will tell you the truth about what you have been disputing.[32]

He adds that "the Koran clearly and categorically excludes coercion in matters of religion and states that 'there is no compulsion in religion.'" Ahmad does not hesitate to add that those Islamic governments today that do otherwise "are clearly in violation of this Koranic injunction." The Prophet allowed Christians to pray in his own mosque, he adds, and accorded full religious liberty to Jews in the constitution of Medina. "There is no Islamic justification whatever for imposing restrictions on non-Muslims" by Muslim governments, whether they are moved by religious or political considerations.[33]

Nowadays, Ahmad goes on (in the same vein as Sachedina), so many Muslims are living abroad and so many Muslim scholars are involved in interfaith dialogue that a wholly new effort is being made to develop a fresh understanding of the Islamic tradition, bringing out the passages that encourage pluralism and respect for individual conscience, alongside those that show how all this suits the will of God and promotes noble human striving.

Sachedina is under no illusions about how distant such scholarship remains from "the major agents of change in Muslim societies, the military and the ulama [the mullahs]." To make matters worse, he notes, such scholars are still not being read or heard even by the ordinary people—or their leaders—in the Muslim communities in the United States and Europe, much less in the fully Muslim nations. In an allusion to the sustained, heavily financed promulgation of the violent Wahhabi tradition of Saudi Arabia, Sachedina bewails "the influence of a narrow-minded and stultified Islamic tradition funded by the petrodollars for over a quarter of a century."[34] Sachedina and Ahmad, in their separate ways, are calling for the scholars in favor of pluralism, religious liberty, and democracy to bring their work into the communities of ordinary Muslim peoples. These scholars have a good chance of being influential, especially in those communities that have suffered grievously under the Taliban, Khomeini, Saddam Hussein, the Sudanese autocrats, and other hyper-Islamicist counterrevolutions.

No matter what their immediate influence, the world is in the end moved by ideas, and a new tide of ideas among Muslim scholars is a very hopeful omen for the future.

Some Sources of New Muslim Thinking

As we have seen, because each human being after death must face his Judge to receive reward or punishment in accord with his deeds in life, Islam teaches in a very vivid way that each human being is free and, in an important sense, self-determining and self-defining. Therefore, there must lurk within Islam a profound theory of human liberty. For example, Ismail al-Faruqi wrote in 1992:

Indeed, fulfillment of his vocation is the only condition Islam knows for man's salvation. Either it is his own doing or it is worthless. Nobody can do the job for him, not even God, without rendering him a puppet. This follows from the nature of moral action, namely, it is not itself moral unless it is freely willed and undertaken to completion by a free agent. Without the initiative and effort of man, all moral worth or value falls to the ground.[35]

Islamic philosophers down the centuries have worked out many of the philosophical implications of this theory, as well as many of the implications for Islamic law and ethics. It seems, however, that they have not worked out in similar depth the *institutional* implications for the political life of pluralistic peoples or for the practices of religious liberty. "What is blatantly missing. . . ," Hamid Enayat writes:

is an adaptation of either the ethical and legal precepts of Islam, or the attitudes and institutions of traditional society, to democracy. This is obviously a much more complex and challenging task than the mere reformulation of democratic principles in Islamic idioms. It is because of this neglect that the hopes of evolving a coherent theory of democracy appropriate to an Islamic context have remained largely unfulfilled.[36]

Since it also took Christian peoples some centuries to work out such institutional implications for themselves, and Catholics longer than Protestants, this delay is not to be wondered at. Indeed, the reason for renewed hope is that so many Muslim scholars of obvious talent and learning are turning their minds to precisely this task, in a way unprecedented in history.

Moreover, some of the facts of Islamic history and geography lean now in their favor. By now, Islam has been practiced under many diverse forms of political regime and in many diverse cultures and climates. Hence, it is widely recognized by even traditional Muslim scholars that the transcendence of Allah precludes identifying Him with any one type of political regime. No one is entitled to say that any particular regime represents the fullness of His will. Furthermore, the study of Islamic history makes clear beyond a doubt that Islam has coexisted with many kinds of regimes and that all, without exception, have had their deficiencies and grievous faults. None completely fulfills the will of Allah. For political leaders, therefore, humility is in order. So also for religious leaders who aspire to political power.

Moreover, despite the fact that early Islam may not have made the same distinction between the "two realms" or "two swords" that the Christian popes were making, dividing political power from spiritual power, Muslims today widely recognize that in practice there are two different powers.[37] Hossein Khomeini, the grandson of the Ayatollah Khomeini, for example, spoke recently at the American Enterprise Institute and said that those Muslims who claim to hold both powers in their hands are "usurpers."[38] Other scholars have made similar points at conferences such as those sponsored by the Islam and Democracy Project at the Ethics and Public Policy Center in Washington, D.C.[39]

But the most important resource in Islamic thought for recognizing religious liberty lies in the basic doctrine of Islam that I have tried to stress throughout this book: namely, the very powerful Islamic insight into the greatness of Allah. Because Allah is absolutely sovereign, utterly transcendent, and uniquely powerful, it is blasphemous for any one man to imitate the divine mode of rulership by arrogating to himself all political power within a community. To put it another way, if all power is located in Allah, then human institutions must disperse power among many parts to avoid pretending to be God.

Let me stress this point a little because it is so important. So great is Allah, so beyond measure, so beyond compare, that his greatness is a warning to any mere mortal spokesman about his own shortsightedness and inadequacy in the face of Allah. In other words, the greatness of Allah relativizes all known pretensions. It opens the human mind to the possibility that only Allah knows all the paths that lead to him and that human agents would do well to respect the freedom of religious conscience both in single individuals and in the public free exercise of other religious groups. For Muslims, Islam is the one true religion, but no single Muslim can claim to know all the mysterious paths along which Allah leads all the other peoples of the Earth. This sense of God's greatness is what lies behind and instructs consciences in matters of religious belief. It is true that, historically, this side of the Islamic doctrine of God has not been made as prominent as it might be. But perhaps it has lain fallow these many years so that its true beauty might flower in, as it were, a delayed springtime for worldwide Islam.

Bernard Lewis himself points to several "elements in Islamic law and tradition that could assist the development of one or another form of democracy."[40] Among these are five in particular: "Islamic tradition strongly disapproves of arbitrary rule." He adds that in Islamic tradition the exercise of political power is conceived of "as a contract, creating bonds of mutual obligation between the ruler and the ruled." Other writers emphasize at this point the great efforts that Muslim rulers are expected to go through to achieve consensus among all branches of society.[41]

The second resource Lewis points to is the need for continuing consent: "The contract can be dissolved if the ruler fails to fulfill or ceases to be capable of fulfilling his obligations." The third resource is the Islamic notion of civil disobedience, namely, that "if the sovereign commands something that is sinful, the duty of obedience lapses." One Hadith says: "Do not obey a creature against his Creator." Another adds: "There is no duty to obedience in sin."

The fourth resource is the principle of accepting diversity. As the Prophet says, "Difference of opinion within my community is a sign of God's mercy." The fifth resource is the traditional stress on the dignity and humility of all citizens. Dignity gives all citizens a place and a right to be taken seriously. Humility applies to the great and the mighty as well as to the ordinary person. The transcendence of the Almighty Creator is an efficient equalizer.

Similarly, in an essay on "Reviving Middle Eastern Liberalism," Saad Eddin Ibrahim points to a hundred-year period, between 1850 and 1952, when there flourished in Egypt a liberal age that was the light of the modern Muslim world. During that time, civil society was defined as "a free space within which people can assemble, work together, express themselves, organize, and pursue shared interests in an open and peaceful manner."[42]

Finally, one of the most important of the young Muslim scholars in the United States, Dr. Khaled Abou El Fadl, now at Yale University and a member of the U.S. President's Commission on Religious Liberty, has summarized many of his writings on Muslim developments in religious liberty, democracy, and human rights in a fairly succinct paragraph that deserves quoting in full:

My argument for democracy draws on six basic ideas: (1) Human beings are God's vicegerents on earth; (2) this vicegerency is the basis of individual responsibility; (3) individual responsibility and vicegerency provide the basis for human rights and equality; (4) human beings in general, and Muslims specifically, have a fundamental obligation to foster justice (and more generally to command right and forbid wrong), and to preserve and promote God's law; (5) divine law must be distinguished from fallible human interpretations; and (6) the state should not pretend to embody divine sovereignty and majesty.[43]

All these, I believe, raise important questions for how we in the more secular West think about democracy. Are our ideas too narrow? Too ideologically secular? In this way, this new intercultural dialogue, while expanding the intellectual and practical possibilities of the Islamic tradition, also enriches the understanding of democracy as we have known it in the West. What Muslim scholars are doing, they do also for us. Their success in building democracies makes the whole world safer and spiritually richer.

Conclusion

Were you to ask me, "What are the probabilities of democracy succeeding, say, in Iraq, as well as in other Arab countries?" I would cite a recent poll from Iraq showing that 50 percent of the respondents believe that democracy, because it comes from the West, automatically cannot succeed, but 40 percent believe it will.[44] Experiences with democracy in Iraq on the village, town, and city levels during the next two years may change these percentages. Even now there is greater optimism in the freer Kurd areas of the North and the Shiite areas of the South than in the Sunni central region, which was loyal to Saddam Hussein and privileged for being so. Finally, since several Muslim nations of Asia have succeeded in launching democratic experiments and in experiencing at least two peaceful successions of leadership through democratic means, it is clear that the problem lies less in Islam than in the political propensities of the Arab states.[45]

A 40 percent chance of success in building successful democracies in some Arab nations during the next 20 years seems to me an unparalleled opportunity that we dare not miss. For how else are Arab peoples likely to prosper, live in peace, and find the opportunity to develop their abundant talents? How else if not under democracy are they to find freedom from torture and tyranny, secret police and arbitrary power, poverty and blocked horizons?

And if you should alter the question and ask me, *"Do you think that we have an obligation* to throw all the energies we can behind the efforts of those brave Muslim political thinkers and doers who are trying to build democracy?"* I will answer with the words of Abdulaziz Sachedina:

> What will happen? That depends on all of us, men and women, Muslim and non-Muslim, working together to make the ideal attain reality.[46]

Professor Sachedina invites us to help. As Christians, as Jews, as humanists, it is our duty to help. In this effort, our own understanding of democracy will be deepened.

EPILOGUE

The Caritapolis Perspective

Many intellectuals look at the world in purely secular terms. This is good as far as it goes, and yet its internal design does not allow it to go very far. For myself, I do not think that faith and reason are at war with one another, or alternatives, or rivals. On the contrary. Jewish and Catholic faith give reasons why reason is to be trusted, cultivated, furthered, celebrated. It is no accident that Western civilization has long been a happy (if not quarrel-free) marriage of Jerusalem and Athens. The God of Abraham has taught us to rejoice in all the knowledge and wisdom that Athens can teach us, and all the organizational practicality of the Romans too. As Alfred North Whitehead once said, the rise of modern science is inconceivable apart from five thousand years of tutoring in the idea that an all-wise and all-powerful Creator knew what He was doing in creating the world. This background assumption makes reasonable—as few other assumptions do—a trust in reason to unravel the secrets of that intelligent creation.

In short, from the point of view of our actual history, it is not reason that is the prolegomenon to faith, but faith that has been the prolegomenon to reason.

Indeed, I would go further. The decline of faith in the God of Abraham, Isaac, Jacob, and Jesus in the contemporary West has brought with it, at accelerating speed, a decline in faith in science, reason, and progress. Visit a university bookstore and observe the shelf space given to astrology, tarot cards, witchcraft, the occult, and the fantastic, as well as to the cult of the absurd in the volumes of postmodernism.

As the cult of the Creator weakens, so it appears does confidence in the possibility of truth. There follows a decline in any nonsubjective measure of progress. There is bound to follow, in due time, a rise in reliance on raw power. And that power will no doubt be wielded with cynicism.

The Contours of the Coming World

What I have tried to do in this book is to imagine a point of practical, civilizational unity toward which the Chinese, Indians, Jews, Eastern Orthodox, Catholics, Muslims, Protestants, Buddhists, Confucianists, agnostics, atheists, and all the other peoples of the world might aspire, without ceasing to be who they are. I have argued for new habits of cross-civilizational respect, based upon the four cardinal virtues spelled out in chapter 2: respect for the regulative ideal of truth; cultural humility; the dignity of the individual person; and human solidarity. These four virtues are quite different from sentimental appeals to "understanding" based upon cultural relativism and moral equivalence. I argue that people should be who they are and present evidence for their unique claims and choices in a way respectful of others—but also respectful of the truths they themselves hold dear. The truth about the human race is larger than any of us—larger than any individual and any civilization—and all of us have much to learn from others. But to learn truly means to make judgments based fairly upon evidence. Mutual respect does not require, and cannot even survive, a disregard of obvious evidence. One need not place a blindfold over one's mind and reduce oneself to oozing sentiment in order to understand others fairly. We pay one another respect by engaging alert minds and wise judgments in the evidence we each present in conversation.

As luck and nature would have it, honest and serious humans in all cultures quickly sense each other out, exchange genuine respect, and go as far together as mutual understanding at that moment will allow them. They understand that today's limits may not be tomorrow's, and after initial exchanges they go to their separate abodes to think some more on what they have heard.

I have tried to show, further, that earthly reality itself teaches all of us, sometimes harshly, and drives us in important respects toward analogous lessons. Ten thousand years ago, there were many fewer human beings on this planet, and even two thousand years ago, or one, there were fewer than a billion alive in any one generation. But as we humans fill up the Earth—now more than six billion of us, and probably heading, despite rapid depopulation on some continents, toward eight billion—our interchanges with one another are becoming much more frequent and much more intimate. Not only contemporary technologies of rapid communication and transport but also huge and continuous migrations from one place to another are teaching even the remotest peoples about the ways of life of others whose very existence only a few decades back was all but unknown to them.

In this way, there is taking shape, slowly and dimly, a kind of universal consciousness of the presence of one another—and even an interpenetration of customs, habits, phrases, and ways of thinking. Moreover, the material success of some, and the political success of others, is slowly breeding emulation. It sometimes brings amazingly swift desires for rapid change, even on a very broad and deep cultural scale, as we have seen in our reflections on India and China and the entire world of Islam in recent decades.

Indeed, I have even dared to try to identify and single out in this sprawling book, and within this broad sprawling world, a world of many burning concerns and dynamic energies heading off in many divers directions, certain fundamental habits of liberty, and even certain fundamental institutions, to which people everywhere are aspiring. These habits and institutions seem shaped by nature itself to serve as necessary gateways to the liberty and prosperity for which there appears to be a universal hunger.

These habits and institutions are rooted in universal human experience; so it seems to me. Perhaps my way of formulating them seems too limited, and someone may formulate them better in a more universal framework. The point of attempts like this one is to prompt a universal conversation, such that tomorrow's findings advance today's.

Let us conclude, then, with brief summary reflections on certain fundamental habits of human liberty, on certain institutions fundamental to liberty, and on some visible connections between faith and reason in our complicated, varied human world.

The Fundamental Virtues of Liberty

To hold that free societies can emerge on Earth in nations whose citizens do not practice the habits necessary for political, economic, and cultural liberty would be reckless. For the free society is not really free if it does not depend upon the freely taken actions of its citizens. Where suspicion, cynicism, greed, ambition, irresponsibility, shoddy workmanship, deliberate deception, and other vicious habits have been allowed to thrive, goals such as the rule of law, respect for the dignity and human rights of others, and public-spirited amity are all but unrealizable, and practices of corruption thrive. Much of daily living is taken up with defensive tactics as every party tries to protect itself against the depredations of others.

The Political Virtues

Democratic institutions call for certain required democratic habits, that is, settled dispositions, inclinations, and modes of acting upon which others can rely. In the same way, a dynamic and inventive economy also depends on certain specific habits, inclinations, and dispositions of character, including a high degree of social trust and faith in the integrity and transparency of patterns of economic transactions.[1] There must be swift and certain justice in the courts; honesty in public speech; codes of ethics in institutions; integrity in ordinary policemen; and a sense of public spirit in the people. When people lose confidence in the integrity of the money supply—to take another sort of example—as the German people did during the massive inflation of the Weimar Republic, money is reduced to being barely worth the paper it is printed on. What gives money value is political faith—faith in the integrity of the system and in the resoluteness of the promise to pay the bearer something reasonably close to the expenditures of labor and effort it cost them to acquire it.[2] When this political faith collapses, social disaster results. A democracy's fiduciary responsibility to protect the value of money is of high moral importance.

The Economic Virtues

In speaking of the economic habits of the free society, we should probably stress economic *initiative* and *creativity*. In the free society, citizens must be self-starters; they must show imagination, develop the habits of enterprise and invention, and bring into being goods and services that do not yet exist in their environment. Without initiative and creativity, economic life is in either stasis or decline. The dynamic force moving economies forward toward prosperity lies coiled within the human mind, heart, and will and is expressed outwardly by sound habits of initiative, risk-taking, creative imagination, and a practical talent for turning dreams into realities.

It goes without saying that habits of trustworthiness, courtesy, reliability, and cooperativeness are also the mark of successful business activities, generating bonds of trust and loyalty among coworkers in the same firm and between the firm and its suppliers, customers, and pensioners. Acts of disloyalty in any of these directions can bring down firms.

Business is a crucial field of moral activity. Great good can be done through it, but also significant evil.

The Cultural Virtues

Obviously, bad habits such as lawbreaking, cutting corners, cheating, lack of self-control, backbiting, envy, and personal greed deeply wound a culture and injure its general sense of community and common purpose. Instead of focusing their energies on new future achievements, citizens in such republics are bound to waste many efforts in defensiveness and self-protection. Such mechanisms penalize the entire society.

Considering the large number of sound habits necessary in the political, economic, and cultural spheres of the free society, it is obvious that the free society must also become an unusually virtuous society, nourishing in all spheres a large number of sound and reliable habits. Where the culture is morally lax, the flag of liberty sags. The frequency with which social vices appear determines the level of police and other regulatory supervision. Low levels not only raise social costs but—if they spiral downwards—precipitate a descent into tyranny.

The more virtuous the habits of its citizenry, the freer a society can be. When for every million citizens there are one million inner policemen (i.e., "consciences"), the number of police in the street can be few. When consciences are not reliable, the number of policemen in the street must necessarily grow.

The Major Institutions of Liberty

The State

Aristotle long ago remarked that the ethos of a nation is deeply affected by the architectonic of its polity. When a nation undergoes occupation by a foreign army, for example, some formerly reliable citizens begin to cooperate with the enemy, perhaps for the rewards that such cooperation promises, perhaps out of fear. Especially when the foreign occupation has a criminal character, it becomes exceedingly difficult for ordinary citizens to maintain their customary honesty and sound moral habits. Cynicism is forced upon them; they must defend themselves on all sides, and they feel great pressure to narrow their sphere of moral action to life within the family and among trusted friends. Just as an unsound ordering of a polity can corrupt or even destroy the moral ethos of a nation, so also a well-shaped architectonic can nourish good habits and sound ethical practices. Where laws are good and reasonable, for instance, and clear and reliable, and when citizens can count on their just administration, then the sphere of personal liberty open to the good habits of citizens expands. The ordinary workings of good habits tend to produce good outcomes in both political life and economic life. Good laws and good habits generate a sort of "beneficent circle," just as bad laws and bad habits generate a "vicious circle."

Nowadays, modern means of communication give government officials an important moral voice. By the legislation of good laws, by the just administration of laws, and by the public promotion of noble examples from the past, governments can do quite a lot to create the sort of political architectonic favorable to a sound human ecology. It is a grievous error for a government either wholly to neglect or thoroughly to dominate the moral ethos of the people. No democracy can long survive the moral decadence of its people, for the abdication of self-control on their part is an invitation to tyranny.

Voluntary Associations

It should be obvious that the cultural formation of the habits necessary to a sound human ecology are much more thoughtfully, successfully, and intensively practiced by associations that are closer than the state to the actual features of daily life: first of all, the home and the family, but secondly, neighborhood associations, schools, fraternal societies, and social groups of all sorts (Red Cross, Boy Scouts, Girl Scouts, Knights of Columbus, Hadassah, Masonic lodges, Sunday schools, church socials, and many more). All these play important roles. Since World War II, great crises in politics and economics seem to have gripped everyone's attention, while moral questions have often been shunted aside as "old-fashioned." Moral capital stored up from previous generations has been swiftly dissipated, and the decline of family life and ordinary moral habits has been rapid and steep. Yet now a corrective rebellion is under way, and even, in the opinion of Nobel Prize–winning historian Robert Fogel, a "Fourth Great Awakening."[3]

An increasingly important player in the world of voluntary associations is the philanthropic foundation. The great number of family fortunes spawned by the long economic boom since World War II is now resulting in the most massive intergenerational transfer of wealth in world history as the oldest living generation disposes of these fortunes to their heirs. Much of this wealth—in the United States, an estimated $20 billion to $30 billion—is likely to be poured into philanthropic foundations, new and old, and into other charitable works. How this money will be spent is of great moment to civilization. Indeed, as more and more nations grow in wealth, the tradition of private philanthropy looms ever larger as a potential source of cultural, moral, intellectual, and artistic renewal throughout the planet.

Supranational Religious Bodies

A third major institutional force is the world's religious bodies. Since the conventional idiom of most scholarly analysis is astringently secular, there are probably no major institutions in the world less commented upon and less studied than religious institutions. It may or may not be true that the great proportion of the world's journalists are not very religious, do not assign religion much importance in world affairs, and do not care enough about religion to study it intensively. It is true that many of them have long and complacently accepted the "secularization thesis," according to which the world is inexorably and inevitably becoming more secular. Perhaps that is why the great explosion of religious energy that has characterized the waning years of the 20th century and the opening years of the 21st has been so startling to Western elites.

By far the largest proportion of the six billion persons upon this planet are religious believers, and only a relatively small proportion are atheists or agnostics. According to various sources, there are two billion Christians in the world, with these numbers growing very rapidly in the Third World, while declining in Western Europe. There are just over one billion Muslims, a large majority of them in Asia, whose numbers are also growing rapidly. There are 700 million Hindus, a smaller number of Buddhists, and hundreds of millions of other believers of various sorts.[4]

Thus, it happens that significantly more than half of the world's population draws most of its signals about moral behavior from religious sources rather than philosophical ones. This is not the place for a thorough investigation of the potential contributions of the world's major religious bodies to human ecology. Yet it would be an unwise observer who thought that religion will not play a prominent role in the formation of human culture during the course of the 21st century.

Business Corporations

Business corporations themselves are important sources of moral teaching. Through their own internal "cultures" and, in many cases, formal "codes of behavior," business corporations embody important moral habits. They are often schools in learning cross-cultural cooperation, habits of teamwork and self-discipline, prudence, modesty, and peaceful methods of persuasion. Long ago, well before the current age of globalization, John Stuart Mill wrote in his often-reprinted *Principles of Political Economy*:

> The economical advantages of commerce are surpassed in importance by those of its effects, which are intellectual and moral. It is hardly possible to overrate the value, in the present low state of human improvement, of placing human beings in contact with persons dissimilar to themselves, and with modes of thought and action unlike those with which they are familiar. Commerce is now, what war once was, the principal source of this contact. There is no nation which does not need to borrow from others,

not merely particular arts or practices, but essential points of character in which its own type is inferior.[5]

Anyone with experience in corporations around the world—Coca-Cola, for instance, or Phillips, or Barclay's—knows the ring of truth in such words. Many with long experience in corporate life speak gratefully about the horizon-expanding opportunities their work has brought them. Nonetheless, it is no doubt true that for too long business schools tended to emphasize the more "scientific" and "value-neutral" aspects of economics rather than the spiritual and moral dimensions of the business vocation. They affected a certain tough-minded "realism" by emphasizing "the bottom line" while neglecting the human dimensions of business reality. At the end of the day, anyone in business who examines his or her conscience can look back on having done much good and, alas, at times on having witnessed (though one hopes not in his or her own firm) certain evil or dishonest or even cruel acts done in the name of business. The vocation of business is noble precisely because it contains within itself capacities for great good or great evil.[6] Evil actions on the part of businessmen have an even greater power to wreak harm than activities in some other fields, because a flagrant wrong can do harm not only in itself but also in stoking public cynicism concerning the free society.

On the other hand, the quiet good that can be done by the intelligent deployment of sound business habits, including keen cultural sensitivities, is likewise of high importance in raising cultural standards all around the world. Not least, it often brings acute instruction in tolerance and cross-cultural understanding, through respect for the talents of coworkers from many different cultures.

Faith and Reason

It would be foolish to ignore the predominant role of religious faith in forming the moral conscience of a substantial majority of the world's citizens. Such terms as "the decline of belief" and a "secular age" may roughly enough describe some elites but do not adequately describe most peoples of the world.

In trying to reach a global moral vision, furthermore, it is not necessary to discover common principles—some "lowest common denominator"—on which everyone can agree. Universal principles need not be univocal. Different traditions may for good reason have somewhat different means of expressing common ideals, yet there may well be "family resemblances" among these statements. It is not necessary to find a single formulation that does full justice to all virtues. For practical cooperation in moral conduct, "family resemblances" may be quite sufficient.

Virtually all of the world's major religious bodies have significant insight to contribute to our understanding of the "cardinal virtues"—cultural humility, respect for the regulative ideal of truth, respect for individual dignity, and solidarity. To a rather remarkable degree, moreover, these diverse traditions point in an analogous or correlative moral direction. The chief concerns of all of them—truth, beauty, being, goodness—are close to such universal human experiences as birth and death, suffering, erring, and trying again.

For this reason, it seems quite feasible to encourage all the world's religious bodies to apply their energies to thinking through a global moral vision in fraternal dialogue with each other. Each tradition might be encouraged to show toward other traditions a welcoming spirit. For good dialogue to take place, it is not necessary that all become homogeneous, or even merely syncretistic. Maintaining a clear awareness of one's own differences in the context of civility and fraternity deepens the conversation.

It also goes without saying that those on whose consciences religion has no personal purchase should address the same questions of a global moral ecology with every resource that reason can bring to bear. For "reason" itself is understood diversely in different traditions; it is itself an analogous, not a univocal, concept. Reason is important to religious people too, it must also be remembered. Religious people do not surrender their capacities for the intelligent and inquiring use of reason by virtue of adding to it the intellectual habit of faith.

The partisans of the free society, marked by a universal respect for human rights, are not too many but too few. In the 19th century, liberals too quickly declared themselves the foes of religion—the "enlightened" against those still living in "darkness"—while religious people in self-defense closed their minds to many of the sensible, practical points that liberals were making. We should not make those mistakes in the new century. The contributions of all persons of goodwill, whether unbeliever or believer, are sorely needed if the universal hunger for liberty is at last to be satisfied.

Zarathushtra Speaks Again

It is the task of our generation, Albert Camus once wrote, to enter into the Absurd, and from it to construct a new ethic, one worthy of human beings. While the buildings of Berlin were crashing down in the flames of the Soviet invasion of 1944 and all of Western civilization seemed to lie in ruins, Camus wrote:

> We are now at the extremities. At the end of this tunnel of darkness, how-ever, there is inevitably a light, which we already divine and for which we have only to fight to ensure its coming. All of us, among the ruins, are preparing a renaissance beyond the limits of nihilism.[7]

And again in *The Myth of Sisyphus*, "Even within nihilism, it is possible to find the means to proceed beyond nihilism."[8]

That conviction has guided all my work, expressly so in early books such as *Belief and Unbelief* (1965) and *The Experience of Nothingness* (1971).

That is why I was so moved by the new sculptures over the doors at the National Cathedral in Washington, D.C., designed and executed by the young sculptor Frederick Hart between 1971 and 1984. The largest of them bears the title *Ex Nihilo*—"out of nothingness."

Hart had a profound vision of the death wish implicit in so much of 20th-century art. It made *things* prominent, and the *thereness* of things, the dead, dull meaninglessness of things. Haphazard fluorescent tubing stuck into sand, iron beams in ugly shapelessness, large boulders rolled into a plaza. Dead things. There. Empty of humanity. In your face.

When man dies, so does God.

Long ago, in one of my first published essays (*Harper's*, 1961), I wrote these words:

> Religion can thrive only in a personal universe; religious faith, hope, and love are personal responses to a personal God. But how can the immense

question of a personal God even be posed and made relevant when fundamental questions about the meaning and limits of personal experience are evaded?

"God is dead. . . . What are these churches if they are not the tombs and sepulchers of God?" Nietzsche asked. But much of Western humanism is dead too. Men do not wander under the silent stars, listen to the wind, learn to know themselves, question, "Where am I going? Why am I here?" They leave aside the mysteries of contingency and transitoriness, for the certainties of research, production, consumption. So that it is nearly possible to say: "Man is dead. . . . What are these buildings, these tunnels, these roads, if they are not the tombs and sepulchers of man?"

God, if there is a God, is not dead. He will come back to the colleges, when man comes back.[9]

NOTES

Introduction

1. A useful journalistic account of the early events of the war on terrorism can be found in Samuel M. Katz, *Relentless Pursuit: The DSS and the Manhunt of the Al Qaeda Terrorists* (New York: Forge, 2002).

2. George W. Bush, address to the nation, March 17, 2003.

3. Fred Barnes, "Mohamed Atta Was Here," *Weekly Standard* 7, no. 46 (August 12, 2002): 10.

4. David Frum and Richard Perle, *An End to Evil: How to Win the War on Terror* (New York: Random House, 2003), 45.

5. "September 11th signaled the arrival of an entirely different era. We suffered massive civilian casualties on our soil. We awakened to dangers even more lethal—the possibility that terrorists could gain weapons of mass destruction from outlaw regimes and inflict catastrophic harm" (Vice President Richard B. Cheney, remarks on war on terror, American Enterprise Institute, July 24, 2003).

6. See Stephen Hayes, "The Imminence Myth," *Weekly Standard* 9, no. 22 (February 16, 2004): 17.

7. "The economic environment in which the founders expected the IMF and the Bank to function no longer exists. . . . Contrary to the initial presumption, most crises in the past quarter century involved not too little but too much lending. . . . The IMF has given too little attention to improving financial structures in developing countries and too much to expensive rescue operations. Its system of short-term crisis management is too costly, its responses too slow, its advice often incorrect, and its efforts to influence policy and practice too intrusive" (Alan H. Meltzer, *International Financial Institutions Reform: Report of the International Financial Institution Advisory Commission*, March 2000 [Washington, D.C.: U.S. Congress, International Financial Institution Advisory Commission (IFIAC), 2000]).

8. *CIA World Factbook 2003*, available at: http://www.cia.gov/cia/publications/factbook/index.html.

9. For an early account of this exchange, see my "Adventure in Asmara," *National Review Online*, September 19, 2002.

10. Newman C. Eberhardt, *A Summary of Catholic History* (St. Louis: B. Herder Book Co., 1961), 215.

11. "The expression, 'City of God,' which I have been using is justified by that Scripture whose divine authority puts it above the literature of all other people and brings under its sway every type of human genius . . . by a disposition of Divine Providence. For in this Scripture, we read: 'Glorious things are said of thee, O city of God' [Ps 86]; and, in another psalm: 'Great is the Lord, and exceedingly to be praised in the city of our God, in His holy mountain, increasing the joy of the whole earth' [Ps 47].. . . Through these and similar passages too numerous to quote, we learn of the existence of a City of God whose Founder has inspired us with a love and longing to become its citizens" (Saint Augustine, *The City of God* [New York: Image Books, 1958], bk. XI, ch. 1).

12. Cf. on democracy and capitalism, see Amy Chua, *World on Fire: How Exporting Free Market Democracy Breeds Ethnic Hatred and Global Instability* (New York: Doubleday, 2003); on globalization, see Benjamin Barber, *Jihad Versus McWorld: How Globalism and Tribalism Are Reshaping the World* (New York: Ballantine Books, 1996); and on Islam, see Robert Spencer, *Islam Unveiled: Disturbing Questions About the World's Fastest-Growing Faith* (San Francisco: Encounter, 2002).

13. *City of God*, bk. XIX, chs. 5 and 6.

14. Atheists constitute about 2 percent of the world's population, Christians 33 percent, Muslims 20 percent, Hindus 14 percent, and Buddhists 6 percent (*The World Almanac and Book of Facts 2004* [New York: World Almanac Education Group, 2004], 612, 856).

15. See Richard John Neuhaus, *Unsecular America* (Grand Rapids, Mich.: William B. Eerdmans Publishing Co., 1986).

16. George Washington, "Thanksgiving Proclamation," City of New York, October 3, 1789.

17. In a chapter of his forthcoming study, as yet untitled, Russell Hittinger, the Warren Professor of Catholic Studies at the University of Tulsa in Oklahoma, has described telegraphically the ordeals of the whole Church in 18th-century France. During the French Revolution itself, all of the Church's property was confiscated and sold; 40,000 were guillotined, in a total of about 200,000 civilian deaths; in occupied Belgium, 8,000 priests were sentenced to deportation to penal colonies. During the century after the Revolution, French law effected the confiscation of Church property in the form of a tax on the sum accruing to a religious order through the death of a member, because the order inherited the dowry. For example, during the outbreak of yellow fever in French Sudan the government demanded 20,000 Francs as a dowry tax from the motherhouse of nuns who died nursing the sick.

18. For example, Hillel Halkin observes that "medieval Jews felt more comfortable with Islam than with Christianity because the former was, like Judaism, a pure monotheistic faith, whereas the latter, with its doctrine of the Trinity and its incarnate God, was tainted by polytheism and paganism" ("Out of Andalusia," *Commentary* 116, no. 2 [September 2003], 40).

19. See *International Religious Freedom Report, 2003* (Washington, D.C.: U.S. Department of State, 2003); and the testimony of Joseph Assad and Erping Zhang of the Center for Religious Freedom (Freedom House, Washington, D.C.) to the UN Special Rapporteur on Religious Intolerance: "Sudan commits religious persecution on a massive scale. Its record includes forced conversion, repression of those who do not subscribe to its version of Islam, the application of its interpretation of Sharia law to the entire population, support for the enslavement of those regarded as opponents of the regime, and the prosecution of a war widely considered 'genocidal'" ("Agenda Item XI: Civil and Political Rights," available at: http://www.freedomhouse.org/media/pressrel/unspeech2.htm).

20. "The condition of civil inferiority, which prevented Christians from attaining public offices, and the condition of religious inferiority, which closed them in an asphyxiated religious life and practice with no possibility of development, put the Christians to the necessity of emigrating, or, more frequently, to the temptation of converting to Islam" (Giuseppe de Rosa, "Christians in Islamic Countries," *La Civiltà Cattolica*, no. 3680 [October 18, 2003]).

21. George Washington, "Farewell Address to the People of the United States," September 17, 1796.

22. For a brief account of these loves, see Michael and Jana Novak, *Tell Me Why: A Father Answers His Daughter's Questions About God* (New York: Pocket Books, 1998), 71–73; see also Michael Novak, William Brailsford, and Cornelis Heesters, eds., *A Free Society Reader: Principles for the New Millennium* (New York: Lexington Books, 2000), 98–99.

23. Roderick Firth, "Ethical Absolutism and the Ideal Observer," *Philosophy and Phenomenological Research* 12 (1952): 317–345.

24. Gerard Manley Hopkins, "The Windhover," in John Pick, ed., *A Hopkins Reader* (Garden City, N.Y.: Image Books, 1966), 50.

25. Samuel Huntington, *The Third Wave: Democratization in the Late 20th Century* (Norman, Okla.: University of Oklahoma Press, 1993).

26. George Washington, "Farewell Orders to the Armies of the United States," November 2, 1783.

Chapter One

1. Richard E. Rubenstein, *Aristotle's Children: How Christians, Muslims, and Jews Rediscovered Ancient Wisdom and Illuminated the Dark Ages* (New York: Harcourt, 2003), 9; cf. John Marenbon, "Medieval Christian and Jewish Europe," in Seyyed Hossein Nasr and Oliver Leaman, eds., *History of Islamic Philosophy, Part II* (London and New York: Routledge, 1996), 1001.

2. Philip F. Esler, *The Early Christian World*, vol. 1 (New York: Routledge, 2000), 296.

3. See articles on each saint in *The Catholic Encyclopedia* (New York: Robert Appleton Co., 1908).

4. Ian Richard Netton, "Islamic Philosophy," in Edward Craig, ed., *The Routledge Encyclopedia of Philosophy* (New York: Routledge, 1998).

5. Cf. Rubenstein, *Aristotle's Children*, 85. Some translators call this book *The Confusion of the Philosophers*, and Frederick Copleston calls it *The Destruction of the Philosophers*; see Copleston, *A History of Philosophy: Medieval Philosophy*, vol. 2 (New York: Image Books, 1993), 195. Copleston also notes that Averroes defended Avicenna in a reply to al-Ghazali, "The Destruction of the Destruction of the Philosophers," ibid., 197.

6. Ibid., 199.

7. Ibid., 197.

8. Copleston recounts: "The *De Anima* was translated from the Greek before 1215, the translation from the Arabic by Michael Scot being somewhat later. William of Moerbeke produced a further version from the Greek or a corrected edition of the first translation from the Greek. Similarly there was a translation of the *Physics* from the Greek before the two translations from the Arabic by Gerard of Cremona and Michael Scot, while a translation of the *De Generatione et Corruptione* from the Greek preceded the translation from the Arabic by Gerard of Cremona. The *Politics* were translated from the Greek about 1260 by William of Moerbeke (there was no translation from the Arabic)" (ibid., 207).

9. Noting the conclusion of historians Etienne Gilson and Fernand Van Steenberghen that "no medieval master held the double-truth theory" (quoting Gilson, emphasis added), Ralph McInerny writes: "Perhaps our historians have adopted their position by deriving a negative historical fact from the demands of coherence. Since it cannot be simultaneously true that Thomas quoted one of his contemporaries and that there was no such contemporary to quote, it must be a historical fact that the double-truth was held by someone in the thirteenth century" (Ralph McInerny, ed., *De unitate intellectus contra Averroistas* [On There Being Only One Intellect] [West Lafayette, Ind.: Purdue University Press, 1993], 212–213, emphasis added).

10. John Henry Newman said, "The prophetic Revelation is a process of development: the earlier prophecies are pregnant texts out of which the succeeding announcements grow; they are types. It is not that first one truth is told, then another; but the whole truth or large portions of it are told at once, yet only in their rudiments, or in miniature, and they are expanded and finished in their parts, as the course of revelation proceeds" (*An Essay on the Development of Christian Doctrine* [New York: Longmans, Green & Co., 1908], 64).

11. Isma'il Raji al-Faruqi, *Al Tawhid: Its Implication for Thought and Life* (Herndon, Va.: The International Institute of Islamic Thought, 1992), 44.

12. Frederick Copleston, *A History of Philosophy*, vol. 2, part I (New York: Image Books, 1962), 219.

13. University of ND Press, 1986. See also his recent brilliant article, "Aquinas and Islam," *Modern Theology* 20, no. 1 (January 2004): 71–89; for a historian's view of differences between Christianity and Islam, see Alain Besanáon, "What Kind of Religion Is Islam?" (a chapter from his forthcoming book *Three Temptations of the Church*), *Commentary* (May 2004): 42–48.

14. According to Aquinas: "Since God is the cause of being, as such He must also be the provider of being, as such. Whatever then in any way is, falls under His providence. But singular things are beings, and indeed more so than universals, because universals do not subsist by themselves, but only in singulars."

He concludes with the example that not even a sparrow falls to the ground without the Creator's knowledge and power being present in it (*III Summa Contra Gentiles*, 75). The best account of Aquinas's view of the theory of God's knowledge and human liberty is Bernard J. Lonergan, *Grace and Freedom: Operative Grace in the Thought of Saint Thomas Aquinas*, edited by Frederick E. Crowe and Robert M. Doran (Toronto: University of Toronto Press, 2000).

15. "For a long time now there has been widespread an error concerning intellect that originates in the writings of Averroes. He seeks to maintain that what Aristotle calls the possible, but he infelicitously calls the material, intellect is a substance which, existing separately from the body, is in no way united to the body as its form, and furthermore that this possible intellect is one for all men" (Aquinas, *De unitate intellectus*, 1).

16. al-Faruqi, *Al Tawhid*, 5–6.

17. "Medieval agricultural productivity was drastically increased by innovations in plowing, crop rotation, the harness and iron horseshoes, and new crops" (Randall Collins, *Weberian Sociological Theory* [Cambridge: Cambridge University Press, 1986], 47).

18. For example, Professor Randall Collins has shown how, from about 1100 to 1350 A.D., the international system of Catholic monasteries put in place an explosion of economically useful inventions, the rule of law, and a rationalized system of responsibilities. "These [Cistercian] monasteries were the most economically effective units that had ever existed in Europe, and perhaps in the world, before that time. The community of monks typically operated a factory. There would be a complex of mills, usually hydraulically powered, for grinding corn as well as for other purposes. In iron-producing regions, they operated forges with water-powered trip-hammers; after 1250 the Cistercians dominated iron production in central France. Iron was produced for their own use but also for sale. In England, the entire monastic economy was geared toward

producing wool for the export market. The Cistercians were the cutting edge of medieval economic growth" (ibid., 52–58); Collins refers to Jean Gimpel, *The Medieval Machine* (New York: Penguin Books, 1976), 46–47, 67–68.

19. "Why this peculiarly European joie de trouver? This pleasure in new and better? This cultivation of invention or what some have called 'the invention of invention'? Different scholars have suggested a variety of reasons, typically related to religious values: The Judeo-Christian respect for manual labor, summed up in a number of biblical injunctions. One example: When God warns Noah of the coming flood and tells him he will be saved, it is not God who saves him. 'Build thee an ark of gopher wood,' he says, and Noah builds an ark to divine specifications" (David Landes, *The Wealth and Poverty of Nations* [New York: W. W. Norton & Co., 1998], 58).

Chapter Two

1. Mary Ann Glendon, A *World Made New: Eleanor Roosevelt and the Universal Declaration of Human Rights* (New York: Random House, 2001).

2. "Long before the encyclical Quadragesimo Anno proclaimed the principle of subsidiarity as 'the most important principle of social philosophy,' Abraham Lincoln had formulated it thus for practical use: 'The legitimate object of government is to do for a community of people whatever they need to have done but cannot do at all, or cannot so well do for themselves in their separate and individual capacities. In all that people can individually do as well for themselves, governments ought not to interfere'" (Oswald Nell-Breuning, "Social Movements: Subsidiarity," in Karl Rahner, *Sacramentum Mundi: An Encyclopedia of Theology*, 6 vols. [New York: Herder & Herder, 1968–1970], 6:115).

3. For criticism of the author's views by Anthony Giddens, John Lloyd, and Paul Ormerod, and his reply, see Michael Novak, *Is There a Third Way?* (London: IEA Health and Welfare Unit, 1998).

4. Ben Wattenberg, *The Birth Dearth: What Happens When People in Free Countries Don't Have Enough Babies?* (New York: Ballantine Books, 1987).

5. Victoria Curzon Price, "La Globalisation et la pensée liberale," unpublished lecture for the Summer University of Aix-en-Provence, 1999.

6. Ibid., citing UNCTAD, *World Investment Report* (various years). Also, the World Bank reports $619 billion in worldwide foreign direct investment for the year 1998 (*World Development Report 2000–2001* [Oxford: Oxford University Press, 2001]); Price, "La Globalisation et la pensée liberale"; Bruce Ross-Larson, ed., *Human Development Report 1999* (New York: United Nations Human Development Programme, 1999), 25.

7. Ibid.

8. Thomas L. Friedman, *The Lexus and the Olive Tree: Understanding Globalization* (New York: Farrar, Straus and Giroux, 1999), 8–9.

9. Richard Jolly and Bruce Ross-Larson, eds., *Globalization with a Human Face: Human Development Report, 1999* (New York: Oxford University Press for United Nations Development Programme, 1999).

10. Thomas A. Mensah, "International and Governmental Structures and Their Relation to Democracy," in Hans Zacher, ed., *Democracy: Some Acute Questions: Proceedings of the Fourth Plenary Session of the Pontifical Academy of Social Sciences, April 22–25, 1998* (Vatican City: Pontificia Academia Scientiarum Socialium, 1999), 354–355.

11. *World Population Prospects: 2000 Revision*, vol. 1, Comprehensive Tables (New York: United Nations, Department of Economic and Social Affairs, Population Division, 2001).

12. Angus Maddison, *The World Economy: A Millennial Perspective* (Paris: Organization for Economic Cooperation and Development, 2001), 28.

13. "Time Warp: 1900 Versus Now," *Time*, April 13, 1998, available at: http://www.time.com/time/time100/timewarp/timewarp.html.

14. World Population Prospects Population Database, available at http://esa.un.org/unpp/.

15. "The theory of moral ecology synthesizes a vast empirical literature . . . into a parsimonious nomological formulation. The philosophical and policy implications of moral ecology, in turn, highlight a poignant Tocquevillian dilemma: How can liberal societies, which leave individuals and companies largely free in the moral arena, shield themselves from cumulative moral depredation?" (Allen D. Hertzke, "The Theory of Moral Ecology," *Review of Politics* [Fall 1988]: 629–659).

16. My own work on moral ecology antedates Hertzke's (1988) essay, as he observes in his notes. While I found his treatment helpful, in what follows I continue my own line of reflection in my own way.

17. Karl R. Popper, *Open Society and Its Enemies*, 2 vols. (Princeton, N.J.: Princeton University Press, 1971); Rocco Pezzimenti, *The Open Society and Its Friends, with Letters from Isaiah Berlin and the Late Karl R. Popper* (Leominster and Rome: Gracewing and Millennium Romae, 1997), 173–178, 182–184.

18. Michael Novak, "'In God We Trust' ovvero il denaro e la sua morale," *Nuntium* (March 1999): 12–20, reprinted as "God and Money," *Catholic Dossier* (May-June 1999): 14–18.

19. Anatoly Shcharansky, *Fear No Evil: The Classic Memoir of One Man's Triumph over a Police State*, translated by Stefani Hoffman (New York: Public Affairs, 1998); Mihajlo Mihajlov, *Underground Notes*, translated by Maria Mihajlov Ivusic and Christopher W. Ivusic (London: Routledge and Kegan Paul, 1977), 105–124.

20. Thomas Aquinas, *Summa theologica* (New York: Blackfriars/McGraw-Hill Book Co., 1966), pt. I, question 29, article 1.

21. Leo XIII, *Rerum novarum* (Boston: Daughters of Saint Paul, [hereafter RN]1891), 11, 16, 17, 19, 27, 45.

22. "It is above all a question of *interdependence*," John Paul II noted, "sensed as a *system determining relationships* in the contemporary world, in its economic, cultural, political and religious elements, and accepted as a moral category. When interdependence becomes recognized in this way, the correlative response as a moral and social attitude, as a 'virtue,' is *solidarity*. This then is not a feeling of vague compassion or shallow distress at the misfortunes of so many people, both near and far. On the contrary, it is a *firm and persevering determination* to commit oneself to the common good; that is to say to the good of all and of each individual, because we are responsible for all" (*Sollicitudo Rei Socialis* [Vatican City: Libreria Editrice Vaticana, 1987], 38, emphasis added).

23. Jolly and Ross-Larson, *Globalization with a Human Face*.

24. "Moreover, it is becoming clearer how a person's work is naturally interrelated with the work of others. More than ever, work is *work with others* and *work for others*: it is a matter of doing something for someone else. Work becomes ever more fruitful and productive to the extent that people become more knowledgeable of the productive potentialities of the earth and more profoundly cognizant of the needs of those for whom their work is done" (John Paul II, *Centesimus Annus*, [London: Catholic Truth Society, 1991; hereafter *CA*], 31).

"Even in recent years it was thought that the poorest countries would develop by isolating themselves from the world market and depending only on their own resources. Recent experience has shown that countries that do this suffer stagnation and recession, while the countries that experience development have been those that succeed in taking part in the general interrelated economic activities at the international level" (ibid., 33).

25. "And where is the mobile-phone market growing most rapidly?" asks Jeremy Lott. "In the developing world, in places like Afghanistan, where such technology has meant the difference between being connected to the world and being cut off. . . . Bangladesh, whose person-to-phone ratio was 275-to–1, has had over 300 villages outfitted with phones." "For Bangladeshi farmers," John Micklethwait and Adrian Wooldridge write, "the phones provide liberation from middlemen. Rather than having to accept a broker's price, Bangladeshi farmers . . . find out the fair value of their rice and vegetables and avoid getting gouged in the process" ("Is Globalization Christian? Why the WTO Protestors Had It Wrong," *Christianity Today* [January-February 2002]); John Micklethwait and Adrian Wooldridge, *A Future Perfect: The Challenge and Promise of Globalization* (London: Heinemann, 2000).

26. *Caritas* is a specific type of love. It is not a sentimental love (as in the Latin word *affectus*), or the generic attraction of the opposite sexes for one another (*amor*), or the love by which one chooses one other to whom to commit oneself (*dilectio*), or even requited *dilectio*, human friendship (*amicitia*), but the suffering love (*caritas*) characteristic of the Persons of the Trinity for One Another, exhibited for humans in the life and death of Christ. For a fuller treatment, see Michael Novak, William Brailsford, and Cornelis Heesters, eds., *A Free Society Reader: Principles for the New Millennium* (New York: Lexington Books, 2000), ch. 10.

27. See, for example, Reinhold Niebuhr, *Nature and Destiny of Man* (New York: Charles Scribner's & Sons, 1964), 2:272–274.

28. Greg Easterbrook, *The Progress Paradox: How Life Gets Better While People Feel Worse* (New York: Random House, 2003), esp. ch. 1.

Chapter Three

1. Michael Novak, *Business as a Calling: Work and the Examined Life* (New York: Free Press, 1996); Michael Novak, "The Moral Heart of Capitalism," *National Review Online*, August 16, 2002.

2. Joerg Rieger, "Theology and Economics," *Religious Studies Review* 28, no. 3 (July 2002).

3. Pierre Bourdieu, "What Is Neoliberalism? A Program for Destroying Collective Structures Which May Impede the Pure Market Logic," and "The Essence of Neoliberalism—Utopia of Endless Exploitation," translated by Jeremy J. Shapiro, *Le Monde Diplomatique* (December 1998).

4. J. Philip Wogaman observed: "Once, following a lecture to students, Paul Tillich was asked whether he still supported socialism. The eminent theologian's answer came quickly: 'That is the only possible economic system from the Christian point of view.' This exchange took place in 1957" (*The Great Economic Debate* [Philadelphia: Westminster Press, 1977], 133).

5. "Nothing is easier than to give Christian asceticism a socialist tinge," noted Karl Marx and Friedrich Engels. "Has not Christianity declaimed against private property, against marriage, against the state? Has it not preached, in the place of these, charity and poverty, celibacy and mortification of the flesh, monastic life and Mother Church? Christian socialism is but the holy water with which the priest consecrates the heart-burnings of the aristocrat" (*The Communist Manifesto*, in Lewis S. Feuer, ed., *Basic Writings on Politics and Philosophy* [Garden City, N.Y.: Anchor Books, 1959], ch. 3).

6. "The world today is divided into ideological camps," he argued. "The adherents of each tell us with great assurance where we're at and what we should do about it. We should not believe any of them.

"Capitalist ideology, as based on the myth of growth, must be debunked.

"Socialist ideology, as based on the myth of revolution, must be debunked" (Peter L. Berger, *Pyramids of Sacrifice* [New York: Basic Books, 1974], xi–xii).

7. See Sidney Hook's essays on Socialism in *Pragmatism and the Tragic Sense of Life* (New York: Basic Books, 1974).

8. Irving Howe, "Introduction," in Irving Howe, ed., *Twenty-five Years of "Dissent": An American Tradition* (New York: Methuen, 1979), xiv.

9. Stuart Hampshire and Leszek Kolakowski, *The Socialist Idea* (New York: Basic Books, 1974).

10. Michael Harrington, *Toward a Democratic Left* (New York: Macmillan, 1968), esp. ch. 2, "The Dynamics of Misery."

11. Robert Heilbroner, *An Inquiry into the Human Prospect* (New York: W. W. Norton & Co., 1974); *Marxism: For and Against* (New York: W. W. Norton & Co., 1980).

12. Peter L. Berger, *The Capitalist Revolution: Fifty Propositions About Prosperity, Equality, and Liberty* (New York: Basic Books, 1986).

13. Friedrich A. von Hayek, *The Intellectuals and Socialism* (Menlo Park, Calif.: Institute for Humane Studies, 1971); *The Road to Serfdom* (Chicago: University of Chicago Press, 1972); Ludwig von Mises, *Socialism: An Economic and Sociological Analysis*, translated by J. Kahane (Indianapolis: Liberty Classics, 1981).

14. "We can see that all elements of the socialist idea . . . could be regarded as a manifestation of one basic principle: the suppression of individuality. . . . People would wear the same clothing and even have similar faces; they would live in barracks. There would be compulsory labor followed by meals and leisure activities in the company of the same labor battalion. Passes would be required for going outside. Doctors and officials would supervise sexual relations, which would be subordinated to only two goals: the satisfaction of physiological needs and the production of healthy offspring. Children would be brought up from infancy in state nurseries and schools. Philosophy and art would be completely politicized and subordinated to the educational goals of the state" (Igor Shafarevich, *The Socialist Phenomenon*, translated by William Tjalsma [New York: Harper & Row, 1980], 269).

15. Michael Novak, *The Spirit of Democratic Capitalism* (New York: Simon & Schuster, 1982), chs. 10–13, 15–17.

16. Ibid.; see also Edward W. Younkins, ed. *Three in One* (Lanham, Md.: Rowman & Littlefield, 2001), ch. 9, "Continuous Revolution."

17. See, for example, Charles Murray, *What It Means to Be a Libertarian: A Personal Interpretation* (New York: Broadway Books, 1997); David Boaz, *Libertarianism: A Primer* (New York: Free Press, 1997); Edmund A. Opitz, *The Libertarian Theology of Freedom* (Tampa, Fla.: Hallberg Publishing, 1999).

18. "Following the impulse for radical simplification, some demonstrators called for 'only one color.' However, the idea of one unifying color was most fully developed by social revolutionaries in their search for a banner to rival the tricolors of national revolutionaries . . . The future banner of international revolution, the red flag, made its modern debut in Paris during riots and demonstrations . . . on June 5, 1832. In a nocturnal scene worthy of his own melodramas, Victor Hugo unfurled the red flag that night on the barricades in the Rue de la Chanverie and lit a torch beside it, which, in his own words, added 'to the scarlet of the flag

I don't know what kind of sinister purple'" James H. Billington, *Fire in the Minds of Men* (New York: Basic Books, 1980), 159; Billington cites Veit Valentin, *Das Hambucher Nationalfest*, (Berlin, 1932), 37 and Maurice Dommanget, *Histoire du drapeau rouge des origins á la guerre de 1939* (Paris: Etoile, 1967), 51, 55.

19. "The influence that Marxism has achieved, far from being the result or proof of its scientific character, is almost entirely due to its prophetic, fantastic, and irrational elements. Marxism is a doctrine of blind confidence that a paradise of universal satisfaction is awaiting us just round the corner. Almost all the prophecies of Marx and his followers have already proved to be false, but this does not disturb the spiritual certainty of the faithful. . . . In this sense Marxism performs the character of a religion, and its efficacy is of a religious character. But it is a caricature and a bogus form of religion" (Leszek Kolakowski, *Main Currents of Marxism: Its Origin, Growth, and Dissolution*, vol. 3, *The Breakdown*, translated by P. S. Falla [Oxford: Clarendon Press, 1978], 525–526).

20. Alexis de Tocqueville, *Democracy in America*, translated by George Lawrence, edited by J. P. Mayer (New York: Anchor Books, 1969), 691–692; cited by Lawrence Harrison in "Culture Matters: Integrating Value and Attitude Change into Development; A Theoretical and Applied Research Project," unpublished paper, December 3, 2001.

21. Gunnar Myrdal, conversation with the author, Center for the Study of Democratic Institutions, Santa Barbara, Calif., published as "The Romantic Myrdal," *The Center Magazine* (May–June 1975).

22. "Skepticism about the link between cultural values and human progress is found particularly in two disciplines: economics and anthropology. For many economists, it is axiomatic that appropriate economic policy effectively implemented will produce the same results without reference to culture. The problem here is the case of multicultural countries in which some ethnic groups do better than others, although all operate with the same economic signals. Examples are the Chinese minorities in Thailand, Malaysia, Indonesia, the Philippines, and the United States; the Japanese minorities in Brazil and the United States; the Basques in Spain and Latin America; and the Jews wherever they have migrated" (Lawrence Harrison, *Culture Matters: How Values Shape Human Progress* [New York: Basic Books, 2000], xxiv.)

23. In conceptual depth and generality, and in the order of being, this level of discourse belongs first, although in my own inquiries (in the order of discovery) I came to it second.

24. On time, see Novak, *The Spirit of Democratic Capitalism*, ch. 5; on history and progress, see ibid., chs. 2–3; on development, see Michael Novak, *This Hemisphere of Liberty: A Philosophy of the Americas* (Washington, D.C.: American Enterprise Institute Press, 1990), chs. 6–7; Michael Novak, *Will It Liberate? Questions About Liberation Theology* (New York: Paulist Press, 1986), ch. 7; Michael Novak, *The Catholic Ethic and the Spirit of Capitalism* (New York: Free Press, 1993), ch. 6; Novak, *Business as a Calling*, chs. 4, 8–10; Michael Novak, *Catholic Social Thought and Liberal Institutions: Freedom with Justice*, 2nd ed. (New Brunswick, N.J.: Transaction, 1989), chs. 7, 9, 10.

25. On family, see Novak, *The Spirit of Democratic Capitalism*, ch. 8; on association, organization, and civil society, see Novak, *The Spirit of Democratic Capitalism*, chs. 2, 6; Novak, *The Catholic Ethic and the Spirit of Capitalism*, ch. 7; Novak, *Business as a Calling*, chs. 6–7; Michael Novak, *On Cultivating Liberty: Reflections on Moral Ecology* edited by Brian C. Anderson (Lanham, Md.: Rowman & Littlefield, 1999), ch. 4; Novak, *Catholic Social Thought and Liberal Institutions*, pt. 3; Michael Novak, *The Fire of Invention, the Fuel of Interest: On Intellectual Property* (Washington, D.C.: American Enterprise Institute Press, 1996), ch. 1; on the state, see Novak, *The Spirit of Democratic Capitalism*, pt. 2; Novak, *On Cultivating Liberty*, ch. 5.

26. On the individual, see Novak, *The Spirit of Democratic Capitalism*, ch. 7; on the person, see Novak, *This Hemisphere of Liberty*, ch. 4; Novak, *The Catholic Ethic and the Spirit of Capitalism*, epilogue; Michael Novak, *Free Persons and the Common Good* (Lanham, Md.: Madison Books, 1989), esp. ch. 1; on liberty, see Novak, *This Hemisphere of Liberty*; Novak, *On Cultivating Liberty*; Novak, *The Catholic Ethic and the Spirit of Capitalism*, ch. 4; on action, see Novak, *The Fire of Invention*, ch. 3; on habits and virtue, see Novak, *This Hemisphere of Liberty*, chs. 4, 5; Novak, *Business as a Calling*, chs. 5–7; Novak, *The Catholic Ethic and the Spirit of Capitalism*, ch. 3; Novak, *Free Persons and the Common Good*, 57–67, 103–107; Novak, *On Cultivating Liberty*, ch. 6; Novak, *Catholic Social Thought and Liberal Institutions*, pt. 3.

27. See Novak, *Business as a Calling*, ch. 5; Novak, *The Spirit of Democratic Capitalism*, ch. 5; Novak, *On Cultivating Liberty*, pt. 1.

28. On happiness and human flourishing, see Novak, *This Hemisphere of Liberty*, chs. 6–7; Novak, *Will It Liberate?* ch. 7; Novak, *The Catholic Ethic and the Spirit of Capitalism*, ch. 6; Novak, *Business as a Calling*, chs. 1, 4, 8–10; Novak, *Catholic Social Thought and Liberal Institutions*, chs. 7, 9, 10; on creativity and in-

vention, see Novak, *Business as a Calling*, ch. 6; Novak, *Will It Liberate?* ch. 5; on common good, public interest, and civility, see Novak, *Free Persons and the Common Good,* esp. ch. 1.

29. See Novak, *The Spirit of Democratic Capitalism*, ch. 11; Novak, *The Fire of Invention*, 108–113; Michael Novak, "Inequality and Ideology," American Enterprise Institute "On the Issues" paper, February 1996.

30. See Novak, *The Spirit of Democratic Capitalism*, ch. 9; Novak, *This Hemisphere of Liberty*, chs. 8–9; Novak, *Will It Liberate?* esp. ch. 10; Novak, *On Cultivating Liberty*.

31. See Novak, *The Spirit of Democratic Capitalism*, ch. 5; Novak, *Business as a Calling*, introduction; Novak, *Will It Liberate?* ch. 3; Novak, *The Catholic Ethic and the Spirit of Capitalism*, ch. 1.

32. See Novak, *Will It Liberate?* ch. 9; Novak, *The Catholic Ethic and the Spirit of Capitalism*, ch. 2; Novak, *Catholic Social Thought and Liberal Institutions*, pt. 2.

33. See Novak, *The Spirit of Democratic Capitalism*, ch. 4; Novak, *This Hemisphere of Liberty*, ch. 5; Novak, *Catholic Social Thought and Liberal Institutions*, ch. 3.

34. Paul Craig Roberts, *Washington Times*, October 23, 2002.

35. Rieger, "Theology and Economics," 215, 218.

36. Voslensky sketches the *nomenklatura* of the Stalinist era: "At the plenary meeting of the Central Committee in 1937, Stalin described the party in military terms: the 'higher command' consisted of between 3,000 and 4,000 'generals' (top-grade leaders), followed by between 30,000 and 40,000 'officers' (middle-grade leaders) and between 100,000 and 150,000 'noncommissioned officers' (junior leaders). This military terminology clearly demonstrates the hierarchical ideas that presided over the creation of the *nomenklatura*" (Michael Voslensky, *Nomenklatura: The Soviet Ruling Class*, translated by Eric Mosbacher [Garden City, N.Y.: Doubleday, 1984], 51).

37. Consider the findings of Stephen Hayward reported in the *2003 Index of Environmental Indicators*: "The national ambient sulfur dioxide (SO_2) level fell 2.9 percent in 2001, and has fallen 67 percent since 1976" [p. 38]. The Environmental Protection Agency's Toxics Release Inventory "shows a 51.2 percent decline in toxic releases since 1988 (and a reduction of 5.1 percent in 2000), a reduction of over 1.7 billion pounds a year" [54]. A study of carbon monoxide emissions in California for the Society of Automotive Engineers found that "between 1994 and 2001, carbon monoxide emissions declined 62 percent, nitrogen oxides fell 49 percent, non-methane organic compounds (ozone precursors) fell 67 percent, and benzene fell 82 percent," Stephen Hayward with Ryan Stowers, *2003 Index of Environmental Indicators* (San Francisco: Pacific Research Institute, 2003), 38, 40, 54.

38. Rieger, "Theology and Economics," 219.

39. Ibid., 218.

40. Ibid., 218–219, emphasis added.

41. "The natural effort of every individual to better his own condition, when suffered to exert itself with freedom and security, is so powerful a principle, that it is alone, and without any assistance, not only capable of carrying on the society to wealth and prosperity, but of surmounting a hundred impertinent obstructions with which the folly of human laws too often incumbers [sic] its operations" (Adam Smith, *An Inquiry into the Nature and Causes of the Wealth of Nations* [New York: Modern Library, 1937], 13, 508).

42. Rieger, "Theology and Economics," 218.

43. In 1982 the IEA/Roper Center Theology Faculty Survey (*This World*, Summer 1982) made clear that 37 percent of professors in theological schools wanted the United States to move in the direction of socialism; 36 percent thought Marxism was consistent with membership in their denomination; 92 percent thought democratic socialism was consistent; 70 percent thought that U.S. multinational corporations hurt the Third World; 70 percent believed that the United States treated the Third World unfairly; 18 percent found the United States to be a force for ill in the world; and only 25 percent thought of the United States as a neutral force. Karl Zinsmeister reported in *The American Enterprise* (August 2002) that in the following university departments the ratio of Democrats to Republicans is: Cornell University—economics, 10:3, history 29:0, political science 16:1; Harvard—economics, 15:1, political science 20:1; Stanford University—economics 21:7, history 22:2, political science 26:4.

44. Rieger, "Theology and Economics," 215.

45. Paul Johnson writes: "Most Domesday predictions, such as (to cite two very characteristic examples) E. J. Mishan's *The Costs of Economic Growth* and the study sponsored by the Club of Rome, *The Limits of Growth* by Dennis and Donella Meadows, J. Randers and W. W. Behrens, leave out of account the magnitude of natural forces. Nature makes man's efforts seem puny. Thus, the Israeli scientists at the Desert Agriculture Station at Beersheba scoff at the theory that destructive Arab methods of cultivation were responsible for the

spread of desert in North Africa and the Middle East: desication on this scale would be beyond even modern technology, let alone the powers of the medieval Arabs. Deserts are usually created by relatively small change in climate. The fact is that nature itself is both a pollutant and a self-cleansing mechanism on a gigantic scale. An average-size hurricane releases the energy of 100,000 H-bombs. Dr. Mishan's estimate that there were (1967) 10 million tons of man-made pollutants in the atmosphere should be set against the 1,600 million tons of methane gas emitted by natural swamps every year. Even cattle produce several million tons of methane gas annually; forests and other vegetation discharge 170 million tons annually of various hydrocarbons. Where artificial pollutants do raise problems, there is a tendency in the ecolobby to confuse questions of local industrial hygiene, which can easily be answered, with the world environment, which is unaffected" (*Enemies of Society* [New York: Atheneum, 1977], 91).

46. Consider the following: Life expectancy throughout the world increased from 1950 to 2000 from about 46 years to 75 years (UNPD, *World Population Prospects: The 1998 Revision*, vol. 1, *Comprehensive Tables*; vol. 2, *Sex and Age* [New York: United Nations Publications, 1999]); infant mortality decreased from 1950 to 2000 from about 155 to 20 per 1,000 live births (ibid.); and the yield in tons per hectare of rice, corn, and wheat in *developing* countries increased from 1950 to 2000 from 1.0 ton to just over 2.5 tons (U.S. Department of Agriculture, *Production Databases from March 1998, March 2000*, and *February 2001*, Washington, D.C.: U.S. Department of Agriculture).

47. "Despite the tremendous expansion of the international grain trade over the past century, for example, the inflation-adjusted, dollar-denominated international price of each of the major cereals—corn, wheat, and rice—fell by over 70 percent between 1900 and 1998" (Nicholas Eberstadt, "Population Sense and Nonsense," *Weekly Standard* 8, no. 1, September 16, 2002, 31).

48. The IRS reports that the top 10 percent of all income earners in the United States earned above $92,144 per annum ("Individual Income Tax Returns with Positive Adjusted Gross Income [AGI]: Tax Years 1986–2000," unpublished Statistics of Income (SOI) data, Excel version 4, September 2002).

49. U.S. Bureau of Labor Statistics, *Civilian Employment-Population Ratio*, series LFS1600000 (Washington, D.C.: U.S. Department of Labor).

Bureau of Economic Analysis, *National Income and Product Accounts Tables: Table 6.8C. Persons Engaged in Production by Industry*.

U.S. Small Business Administration, *Small Business Economic Indicators, 2000* (Washington, D.C.: U.S. Small Business Administration, 2001). Fortune, unpublished figures obtained directly from editors, November 6, 2002.

50. Maritain notes several qualities of the American character that "give the lie to the fable of American materialism": "what I know is that the basic characteristics of the American people are generosity, good will, the sense of human fellowship" (*Reflections on America* [New York: Charles Scribner's Sons, 1958], 33).

Chapter Four

1. Thomas Sowell, *A Conflict of Visions: Ideological Origins of Political Struggles* (New York: Basic Books, 2002).

2. Thomas Sowell, *A Personal Odyssey* (New York: Free Press, 2000).

3. Thomas Sowell, *The Vision of the Anointed* (New York: Basic Books, 1995).

4. Thomas Sowell, *Basic Economics: A Citizen's Guide to the Economy* (New York: Basic Books, 2000).

5. U.S. Bureau of Economic Analysis, "GDP and Other Major Series, 1929–2003," *Survey of Current Business* 84 (February 2004): 152–176, available at: http://www.bea.gov/bea/ARTICLES/2004/02february/0204GDP&Other.pdf.

6. James H. Billington, *Fire in the Minds of Men*, 159.

7. Thomas Jefferson, "A Bill for Establishing Religious Freedom," 1779.

8. See Michael Novak, *Awakening from Nihilism* (Washington, D.C.: Crisis Books, 1995).

9. Nicholas Eberstadt, memo to the author, March 5, 2004.

10. "A Survey of India" (magazine insert), *The Economist* (February 21, 2004), 13.

11. Jagdish Bhagwati, *In Defense of Globalization* (New York: Oxford University Press, 2004), 65.

12. "The Hungry Dragon," *The Economist* (February 21, 2004), 59–60.

13. "China Acts to Protect Private Property," *International Herald Tribune*, Dec. 22, 2003.

Chapter Five

1. Samuel P. Huntington, *The Third Wave: Democratization in the Late Twentieth Century* (Norman, Okla.: University of Oklahoma Press, 1991), 76.

2. Philip Jenkins projects in *The Next Christendom: The Coming of Global Christianity* (New York: Oxford University Press, 2002), that in 2025 there will be 2.6 billion Christians. His projections for the number of Catholics rely on information from David B. Barrett, George T. Kurian, and Todd M. Johnson, eds., *World Christian Encyclopedia*, 2nd ed. (New York: Oxford University Press, 2001), 195.

3. Drawing from eyewitness accounts of the persecution of Christians around the globe, Nina Shea writes: "The shocking, untold story of our time is that more Christians have died this century simply for being Christians than in the first nineteen centuries after the birth of Christ" (*In the Lion's Den* [Nashville: Broadman & Holman Publishers, 1997], 1).

One of the best governmental sources documenting religious persecution is U.S. Department of State, *Annual Report on International Religious Freedom* (Washington, D.C.: U.S. Government Printing Office).

4. Robert Royal, *The Catholic Martyrs of the Twentieth Century: A Comprehensive World History* (New York: Crossroad/Herder & Herder, 2000), 1.

5. "Man is understood in a more complete way," John Paul II tells us, "when he is situated within the sphere of culture through his language, history, and the position he takes towards the fundamental events of life, such as birth, love, work and death. At the heart of every culture lies the attitude man takes to the greatest mystery: the mystery of God" (*CA*, 24).

6. "Accordingly, two cities have been formed by two loves: the earthly by the love of self, even to the contempt of God; the heavenly by the love of God, even to the contempt of self. The former, in a word, glories in itself, the latter in the Lord. For the one seeks glory from men; but the greatest glory of the other is God, the witness of conscience" (Saint Augustine, *City of God* [New York: Alfred A. Knopf, 2001], bk. 14, ch. 28).

7. Cf. *Catechism of the Catholic Church* (1359): "The Eucharist, the sacrament of our salvation accomplished by Christ on the cross, is also a sacrifice of praise in thanksgiving for . . . all that God has made good, beautiful, and just in creation and in humanity" (Vatican City: Libreria Editrice Vaticana, 2000).

8. Following a principle traditionally attributed to Saint Augustine: "In necessary things, unity; in doubtful things, liberty; in all things, charity."

9. John Paul II: "The Church has no models to present; models that are real and truly effective can only arise within the framework of different historical situations, through the efforts of all those who responsibly confront concrete problems in all their social, economic, political and cultural aspects, as these interact with one another" (*CA*, 43).

10. "Each person collaborates in the work of others and for their good. Man works in order to provide for the needs of his family, his community, his nation, and ultimately all humanity. . . . Moreover, he collaborates in the work of his fellow employees, as well as in the work of suppliers and in the customers' use of goods, in a progressively expanding chain of solidarity" (*CA*, 43; see also 10, 15, 49, 51).

11. "The common good is not simply the sum total of particular interests; rather it involves an assessment and integration of those interests on the basis of a balanced hierarchy of values; ultimately, it demands a correct understanding of the dignity and the rights of the person" (*CA*, 47).

12. "We see in some countries and under certain aspects a positive effort to rebuild a democratic society inspired by social justice, so as to deprive Communism of the revolutionary potential represented by masses of people subjected to exploitation and oppression. In general, such attempts endeavor to preserve free market mechanisms, ensuring . . . the conditions for steady and healthy economic growth in which people through their own work can build a better future for themselves and their families. At the same time, these attempts try to avoid making market mechanisms the only point of reference for social life, and they tend to subject them to public control which upholds the principle of the common destination of material goods" (*CA*, 19).

13. "God gave the earth to the whole human race for the sustenance of all its members, without excluding or favoring anyone. This is the foundation of the universal destination of the earth's goods. The earth, by reason of its fruitfulness and its capacity to satisfy human needs, is God's first gift for the sustenance of human life. But the earth does not yield its fruits without a particular human response to God's gift, that is to say, without work" (*CA*, 31).

14. "The root of modern totalitarianism is to be found in the denial of the transcendent dignity of the human person who, as the visible image of the invisible God, is therefore by his very nature the subject of

rights which no one may violate . . . not even the majority of a social body . . . by isolating, oppressing, or exploiting [the minority], or by attempting to annihilate it" (*CA*, 44).

15. "The principle of subsidiarity must be respected: a community of a higher order should not interfere in the internal life of a community of a lower order, depriving the latter of its functions, but rather should support it in case of need and help to coordinate its activity with the activities of the rest of society, always with a view to the common good" (*CA*, 48).

16. "According to *Rerum novarum* and the whole social doctrine of the Church, the social nature of man is not completely fulfilled in the State, but is realized in various intermediary groups, beginning with the family and including economic, social, political and cultural groups which stem from human nature itself and have their own autonomy, always with a view to the common good. This is what I have called the 'subjectivity' of society which, together with the subjectivity of the individual, was canceled out by 'Real Socialism'" (*CA*, 13).

17. "It is by responding to the call of God contained in the being of things that man became aware of his transcendent dignity. Every individual must give this response, which constitutes the apex of his humanity, and no social mechanism or collective subject can substitute for it" (*CA*, 13).

18. "The first and fundamental structure for 'human ecology' is the family, in which man receives his first formative ideas about truth and goodness, and learns what it means to love and to be loved, and thus what it actually means to be a person" (*CA*, 39).

19. Pierre Manent, "Christianity and Democracy," *Crisis* (February 1995), reprinted in Michael Novak, William Brailsford, and Cornelius Heesters, eds., *A Free Society Reader: Principles for the New Millennium* (Lanham, Md.: Lexington Books, 2000).

20. Felix Sarda y Salvany, *El Liberalismo es pecado* (Barcelona: Libreria e Typografia Católica, 1887); originally published in English as *What Is Liberalism?* (St. Louis: B. Herder Book Co., 1899); reprinted 1979, 1989, 1993 (as *Liberalism Is a Sin*) by TAN Books and Publishers, Inc.

21. Luca Diotallevi, "Cultura politica e cultura religiosa, oggi, in Italia: il caso degli intellettuali," paper presented to the annual meeting of the Associazione Italiana di Sociologia, session on sociology in religion, Padova, Italy (November 28, 2003); cited by Sandro Magister in "Interventionists and Resisters: The Preview of a Study on the Catholic Intellectual Class," available at www.Chiesa, http://213.92.16.98/ESW_articolo/0,2393,42124,00.html.

22. Hernando de Soto, *The Other Path: The Invisible Revolution in the Third World* (New York: HarperCollins, 1989), 11–13.

23. For Jenkins's full discussion of the Catholic Church in Latin America, see *The Next Christendom*, 142–147, 194–198.

24. John Paul II, *CA*, 42.

25. See the discussion of both the Pope's reservations and his appropriations in Michael Novak, *The Catholic Ethic and the Spirit of Capitalism* (New York: Free Press, 1993), 114–144 (ch. 5, "Capitalism Rightly Understood").

26. Juan Forero, "Latin America's Political Compass Veers Toward the Left," *New York Times*, January 19, 2003.

27. Lawrence Harrison et al., *Culture Matters: Integrating Value and Attitude Change into Development: a Theoretical and Applied Research Project, Proposal to the Smith Richardson Foundation* (December 3, 2001). See also Lawrence Harrison, *Culture Matters: How Values Shape Human Progress* (New York: Basic Books, 2000), 299–300.

28. John Paul II, *CA*, 34.

29. The writings of many of these leaders have been compiled in Novak et al., *A Free Society Reader*. In Italy, see the works of Dario Antiseri and Flavio Felice; in Slovakia, Juraj Kohutiar; in Poland, Ryzard Legutko.

30. A full treatment of this concept can be found in Francis Fukuyama, *Trust: The Social Virtues and the Creation of Prosperity* (New York: Free Press, 1995). See also Novak, *The Catholic Ethic and the Spirit of Capitalism*, 203–206.

31. See Novak, *The Catholic Ethic and the Spirit of Capitalism*, "Epilogue: The Creative Person," esp. 232–237, and Michael Novak, *Business as a Calling* (New York: Free Press, 1996), ch. 5.

32. For the virtue of enterprise, see Michael Novak, *This Hemisphere of Liberty: A Philosophy of the Americas* (Washington, D.C.: American Enterprise Institute Press, 1990), ch. 4; for the virtues of enterprise, building community, and practical realism, see Novak, *Business as a Calling*, 119–133.

33. For a discussion of self-government and social justice, see Novak, *The Catholic Ethic and the Spirit of Capitalism*, 62–86, 185–194; Novak, *On Cultivating Liberty*, 14–17, 103–106; and Novak, *Business as a Calling*, 148–149.

34. See Novak, *This Hemisphere of Liberty*, 41–43; Michael Novak, *Free Persons and the Common Good* (Lanham, Md.: Madison Books, 1989), 65–69. Alexis de Tocqueville wrote: "Americans are pleased to explain almost all the actions of their life with the aid of self-interest well understood; they complacently show how the enlightened love of themselves constantly brings them to aid each other and disposes them willingly to sacrifice a part of their time and their wealth to the good of the state. I think that in this it often happens that they do not do themselves justice.

"The doctrine of self-interest well understood does not produce great devotion; but it suggests little sacrifices each day; by itself it cannot make a man virtuous; but it forms a multitude of citizens who are regulated, temperate, moderate, farsighted, masters of themselves; and if it does not lead directly to virtue through the will, it brings them near to it insensibly through habits.

"If the doctrine of self-interest well understood came to dominate the moral world entirely, extraordinary virtues would without doubt be rarer. But I also think that gross depravity would then be less common. The doctrine of self-interest well understood perhaps prevents some men from mounting far above the ordinary level of humanity; but many others who were falling below do attain it and are kept there. Consider some individuals, they are lowered. View the species, it is elevated" (*Democracy in America* [Chicago: University of Chicago Press, 2000], 501).

35. See Novak, *This Hemisphere of Liberty*, 21–24, 103–105; Michael Novak, *Will It Liberate? Questions About Liberation Theology* (New York: Paulist Press, 1986), 202–217.

36. William E. Simon, former Secretary of the Treasury, cofounded Wesray Corporation, a successful pioneer in mergers and acquisitions, and launched WSGP International, which concentrated on investments in real estate and financial service organizations in the western United States and on the Pacific Rim. In 1988 he founded William E. Simon & Sons, a global merchant bank with offices in New Jersey, Los Angeles, and Hong Kong. See http://www.ustreas.gov/education/history/secretaries/wesimon.html. William H. Brady was a prominent Milwaukee industrialist and philanthropist with wide-ranging interests in politics, culture, and art. He was for many years the chief executive officer of the W. H. Brady Company, recently renamed the Brady Corporation, a leading producer of industrial labels, fasteners, adhesives, and software with annual sales of more than $500 million (NYSE symbol BRC).

37. Information on the Sovereign Military Hospitaller Order of Malta may be found at: www.chivalri-corders.org/orders/smom/main3.htm.

38. This story, with the woman's name changed, was told to the author by an American missionary.

39. This story was adapted from Jeremy Lott, "Is Globalization Christian? Why the WTO Protestors Had It Wrong," *Christianity Today* (January-February 2002), available at: http://www.christianitytoday.com/bc/2002/001/12.32.html.

40. See for example, Steve Forbes, "Fact and Comment," *Forbes* (August 11, 2003): 21.

Chapter Six

1. "It is entirely possible that when the history of the 20th century is finally written, the single most important social movement of the period will be judged to be environmentalism" (Robert A. Nisbet, *Prejudices: A Philosophical Dictionary* [Cambridge, Mass.: Harvard University Press, 1982], 101).

2. "Writing in Scientific American in 1993, the volcanologists Millard Coffin and Olav Eldholm estimated that a single flood-basalt eruption placed into the air 17 billion tons of carbon dioxide, about 2.5 times the current annual human-caused emission; 3.5 billion tons of sulfur, some 30 times current annual artificial emissions; and 28 billion tons of halogen gases, one hundred times more than total artificial release of these ozone-depleting chemicals" (Gregg Easterbrook, *A Moment on the Earth* [New York: Viking, 1995], 32, citing Millard Coffin and Olav Eldholm, "Large Igneous Provinces," *Scientific American* [October 1993]).

3. See, for example, a new study of how wildfires release carbon dioxide into the atmosphere, reported by Tom Clarke, "Burning Bogs Belch Carbon," *Nature* (November 7, 2002).

4. Al Gore, *Earth in the Balance: Ecology and the Human Spirit* (Boston: Houghton Mifflin, 1992), 14.

5. United Nations, Division for Sustainable Development, Agenda 21, July 29, 2000.

6. See Joel Tarr, "Urban Pollution—Many Long Years Ago," *American Heritage*, October 1971, 65; U.S. Census Bureau, *Historical Statistics of the United States, Colonial Times to 1970* (Washington, D.C.: U.S. Gov-

ernment Printing Office, 1975), series S–4, 818, series P–362, 702, series K–498, 510; "50, 100 & 150 Years Ago: Septicwear," *Scientific American*, August 2000, 14.

7. "As Forest Reclaims American East, It's Man Versus Beast," *Wall Street Journal*, May 21, 2002: "The Great Eastern Forest has been coming back since the middle of the 19th century. It's not all back and it's not the same forest. But about 70 percent of the land that was forested in 1600 is forest again today.

"Massachusetts and Connecticut—once a virtually unbroken sea of trees—had lost 70 percent of their forests by the Civil War. Today, nearly two-thirds of their land is covered with trees. Similarly deforested, Vermont is now 80 percent woods, New Hampshire 90 percent . . . New York, 66 percent.

"Between 1901 and 1907, New York moved 34 beavers into the Adirondacks. Without predators, these original 34 resettlers—reproducing at a rate of between 3 and 5 kits annually—multiplied to around 15,000 by 1915. . . . Today, beavers number an estimated 15 million to 25 million in Canada and the U.S."

8. Curtis H. Flather, Stephen J. Brady, and Michael S. Knowles, *Wildlife Resource Trends in the United States* (Washington, D.C.: U.S. Department of Agriculture, Forest Service, Rocky Mountain Research Station, 2001).

9. Steven Hayward and Julie Majeres, *Index of Leading Environmental Indicators*, 7th ed. (San Francisco: Pacific Research Institute, 2002), 16.

10. Paul Johnson, *Enemies of Society* (New York: Atheneum, 1977), 95.

11. Hayward and Majeres, *Index of Leading Environmental Indicators*, 4, table 1, 16, and 19–23.

12. Steven Hayward and Julie Majeres, *Index of Leading Environmental Indicators*, 6th ed. (San Francisco: Pacific Research Institute, 2001); Steven Hayward, Elizabeth Fowler, and Laura Steadman, *Index of Leading Environmental Indicators*, 5th ed. (San Francisco: Pacific Research Institute, 2000).

13. Hayward and Majeres, *Index of Leading Environmental Indicators*, 7th ed., 5, citing Bjorn Lomborg, *The Skeptical Environmentalist* (Cambridge: Cambridge University Press, 2001), 3. Of the well-known controversy sparked by Lomborg's book, Hayward writes, "This level of vituperation belies either a disturbing self-righteousness that brooks no criticism and/or a lack of confidence that supposedly superior science can win out in a sustained debate" (6).

14. See "Julian Simon's Bet with Paul Ehrlich," available at: http://www.overpopulation.com/faq/People/julian_simon.html.

15. *Sapere* is the verb for *to taste*, and the most significant element in tasting things is the order in which tastes are arranged; serving vanilla ice cream with pickles disrupts the good tastes of both. A sign of *sapientia* is to put things in their right order so well that a better order is difficult to discern. Thus, King Solomon devised a simple test to discern the true order in the hidden desires of the two contesting mothers, who each claimed the infant was hers. "Split it with a sword," he ordered, and one mother instantly cried out in protest, "No!"

16. World Health Organization and United Nations Children's Fund, *Global Water Supply and Sanitation Assessment: 2000 Report* (Geneva: WHO and UN Children's Fund, 2000), 8.

17. Ibid.

18. United Nations Environment Programme, *Africa Environment Outlook: Past, Present, and Future Perspectives* (New York: United Nations Environment Programme, 2002), ch. 2, pt. E.

19. "At huge cost and great risk to the environment, the government plans to rechannel vast rivers of water from the Yangtze basin to the thirsty north, over three pathways of nearly 1,000 miles each. The official price tag of $58 billion, nearly half to be spent in the next eight years, is more than twice that of the Three Gorges Dam, China's most recent megaproject now nearing completion" (Erik Eckholm, "Chinese Will Have Water to Quench the Thirst of Cities," *New York Times*, August 27, 2002).

20. United Nations, *World Population Prospects: 1998 Revision* (New York: United Nations, 1998).

21. See James C. Riley, *Rising Life Expectancy: A Global History* (Cambridge: Cambridge University Press, 2001), 35–36.

22. Henry Adams, *The Education of Henry Adams* (Boston: Houghton Mifflin, 1961), ch. 15, "The Dynamo and the Virgin."

23. Ibid., 384–385. See the discussion by Robert Royal, *The Virgin and the Dynamo: Use and Abuse of Religion in Environmental Debates* (Washington, D.C.: Ethics and Public Policy Center, 1999), 1–30.

24. I owe this insight to Royal, *The Virgin and the Dynamo*, 12–13.

25. See Ron Bailey, ed., *Global Warming and Other Eco-myths: How the Environmental Movement Uses False Science to Scare Us to Death* (Roseville, Calif.: Prima Publishing, 2002), xx.

26. "At its modern founding, ideological environmentalists made sweeping claims about the impending fate of humanity and the Earth. . . . Not a single major prediction of ideological environmentalism has come true—no global famines, no cancer epidemics, and no resource depletion crisis" (ibid., xx, xxiii).

27. H. John Heinz II Center for Science, Economics, and the Environment, *The State of the Nation's Ecosystems: Measuring the Lands, Waters, and Living Resources of the United States* (New York: Cambridge University Press, 2002).

28. The introduction to the report's first part states: "This volume is intended as the first in a series of periodic reports on the extent, condition, and use of the lands, waters, and living resources of the United States. The 'ecosystem indicators' that form the heart of The State of the Nation's Ecosystems have been selected through a nonpartisan collaboration among government, environmental organizations, the private sector, and the academic community. The indicators thus represent a unique consensus on how the nation's ecosystems can be described—and their status tracked over time—in a fair and balanced way. They characterize what is most important to know about the nation's ecosystems, rather than merely reflecting what happens to have been measured. Finally, the data presented for each indicator are based on solid science—on verified measurements, not opinion—that have been reviewed by experts from all sectors of society" (ibid., 1).

29. Ibid., 181.

30. World Health Organization and United Nations Children's Fund, *Global Water Supply and Sanitation Assessment: 2000 Report*, 8.

31. CNN, "'Asian Brown Cloud' Poses Global Threat," August 12, 2002, available at: http://www.cnn.com/2002/WORLD/asiapcf/south/08/12/asia.haze. In a press release the same day of the CNN report, the United Nations Environmental Programme reported a new study of the effects of the "Asian Brown Cloud" in "Regional and Global Impacts of Vast Pollution Cloud Detailed in New Scientific Study," available at: http://www.unep.org/Documents/Default.asp?DocumentID=259&ArticleID=3103.

32. "In today's world, among other rights, the right of economic initiative is often suppressed. Yet it is a right which is important not only for the individual but also for the common good. Experience shows us that the denial of this right, or its limitation in the name of an alleged 'equality' of everyone in society, diminishes, or in practice absolutely destroys the spirit of initiative, that is to say the creative subjectivity of the citizen" (John Paul II, *Sollicitudo Rei Socialis*, [Boston: Pauline Books and Media,1987], 15).

33. Hernando de Soto, *The Mystery of Capital: Why Capitalism Triumphs in the West and Fails Everywhere Else* (New York: Basic Books, 2000).

34. Hernando de Soto, The *Other Path: The Invisible Revolution in the Third World* (New York: HarperCollins, 1989).

35. "Indeed, besides the earth, man's principal resource is man himself. His intelligence enables him to discover the earth's productive potential and the many different ways in which human needs can be satisfied. It is his disciplined work in close collaboration with others that makes possible the creation of ever more extensive working communities which can be relied upon to transform man's natural and human environments" (John Paul II, *CA*, 32).

36. "The original source of all that is good is the very act of God, who created both the earth and man, and who gave the earth to man, so that he might have dominion over it by his work and enjoy its fruits (Genesis 1:28). God gave the earth to the whole human race for the sustenance of all its members, without excluding or favoring anyone. This is the foundation of the universal destination of the earth's goods" (John Paul II, *CA*, 31).

Chapter Seven

1. "If patient observation and sincere meditation have led men of the present day to recognize that both the past and the future of their history consist in the gradual and measured advance of equality, that discovery in itself gives this progress the sacred character of the will of the Sovereign Master. In that case effort to halt democracy appears as a fight against God Himself, and nations have no alternative but to acquiesce in the social state imposed by Providence" (Alexis de Tocqueville, "Author's Introduction," *Democracy in America*, translated by George Lawrence and edited by J. P. Mayer [New York: Anchor Books, 1969], 12).

2. The English translations of *Democracy in America* are the Henry Reeve (1853) text, revised by Francis Bowen and further corrected and edited with a historical essay, editorial notes, and bibliographies by Philip Bradley (New York: Vintage Books, 1945); the version translated by George Lawrence and edited by J. P. Mayer (New York: Anchor Books, 1969); the version translated and edited by Harvey C. Mansfield and Delba

Winthrop (Chicago: University of Chicago Press, 2000); and Arthur Goldhammer, trans. and ed. (New York: Library of America, 2004).

3. For example: "Among democratic peoples new families continually rise from nothing while others fall, and nobody's position is quite stable. The woof of time is ever being broken and the track of past generations lost.

"As each class catches up with the next and gets mixed with it, its members do not care about one another as strangers. Aristocracy links everybody, from peasant to king, in one long chain. Democracy breaks the chain and frees each link.

"As social equality spreads there are more and more people who, though neither rich nor powerful enough to have much hold over others, have gained or kept enough wealth and enough understanding to look after their own needs. Such folk owe no man anything and hardly expect anything from anybody. They form the habit of thinking of themselves in isolation and imagine that their whole destiny is in their own hands" (Lawrence, *Democracy in America*, 507–508).

4. Tocqueville's focus on "equality" begins early in his volume and pervades the whole: "[T]he gradual progress of equality is something fated. The main features of this progress are the following: it is universal and permanent, it is daily passing beyond human control, and every event and every man helps it along" (Lawrence, *Democracy in America*, 12).

5. "Individualism" is a word recently coined to express a new idea. Our fathers only knew about egoism: "Egoism is a passionate and exaggerated love of self which leads a man to think of all things in terms of himself and to prefer himself to all.

"Individualism is a calm and considered feeling which disposes each citizen to isolate himself from the mass of his fellows and withdraw into the circle of family and friends; with this little society formed to his taste, he gladly leaves the greater society to look after itself" (Lawrence, *Democracy in America*, 506).

6. Ibid., 517.

7. "Nothing, in my view," Tocqueville wrote, "more deserves attention than the intellectual and moral associations in America.

"In democratic countries knowledge of how to combine is the mother of all other forms of knowledge; on its progress depends that of all the others.

"Among laws controlling human societies there is one more precise and clearer, it seems to me, than all the others. If men are to remain civilized or to become civilized, the art of association must develop and improve among them at the same speed as equality of conditions spreads" (ibid., 517).

8. Alexis de Tocqueville, *The Old Regime and the French Revolution*, translated by Stuart Gilbert (Garden City, N.Y.: Doubleday, 1955), 206.

9. "I am trying to imagine under what novel features despotism may appear in the world. In the first place, I see an innumerable multitude of men, alike and equal, constantly circling around in pursuit of the petty and banal pleasures with which they glut their souls. Each one of them, withdrawn into himself, is almost unaware of the fate of the rest.

"Over this kind of men stands an immense, protective power which is alone responsible for securing their enjoyment and watching over their fate. That power is absolute, thoughtful of detail, orderly, provident, and gentle. It would resemble parental authority if, fatherlike, it tried to prepare its charges for a man's life, but on the contrary, it only tries to keep them in perpetual childhood. . . . Why should it not entirely relieve them from the trouble of thinking and all the cares of living?

"Thus it daily makes the exercise of free choice less useful and rarer, restricts the activity of free will within a narrower compass, and little by little robs each citizen of the proper use of his own faculties. Equality has prepared men for all this, predisposing them to endure it and often even regard it as beneficial.

"Having thus taken each citizen in turn in its powerful grasp and shaped him to its will, government then extends its embrace to include the whole of society. It covers the whole of social life with a network of petty, complicated rules that are both minute and uniform, through which even men of the greatest originality and the most vigorous temperament cannot force their heads above the crowd. It does not break men's will, but softens, bends, and guides it; it seldom enjoins, but often inhibits, action; it does not destroy anything, but prevents much being born; it is not at all tyrannical, but it hinders, restrains, enervates, stifles, and stultifies so much that in the end each nation is no more than a flock of timid and hardworking animals with the government as its shepherd" (Lawrence, *Democracy in America*, 691–692, emphasis added).

10. The necessity of the free market, the limited priority of politics over economics, and the primacy of the spirit—this is a fairly good summary of the neoconservative position, as outlined in Irving Kristol's *Re-*

flections of a Neoconservative: Looking Back, Looking Ahead (New York: Basic Books, 1983). See also his *Neoconservatism: Selected Essays 1949–1995* (New York: Free Press, 1995).

11. For more on the Catholic Whig tradition, see Michael Novak, "Thomas Aquinas, the First Whig," in Novak, *This Hemisphere of Liberty* (Washington, D.C.: AEI Press, 1992), 107–112. See also Michael Novak, "The Catholic Whig Revisited," *First Things* (March 1990), reprinted in Michael Novak, *On Cultivating Liberty*, 145–160.

12. "When the world was under the control of a few rich and powerful men, they liked to entertain a sublime conception of the duties of man. It gratified them to make out that it is a glorious thing to forget oneself and that one should do good without self-interest, as God himself does. That was the official doctrine of morality at the time.

"I doubt whether men were better in times of aristocracy than at other times, but certainly they talked continually about the beauties of virtue. Only in secret did they study its utility. But since imagination has been taking less lofty flights, and every man's thoughts are centered on himself, moralists take fright at this idea of sacrifice and no longer venture to suggest it for consideration. So they are reduced to inquiring whether it is not to the individual advantage of each to work for the good of all, and when they have found one of those points where private advantage does meet and coincide with the general interest, they eagerly call attention thereto. Thus what was an isolated observation becomes a general doctrine, and in the end one comes to believe that one sees that by serving his fellows man serves himself and that doing good is to his private advantage" (Lawrence, *Democracy in America*, 525; see also Michael Novak on Madison and Tocqueville on "self-interest" in Michael Novak, *Free Persons and the Common Good* [Lanham, Md.: Madison Books, 1989], ch. 2).

13. "The Americans, on the other hand, enjoy explaining almost every act of their lives on the principle of self-interest properly understood. It gives them pleasure to point out how an enlightened self-love continually leads them to help one another and disposes them freely to give part of their time and wealth for the good of the state. I think that in this they often do themselves less than justice, for sometimes in the United States, as elsewhere, one sees people carried away by the disinterested, spontaneous impulses natural to man. But the Americans are hardly prepared to admit that they do give way to emotions of this sort. They prefer to give the credit to their philosophy rather than to themselves" (ibid., 526).

14. "In the United States there is hardly any talk of the beauty of virtue. But they maintain that virtue is useful and prove it every day. American moralists do not pretend that one must sacrifice himself for his fellows because it is a fine thing to do so. But they boldly assert that such sacrifice is as necessary for the man who makes it as for the beneficiaries" (ibid., 525).

15. Ibid., 502.

16. "I questioned the faithful of all communions; I particularly sought the society of clergymen, who are the depositaries of the various creeds and have a personal interest in their survival. As a practicing Catholic I was particularly close to the Catholic priests, with some of whom I soon established a certain intimacy. I expressed my astonishment and revealed my doubts to each of them; I found that they all agreed with each other except about details; all thought that the main reason for the quiet sway of religion over their country was the complete separation of church and state. I have no hesitation in stating that throughout my stay in America I met nobody, lay or cleric, who did not agree about that" (ibid., 295, emphasis added).

17. "Person signifies what is noblest in the whole of nature," wrote Thomas Aquinas (*Summa theologica*, Ia. xxix. 2). And elsewhere: "An individual who is governed for the sake of the species is not governed because of any inherent worth. But human persons come under divine providence in their own right, for the activities of rational creatures alone are divinely directed for the sake of the individual as well as of the species" (*III Summa Contra Gentiles*, 113; both quotations from Saint Thomas Aquinas: *Philosophical Texts*, translated by Thomas Gilby [New York: Oxford University Press, 1960], 389, 392). The historical emergence of personal dignity was beautifully treated by Jacques Maritain with respect to the arts in *Creative Intuition in Art and Poetry*, Bollingen Series (New York: Pantheon, 1953), and with respect to politics in *The Person and the Common Good*, translated by John J. Fitzgerald (New York: Charles Scribner's Sons, 1947).

18. Two important books on this theme are Jacques Maritain, *Reflections on America* (New York: Charles Scribner's Sons, 1958), and Raymond-Lèopold Bruckberger, *Image of America* (New York: Viking Press, 1959).

19. The first major summary of the evidence against the secularization thesis is found in Richard John Neuhaus, *Unsecular America* (Grand Rapids, Mich.: William B. Eerdmans Publishing Co., 1986).

20. Michael Medved's summary is apt: "As *Newsweek* magazine reported in January 1992: 'This week, if you believe at all in opinion surveys, more of us will pray than will go to work, or exercise, or have sexual re-

lations.' According to *Newsweek's* research, 78 percent of Americans pray at least once a week, and more than 40 percent attend worship services on a weekly basis. This means that the number of people who go to church in a given week is more than five times larger than the number of people who go to the movies. . . .

"Perhaps most astonishing of all, a poll reported in *U.S. News and World Report* (December 1991) asked American voters to describe 'their greatest objective in life'; fully 56 percent listed 'a closer relationship to God' as their top personal priority" (*Hollywood Versus America: Popular Culture and the War on Traditional Values* [New York: HarperCollins, 1992], 71). Medved also cites Gallup and other polling data.

21. The survey done of the 1992 election by John Green for the Pew Charitable trust shows that religious traditions do matter in politics. He summarizes the result: "84 percent of observant white evangelical Protestants voted for Bush. . . . Less observant white evangelical Protestants did not vote as strongly Republican, just 55 percent. . . . With Roman Catholics, a pattern continues that had been developing all through the 1990s: *more observant Roman Catholics voted more Republican, less observant more Democratic.* . . . In contrast to their white counterparts, black Protestants voted overwhelmingly for Gore: 96 percent. Of course, African Americans generally vote Democratic, but the black Protestant church is the strongest Democratic component of the African American community. Hispanics voted for Gore as well, particularly Hispanic Catholics, at 76 percent. Hispanic Protestants were a little more divided but still gave Gore 67 percent of their votes" (John Green, "How the Faithful Voted," *Center Conversations* [Ethics and Public Policy Center] 10 [March 2001]: 2, emphasis added). On the Catholic vote, see Steve Wagner, "Election 2000," *Crisis* (January 2001): 10–16.

22. Lawrence and Mayer, *Democracy in America*, 450.

23. Barry Moreno, *The Statue of Liberty Encyclopedia* (New York: Simon & Schuster, 2000).

24. Thucydides, *The Peloponnesian Wars* (New York: Modern Library, 1951), 331.

25. Lawrence and Mayer, *Democracy in America*, 288.

26. Alexander Hamilton, "The Farmer Refuted" (1775), in Harold C. Syrett, ed., *Papers of Alexander Hamilton* (New York: Columbia University Press, 1961).

27. George Washington, "Farewell Address," W. B. Allen, ed., *George Washington: A Collection*, (Indianapolis: Liberty Classics, 1988).

28. From "A Bill Establishing a Provision for Teachers of the Christian Religion," quoted in John Eidsmoe, *Christianity and the Constitution: The Faith of Our Founding Fathers* (Grand Rapids, Mich.: Baker Books, 1987), 310.

29. Lawrence, *Democracy in America*, vol. 1, pt. 2, 9, 292. It is here that Tocqueville called religion "the first of their political institutions."

30. Ibid.

31. Ibid., 293.

32. Ibid., Vol. II, 443.

33. Ibid., 442–446.

34. Ibid., 542ff.

35. Quoted in James Madison, *Notes of Debates in the Federal Convention of 1787* (New York: W. W. Norton and Co., 1987), 209–210, emphasis in the original.

36. Lawrence, *Democracy in America*, 291.

37. Ibid.

38. *Planned Parenthood of Southeastern Pennsylvania. v. Casey* (91–744), 505 U.S. 833 (1992).

39. "It was fitting that the Divine law [the Ten Commandments] should come to man's assistance not only in those things for which reason is insufficient, but also in those things in which human reason may happen to be impeded" (Thomas Aquinas, *Summa theologica* I-II, question 99, article 2, response 2).

40. Lawrence, *Democracy in America*, 46–47.

41. Justice Kennedy repeated the maxim of *Casey* in *Lawrence v. Texas* (02–102) 1 S. W. 3d 349.

42. Fifty-three countries have more than a 60 percent Catholic population, according to Matthew Bunson, 2003: *Our Sunday Visitor's Catholic Almanac* (Huntington, Ind.: Our Sunday Visitor, November 2002).

43. The constitutions of these 18 countries name Islam as the religion of the state: Pakistan, Iran, Saudi Arabia, Sudan, Malaysia, Iraq, Egypt, Jordan, Tunisia, Morocco, Kuwait, Afghanistan, Yemen, Syria, Bahrain, Libya, Oman, and Bangladesh (see http://islamic-world.net/islamic-state/assessing_consti.htm).

The Organization of Islamic Conferences (OIC) has 56 members, including countries that are not officially Muslim but whose Muslim populations want their country to participate (see http://www.oic-oci.org).

Chapter Eight

1. Professor Russell Hittinger, chair of Catholic studies at the University of Tulsa in Oklahoma, has described the situation crisply: "Leo XIII was born in 1810; became pope in 1878, and died in 1903. The first thing that needs to be said is that his entire life and ecclesiastical career was dominated by persecution of the church. The century began with the death of Pius VI who died in captivity in France after being kidnapped by the 'moderate' French government. The French Directory declared him to be 'the last Pope.' During his lifetime, Leo XIII had seen yet another pope kidnapped (Pius VII, in 1809–1814), three archbishops of Paris murdered, and half of the Prussian hierarchy imprisoned by Bismarck for refusing to cooperate in state control of the Church. Priests, monks, and nuns, by the tens of thousands throughout Europe, were expelled from their countries. Just one year after the 1900 Jubilee, the French government would pass a law that closed 2,500 Catholic schools" (lecture for the Slovak Summer Seminar on the Free Society, 2001).

2. See, for example, Robert Nisbet: "Bear in mind, too, that the first objects of the Jacobins' reforming zeal when they achieved power anywhere were representatives of the church: bishops, priests, monks, nuns, and others. The celebrated dechristianization decrees of 1793–94 had as their declared aim the extermination from France of Christianity in all its aspects" (*The Social Philosophers* [New York: Thomas Y. Crowell, 1973], 215).

3. "The magisterium of the Church was slow to speak about democracy, and did so even then with considerable circumspection, if not suspicion." Also, "The word 'democracy' was very little used in papal documents before 1965, and does not appear in any of the conciliar documents!" (Michel Schooyans, "Democracy in the Teaching of the Popes," *Proceedings of the Workshop on Democracy* [Vatican City: Pontificia Academia Scientiarum Socialium, 1996; hereafter *DEM*], 11, 26).

4. In that message, *Benignitas* (Christmas 1944), Pius XII wrote: "Gripped in the grim light of war, *peoples have awakened* as if from a long slumber. They have taken up a new stance toward the State and governments, questioning, criticizing and mistrusting them. Educated through bitter experience, they view the monopoly of dictatorial, uncontrollable and intangible power with mounting repugnance and rejection. They demand a system of government more compatible with the dignity and freedom of citizens" (Schooyans, *DEM*, 22, emphasis added).

5. "When we try to study democracy in the teaching of the Church, we are most struck by the rarity of systematic statements—a rarity in contrast with the large amount of scattered but relatively uncoordinated material on the subject. It is with John Paul II that the topic starts to appear fairly regularly—and more particularly that the spotlight is really focused on it" (Schooyans, *DEM*, 31).

6. "It must be admitted that nowhere is there a detailed discussion of the problems raised by different conceptions and contemporary models of democracy. In the last analysis, teaching on this subject seems somewhat sketchy and in urgent need of development" (Schooyans, *DEM*, 32).

7. For the first volume (*DEM*), see note 3; *Democracy: Some Acute Questions—Proceedings of the Fourth Plenary Session of the Pontifical Academy of Social Sciences, April 22–25, 1998* (Vatican City: Pontificia Academia Scientiarum Socialium, 1999; hereafter *DAQ*); and *Democracy: Reality and Responsibility—Proceedings of the Sixth Plenary Session of the Pontifical Academy of Social Sciences, February 23–26, 2000* (Vatican City: Pontificia Academia Scientiarum Socialium, 2001; hereafter *DRR*).

8. John Paul II, *CA*, 46.

9. Leo XIII, letter to Cardinal Gibbons (1888): "We desire that you should assure the President of our admiration for the Constitution of the United States, not only because it enables industrious and enterprising citizens to attain so high a level of prosperity, but also because under its protection your countrymen have enjoyed a liberty which has so confessedly promoted the astonishing growth of religion in the past and will, we trust, enable it in the future to be of the highest advantage to the civil order as well" (a copy of the letter is in the Cathedral Archives, Baltimore; see Allen Sinclair Will, *Life of Cardinal Gibbons* [New York: E. P. Dutton & Co., 1922] 1:412).

10. Schooyans, *DEM*, 22–27.

11. "A full examination of the teaching of the Church on democracy would require study of the involvement of lay people and/or priests who have fought for social and then political democracy, albeit without formulating the theory. We would have to mention such figures as Buchez, Lamennais, Toniolo, Fathers Lennie, Naudet, Taparelli d'Azeglio, Liberatore, Romolo Murri and Luigi Sturzo. . . . We would have to study the origin and action of Christian democratic parties—the Belgian Catholic Party, the Dutch Catholic Party, the German Zentrum Party, the Italian Popular Party, the Czechoslovakian Populist Catholic Party, etc. Closer to our own times, we would have to recall the influence of philosophers such as Maritain, Mounier and Jacques

Leclercq, and the activity of Marc Sangnier, De Gasperi, Robert Schuman, Adenauer, and de Gaulle. We would have to assess the political impact of the positions taken up by Archbishop John Ireland of St. Paul, Cardinal Gibbons in Baltimore and Cardinal Manning in London, or, more recently still, Cardinal Cardijn in many parts of the world (Schooyans, *DEM*, 15).

12. Mary Ann Glendon, A *World Made New: Eleanor Roosevelt and the Universal Declaration of Human Rights* (New York: Random House, 2001).

13. *Gaudium et Spes* in *Vatican Council II: The Conciliar and Post Conciliar Documents*, new revised edition 1992 (Northport, NY: Costello Publishing Company, 1992 [hereafter *GS*]), 73.

14. "The Synod further declares that the right to religious freedom has its foundation in the very dignity of the human person, as this dignity is known through the revealed Word of God and by reason itself. This right of the human person to religious freedom is to be recognized in the constitutional law whereby society is governed, and thus it is to become a civil right. It is in accordance with their dignity as persons, that is, beings endowed with reason and free will and therefore privileged to bear personal responsibility, that all men should be once impelled by nature and also bound by a moral obligation to seek the truth, especially religious truth" (*Dignitatis Humanae* in *Vatican Council II: The Conciliar and Post Conciliar Documents*, new revised edition 1992 [Northport, N.Y.: Costello Publishing Company, 1992 (hereafter *DH*)], 2.)

15. Michael Zuckert writes that "the state of nature, according to Hobbes, is the home of the right of nature (jus naturale), or the right of all men to everything, including one another's bodies." He adds that, according to Locke, "in the state of nature, human beings possess 'a title to perfect freedom, and an uncontrolled enjoyment of all the rights and privileges of the law of nature'" (Michael Zuckert, *Natural Rights and the New Republicanism* [Princeton, N.J.: Princeton University Press, 1994], 138, 83).

16. "The idea of natural rights grew up—perhaps could only have grown up in the first place—in a religious culture that supplemented rational argumentation about human nature with a faith in which humans were seen as children of a caring God. But the idea was not necessarily dependent on divine revelation, and later it proved capable of surviving into a more secular epoch" (Brian Tierney, *The Idea of Natural Rights* [Grand Rapids, Mich.: William B. Eerdmans Publishing Co., 1997], 343).

17. "It should be noted that in today's world, among other rights, the right of economic initiative is often suppressed. Yet it is a right which is important not only for the individual but also for the common good. Experience shows us that the denial of this right, or its limitation in the name of an alleged 'equality' of everyone in society, diminishes, or in practice absolutely destroys the spirit of initiative, that is to say the creative subjectivity of the citizen" (John Paul II, *Sollicitudo Rei Socialis*, 15).

18. "At no time have men had such a keen sense of freedom" (*GS*, 4).

19. Partha Dasgupta, "Democracy and Other Goods," *DRR*, 26.

20. Michel Schooyans, "Democracy in the Teaching of the Popes," *DEM*, 17.

21. Nicholas J. McNally, "Democracy in Africa," *DEM*, 101–102; Göran Therborn, "Ambiguous Ideals and Problematic Outcomes: Democracy, Civil Society, Human Rights, and Social Justice," *DRR*, 148–155; and Habib Malik, "Democracy and Religious Communities: The Riddle of Pluralism," *DRR*, 381–399.

22. McNally, *DEM*, 102.

23. Michel Schooyans, "Démocratie et Valeurs: Quelle stratégie dans une société pluraliste?" *DRR*, 46.

24. Taketoshi Nojiri, "Values as a Precondition of Democracy," *DAQ*, 92, emphasis added.

25. Ibid., 98, emphasis added.

26. Schooyans, "Democracy in the Teaching of the Popes," *DEM*, 13.

27. John Paul II, *CA*, 44. According to Schooyans, without checks and balances, the United Nations, for instance, now threatens the very rights that its Universal Declaration of Human Rights sought to protect: "The conception of value which predominates today in UN circles is resolutely empiricist. According to UN technocrats, the values are the result of a utilitarian calculus obtained by consensus or majority decision. The values are values of preference; they are expressed in the frequency of choice and are measured in histograms: a triumph for the Gauss Curve. Whence comes the tyranny of the majority, already denounced by Tocqueville [*Democracy in America*, II, 3]. What counts is the satisfaction of man's passions. The fundamental right of man is the right to satisfy his individual passions, even to the point of suicide. That is what ought to confirm positive law" (*DRR*, 38, translated from the French).

28. John Paul II observed: "Another task of the State is that of overseeing and directing the exercise of human rights in the economic sector. However, primary responsibility in this area belongs not to the State but to individuals and to the various groups and associations which make up society. The State could not directly ensure the rights to work for all its citizens unless it controlled every aspect of economic life and restricted the free initiative of individuals" (*CA*, 48).

29. "The principle of subsidiarity must be respected: a community of a higher order should not interfere in the internal life of a community of a lower order, depriving the latter of its functions, but rather should support it in case of need and help to coordinate its activity with the activities of the rest of society, always with a view to the common good" (John Paul II, *CA*, 48).

30. "In the world of 1800, one democracy existed, the small United States of America. If we look next at 1850, America had been joined in the democratic camp by Belgium, Switzerland, and to some extent England" (Joshua Muravchik, *Exporting Democracy* [Washington, D.C.: AEI Press, 1991], 79).

31. Genesis 1:26a–27: "Then God said: 'Let us make man in our image, after our likeness.' God created man in his image; in the divine image he created him; male and female he created them." Deuteronomy 10:17–19: "For the LORD, your God, is the God of gods, the LORD of lords, the great God, mighty and awesome, who has no favorites, accepts no bribes; who executes justice for the orphan and the widow, and befriends the alien, feeding and clothing him. So you too must befriend the alien, for you were once aliens yourselves in the land of Egypt." Jeremiah 1:4–5a: "Before I formed you in the womb I knew you, before you were born I dedicated you."

32. Robert Nisbet writes on "progress": "There are at least two misconceptions about this historic idea: first, that it is a uniquely modern idea, and second, that its rise is the consequence of secularism, of Western thought's liberation from Christian theology. But the truth is that the idea originated in classical Greece and subsequently achieved its fullest expression in Christian philosophy of history. It is in fact the general weakening of the Christian foundations of Western culture that explains much of the parlous state in which this once-grand idea now lies" (*Prejudices: A Philosophical Dictionary* [Cambridge, Mass.: Harvard University Press, 1982], 238–239).

33. Article 16 of the "Virginia Declaration of Rights" acknowledges: "That Religion, or the duty which we owe to our Creator, and the manner of discharging it, can be directed only by reason and conviction, not by force or violence; and, therefore, all men are equally entitled to the free exercise of religion, according to the dictates of conscience; and that it is the mutual duty of all to practice Christian forbearance, love, and charity, towards each other" ("The Virginia Declaration of Rights" [1776], in *The Founders' Constitution*, Philip B. Kurland and Ralph Lerner, eds. [Chicago: University of Chicago Press, 1987], 1:7, emphasis in the original).

A similar principle animates James Madison's *Memorial and Remonstrance Against Religious Assessments*: "The religion then of every man must be left to the conviction and conscience of every man; and it is the right of every man to exercise it as these may dictate" (Ibid., vol. 5, 82).

34. Brian Tierney notes: "The doctrine of rights shaped by the experience of previous centuries turned out to be still of value in addressing the problems of a new era. The proponents of the secularized rights theories of the Enlightenment had often forgotten the remoter origins of the doctrines they embraced; but their rhetoric about the rights of man becomes fully intelligible only when it is seen as the end product of a long process of historical evolution" (*The Idea of Natural Rights*, 343; see also Russell Kirk, *The Roots of American Order* [Washington, D.C.: Regnery Gateway, 1991], esp. chs. 3 and 4 on the Greek and Roman worlds).

35. Kaufmann, Franz-Xavier, "Democracy Versus Values," *DAQ*, 116.

36. Ibid., 116–117.

37. The 1996 conference studied the following regions: Western Europe, post-Communist countries, Latin America, Asia, and Africa. The 1998 conference considered the interaction of regional states and globalization.

38. As John Paul II has noted: "If one does not acknowledge transcendent truth, then the force of power takes over, and each person tends to make full use of the means at his disposal in order to impose his own interests or his own opinion, with no regard for the rights of others. People are then respected only to the extent that they can be exploited for selfish ends" (*CA*, 44).

39. "Those who are convinced that they know the truth and firmly adhere to it are considered unreliable from a democratic point of view, since they do not accept that truth is determined by the majority, or that it is subject to variation according to different political trends" (John Paul II, *CA*, 46; see also Schooyans, *DEM*, 30).

40. "Democracy seeks to bring about the participation of all people in all spheres of the life of society—participation in the twofold sense of sharing in the benefits and drawbacks offered by society, and making a personal contribution to building up the common good" (Schooyans, *DEM*, 13).

41. Stefano Bartolini, "European Integration and Democracy: Some Skeptical Reflections," *DAQ*, 315.

42. James Madison observed: "The latent causes of faction are thus sown in the nature of man; But the most common and durable source of factions has been the various and unequal distribution of property. A

landed interest, a manufacturing interest, a mercantile interest, a moneyed interest, with many lesser interests, grow up of necessity in civilized nations, and divide them into different classes, actuated by different sentiments and views. Extend the sphere [of the society, i.e., the territory and the number of its citizens] and you take in a greater variety of parties and interests; you make it less probable that a majority of the whole will have a common motive to invade the rights of other citizens" (*The Federalist Papers* 10 [New York: New American Library, 1961], pp. 45, 51).

43. Nojiri, *DAQ,* 100.

44. Joachim Bony, "Culture et Democratie," *DAQ,* 263.

45. "Fundamental conceptions of democracy from Plato and Aristotle to Thomas Aquinas and Gramsci are premised on an education designed to develop in each individual the fundamental capacity to think critically and an ability to find one's way in life" (Paulus Zulu, "Education as a Precondition for Democracy," *DRR,* 170, emphasis added).

46. Isaiah Berlin, "Two Concepts of Liberty" in *The Proper Study of Mankind* (New York: Farrar, Straus, and Giroux, 2000).

47. "Man's capacity for justice makes democracy possible; but man's inclination to injustice makes democracy necessary" (Reinhold Niebuhr, *The Children of Light and the Children of Darkness* [New York: Charles Scribner's & Sons, 1944], xiii–xv).

48. "In modern societies the apparent 'decay of values' at the level of individual attitudes is compensated for by the institutionalization of rules and procedures by which comparable effects are achieved at the level of behavior" (Kaufmann, *DAQ,* 133–134, emphasis added).

49. Kaufmann, *DAQ,* 124. Churchill said: "No one pretends that democracy is perfect or all-wise. Indeed, it has been said that democracy is the worst form of Government except all those other forms that have been tried from time to time" (speech, Hansard, November 11, 1947, col. 206, reprinted in *The Oxford Dictionary of Quotations,* 4th ed., edited by Angela Parthington [Oxford: Oxford University Press, 1992], 202).

50. "Equating democracy solely, or even principally, with majority rule becomes therefore a ready recipe for persecution of ethno-religious minorities" (Malik, *DRR,* 391–392).

51. "The two great points of difference between a democracy and a republic are: first, the delegation of the government, in the latter, to a small number of citizens elected by the rest; secondly, the greater number of citizens and greater sphere of country over which the latter may be extended.

"In the first place it is to be remarked that however small the republic may be the representatives must be raised to a certain number in order to guard against the cabals of a few; and that however large it may be they must be limited to a certain number in order to guard against the confusion of a multitude" (James Madison, *The Federalist Papers* 10, p. 50).

52. "To that end, it is preferable that each power be balanced by other powers and by other spheres of responsibility which keep it within proper bounds" (John Paul II, *CA,* 42; see also note 27).

53. "Civil society exists for the common good, and hence is concerned with the interests of all in general, albeit with individual interests also in their due place and degree. It is therefore called a public society. . . . But societies which are formed in the bosom of the commonwealth are styled private, and rightly so, since their immediate purpose is the private advantage of the associates" (Leo XIII, *RN,* 51).

54. "The totalitarian State tends to absorb within itself the nation, society, the family, religious groups and individuals themselves" (John Paul II, *CA,* 45).

55. "The policy of supplying, by opposite and rival interests, the defect of better motives, might be traced through the whole system of human affairs, private as well as public. We see it particularly displayed in all the subordinate distributions of power, where the constant aim is to divide and arrange the several offices in such a manner as that each may be a check on the other—that the private interest of every individual may be a sentinel over the public rights" (James Madison, *The Federalist Papers* 51, p. 290).

56. Hans F. Zacher, "Democracy: Common Questions," *DEM,* 126.

57. See Malik, *DRR,* 387–400.

58. "An independent judiciary with adequate integrity and power to maintain the rule of law and to protect basic human rights" (McNally, *DEM,* 102).

59. Zacher, *DEM,* 126.

60. Bartolini, *DAQ,* 313.

61. "State machinery, in particular the administration . . . may not be viewed and acted upon only as an instrument of the current government. The legal order can and should also subject it to a direct obligation—under the ultimate responsibility of the government" (Zacher, *DEM,* 126).

62. Nojiri, *DAQ,* 96.

63. Alexis de Tocqueville, *Democracy in America*, translated by George Lawrence and edited by J. P. Mayer (New York: Anchor Books, 1969) vol. I, pt. 2, ch. 9, 292.

64. McNally, *DEM*, 102.

65. Dasgupta emphasizes that "the *demos* must include all adult members of the association except transients and persons proved to be mentally defective" (*DRR*, 22). Dasgupta draws this essential element, and four others, from the work of Robert Dahl, *Democracy and Its Critics* (New Haven, Conn.: Yale University Press, 1989), 119–131.

66. "Differences arising from the existing pluralism in society are to be aired under the sway of three non-negotiable premises: the rule of law, a tolerant civility, and a modicum of universally accepted moral norms of conduct" (Malik, *DRR*, 376).

67. "The Church thus follows a tradition going back to Aristotle, recommending the moral virtues whose practice is a necessary condition—albeit only partial—for democracy: justice, a social sense, solidarity, prudence, fortitude, moderation, respect for others, etc." (Schooyans, *DEM*, 33).

68. "There should be recognized and acknowledged equality among participants so that views expressed by the various parties are accepted as being of equal value" (Zulu, *DRR*, 164).

69. "The cultural cross-fertilization tied to the expansion of democracy demands that we remain firm upon some crucial requirements, some timeless imperatives: the rights of man, justice, tolerance, solidarity, democratic values and Christian values whose defense and practical application always and everywhere oblige every responsible person" (Bony, *DAQ*, 280, translated from the French).

70. "An authentic public sphere capable of transcendentality (that is to say as a sphere of the transcendental as an expression of the shared values of religions and of their transcendental truths) must be able to transmit values and trust to the democratic political system" (Pierpaolo Donati, "Religion and Democracy in the Post-Modern World: the Possibility of a 'Religiously Qualified' Public Sphere," *DRR*, 355).

71. "Civic engagement creates trust by reducing the uncertainties each party harbors about others' predilections and dispositions. . . . Recent empirical work on common-property resource management supports this reasoning by showing that trust can indeed be 'habit forming'" (Dasgupta, *DRR*, 25–26).

72. "The person, politically refined or reflecting profoundly upon the facts of the past and present, finds a path, an alternative permitting the creative imagination to bring forth an original decision" (Bony, *DAQ*, 263, translated from the French).

73. The disastrous outcomes of unreasonableness can be seen throughout the PASS studies when authors speak of demagoguery, the oppression of minorities by majority decisions, and the manipulation of the common good by powerful minority groups.

74. Therborn, *DRR*, 143.

75. Paul Kirchhof, *DRR*, 66; and especially Zampetti: "The nurture and education of children is an important aspect of the formation of human capital, which in an information society is superior to economic-financial capital" ("Il Concetto di Stato Democratico e 'la Societa Civile,'" *DRR*, 205), translated from the Italian.

76. "The German conception of values ('werte') has strong normative or moral connotations. The history of this term originated only in the nineteenth century in the tradition of Kantian philosophy and is thus meant in a strictly anti-utilitarian sense. 'Werte' has become a central concept for discussing problems of human order, and it is obviously in this sense that the concept is used in the program of this meeting" (Kaufmann, *DAQ*, 118).

77. Jean Bethke Elshtain, "What is 'Civil Society' and How Does It Develop?" *DAQ*, 211, 212.

78. Lawrence, *Democracy in America*, 308, emphasis added.

79. "Embedded in the civil society framework is a recognition that our social and political worlds are enormously complex and that they emerge and take shape concretely over time. No social engineer can 'design' a civil society. No linear model can explain one. Civil society is a repository of human actions and reactions to a material and moral environment. A sturdy yet supple civil society embodies the decocted wisdom of the ages yet remains open to new insights and challenges. A civil society is a system, but it is an open system" (Elshtain, *DAQ*, 209–210).

80. "Private societies, then, although they exist within the body politic, and are severally part of the commonwealth, cannot nevertheless be absolutely, and as such, prohibited by public authority. For, to enter into a 'society' of this kind is the natural right of man; and the State has for its office to protect natural rights, not to destroy them" (Leo XIII, *RN*, 51). The locus classicus is the defense of the associations of Dominicans and Franciscans at the University of Paris by Thomas Aquinas (*Contra impugnantes Dei cultum et religionem*, 1257).

81. "The political society exists to serve the people who belong to it; its role should be subsidiary; it should help people to flourish, which cannot be done without respect for families, for intermediary associations and notably for the nation" (Schooyans, *DAQ*, 48).

82. Klaus Von Beyme, "Democracy as Civil Society: the Mediating Structures," *DAQ*, 230.

83. Zampetti, *DAQ*, 182–183.

84. "Among laws controlling human societies there is one more precise and clearer, it seems to me, than all the others. If men are to remain civilized or to become civilized, the art of association must develop and improve among them at the same speed as equality of conditions spreads" Lawrence, *Democracy in America*, 517.

85. Mary Ann Glendon, "The Ever-Changing Interplay Between Democracy and Civil Society," *DRR*, 97.

86. Elshtain, *DAQ*, 209.

87. "What is referred to here as value-absolutism is the view that there is an absolute and universal truth and that it can be accepted without reservation by anyone. With such a point of view, dialogue itself would become quite unnecessary. A man who completely grasped the universal truth might be allowed to decide the will of the whole and to enforce it. Such a viewpoint, then, has a tendency to lead to autocracy" (Nojiri, *DAQ*, 95).

88. "Africa is volatile, because of poverty, because of tribal loyalties, because simple cultures react in ways unexpected by Westerners. Extravagant oratory can lead to loss of life in rioting and disturbances. Thus in a hierarchy of values, stability and unity may be seen to rank higher than freedom of expression. This again causes conflict with the West" (McNally, *DEM*, 106).

89. See Schooyans, *DRR*, 46.

90. Elshtain, *DAQ*, 216–218; Glendon, *DRR*, 110–114. Glendon lists five damaging aspects of contemporary American culture: the centralization of government; the decline of the mediating structures; the specter of new forms of oligarchy; materialism and extreme individualism; and lack of confidence that there are any common truths.

91. Donati, *DRR*, 309.

92. Donati, *DRR*, 318–321.

93. Donati, *DRR*, 329. Donati cites R. Collins, "The Rise and Fall of Modernism in Politics and Religion," *Acta Sociologica* 35, no. 3 (1992): 171–186.

94. Donati, *DRR*, 333.

95. Zulu, *DRR*, 169.

96. Ibid., 170.

97. "That no free government, or the blessings of liberty, can be preserved to any people but by a firm adherence to justice, moderation, temperance, frugality, and virtue and by frequent recurrence to fundamental principles" ("The Virginia Declaration of Rights," in Kurland and Lerner, *The Founders' Constitution*, vol. 1, p. 7).

98. Janusz Ziolkowski, "Democracy, Public Opinion and the Media," *DRR*, 185.

99. Ziolkowski quotes Robert Nisbet: "It does not seem to have occurred to [Tocqueville] that public opinion is something that can be manufactured as well by minority pressure groups" (*DRR*, 179, from the entry on Tocqueville in *International Encyclopedia*).

100. Ziolkowski, *DRR*, 181.

101. Ibid., 184.

102. Ibid., 185.

103. Ibid., 181.

104. Ibid., 197.

105. Ibid., 198.

106. See note 76.

107. Nojiri, *DAQ*, 95.

108. Ibid.

109. Ibid., 96.

110. "Each seeker may be moved by one fragment of truth; other fragments emerge in the open contestation of ideas, under fair rules of argument. As Reinhold Niebuhr used to warn himself: There is always some truth in the errors of others and some error in my truth [see Reinhold Niebuhr, "Having, and Not Having the Truth," in *The Nature and Destiny of Man* (New York: Macmillan, 1943)]. The standard of evidence is beyond all of us. We need to listen hard—even where we would rather not listen—to learn all that we might learn

about reality, especially moral reality" (Michael Novak, *On Cultivating Liberty* [New York: Rowman & Little-field, 1999], 25).

111. "It seems to have been reserved to the people of this country, by their conduct and example, to decide the important question, whether societies of men are really capable or not of establishing good government from reflection and choice, or whether they are forever destined to depend for their political constitutions on accident and force" (James Madison, *The Federalist Papers* 1, p. 1).

112. "To live together, men need truth, of a truth which does not follow caprice, opinion, or opportunity. When a society gives up its concern for that value which is the truth, it is ripe for giving itself over to all manner of ideology" (Schooyans, *DRR*, 354).

113. According to the founder of the "Common Sense" school of Scottish philosophers, Thomas Reid, common sense is formed by our experience of nature itself: "If there are certain principles, as I think there are, which the constitution of our nature leads us to believe, and which we are under a necessity to take for granted in the common concerns of life, without being able to give a reason for them; these are what we call the principles of common sense; and what is manifestly contrary to them, is what we call absurd" (Thomas Reid, *An Inquiry into the Human Mind: On the Principles of Common Sense* [1764], edited by Derek R. Brookes [University Park: Pennsylvania State University Press, 1997], ch. 2, sect. 6, p. 33; quoted in Daniel J. Robinson, lecture for the James Madison Program, Princeton University, October 10, 2001).

114. Malik, *DRR*, 372.

115. "Since no one knows the absolute truth, it is thus entirely possible that the truth can in fact have been grasped by the minority. A decision-making process by a majority that disregards this point could result in dominance by a powerful majority and thus in a kind of autocracy" (Nojiri, *DAQ*, 96).

116. "The present-day problems of orientation in Western democracies are not due to a decay of values but rather to an excess of values. There are so many institutionalized options, and these interact often in rather confusing ways, that it becomes more and more difficult to find out what the best way to solve a problem really is. This is true not only at the level of individual but also at that of collective decisions. This presents substantial challenges for democratic practice as well as for democratic theory" (Kaufmann, *DAQ*, 134).

To choose another example of my own, today's hectic schedules and rushed eating periods provide countless acts of sensory deprivation (and actual discomfort) throughout the day, so that what the soul often needs most is a little quiet and calm sensory pleasure. Modern life, far from being entirely hedonistic (as its advertising certainly is), is in fact often quite ascetical in its pace and its demands. Preaching apposite for earlier ages often misses the mark today.

117. Nojiri, for instance, wrote: "Democracy denotes a way of thinking where everyone is equally a person, precisely because they are human beings. Democracy in this sense is good in its own right, i.e., as an end in itself, beyond being merely an instrumental value" (*DAQ*, 98, emphasis added).

Also Remond: "Democracy, more than institutions and principles, is a state of mind. It is the willingness of each one to prefer the good of the whole to particular interests. It is the fruit of an education" ("Democracy in Western Europe," *DEM*, 51–52, emphasis added).

118. "As has often been the case, the Church showed an openness first to social democracy, which can be summed up in the formula 'Everything for the people,' and only later to political democracy, which can be summed up in the formula 'Everything for the people and by the people'" (Schooyans, *DEM*, 12).

119. Zacher, *DEM*, 134.

120. See *CA*, paragraph 42.

121. Thomas A. Mensah, "International and Governmental Structures and their Relation to Democracy: Common Report on Africa, America and Asia," *DAQ*, 355.

122. "One must not overlook that special form of poverty which consists in being deprived of fundamental human rights, in particular the right to religious freedom and also the right to freedom of economic initiative" (John Paul II, *Sollicitudo Rei socialis*, 42). "Indeed, besides the earth, man's principal resource is man himself. His intelligence enables him to discover the earth's productive potential and the many different ways in which human needs can be satisfied" (John Paul II, *CA*, 32).

123. "A mature democratic welfare state can pride itself on major successes. . . . protecting people against material impoverishment and securing people against the risks of income loss caused by unemployment, disability, old age, sickness, motherhood, or the provision of care. . . . [reducing] the level of social inequality to a considerable degree. . . . [protecting] not only the individual from hardship, [but also] the polity and society as a whole from the destabilizing effects of economic shocks and economic recessions. . . . [incorporating] a significant 'economic value' despite the considerable costs which it places on employers and employees. . . .

[becoming] a highly popular institution, if not, indeed, regarded as an inalienable good" (Manfred Schmidt, "The Democratic Welfare State," *DRR*, 267–268).

124. "By intervening directly and depriving society of its responsibility, the Social Assistance State leads to a loss of human energies and an inordinate increase of public agencies, which are dominated more by bureaucratic ways of thinking than by concern for serving their clients, and which are accompanied by an enormous increase in spending. In fact, it would appear that needs are best understood and satisfied by people who are closest to them and who act as neighbors to those in need" (John Paul II, *CA*, 48).

125. Colin Crouch, "Democracy and Labor," *DRR*, 236, 239, 241. On the final point: "The particular problem that unions have in reaching out to the new groups of marginal and insecure workers creates both a problem of socio-political exclusion for these latter, and an awkward position of relative position for the unions" (Ibid., 247).

126. Therborn, *DRR*, 155.

127. Ziolkowski, *DRR*, 188.

128. Ibid.

129. John P. Hittinger, "The Munus Regale in John Paul II's Political Theology," in his forthcoming book on papal social teaching (as yet untitled).

130. Louis Sabourin, "La Mondialisation en Quête de Gouvernance Democratique: Contradictions Nationales, Contraintes Internationales," *DAQ*, 376–377. Translated from the French.

131. "[When] Westerners and more particularly the United States and France, . . . [proclaim] themselves repositories of universal values and guidelights destined to enlighten the whole planet, that pretention can seem, in the eyes of the majority of people, to manifest an arrogance that is difficult to tolerate. Other civilizations also participated in the edification of the patrimony of human wisdom. As long as international institutions fail to recognize the distinguishing features of their contributions and continue to reflect a sort of cultural neo-colonialism, their legitimacy will not be completely assured" (Thierry de Montbrial, "Interventions Internationales, Soueraineté des Etats et Democratie," *DAQ*, 422, translated from the French).

132. Mensah, *DAQ*, 354–355. This passage is so good I have used it twice. See p. 29 for first reference.

133. "Is there no virtue among us?" asked Madison defiantly. "If there be not, we are in a wretched situation. No theoretical checks, no form of government, can render us secure. To suppose any form of government will secure liberty or happiness without any virtue in the people, is a chimerical idea" (Jonathan Elliot, ed., *Debates in the Several State Conventions on the Adoption of the Federal Constitution*, 2nd edition, Virginia, June 20, 1788 [Washington, D.C.: U.S. Congress, 1836], 536–537).

134. Carlos A. Floria, citing a definition from Fr. Jean-Yves Calvez, S.J., *DEM*, 80.

135. "Democracy is a form of government that is always under attack. . . . Again and again political challenges may be greater than the ability of the complicated democratic government machinery to react. Other reasons are that democracy relies on being supported by a 'civil society,' the development of which is however largely a 'natural phenomenon' of society and history that can only be steered marginally if at all. The result is continued crises, in which the 'governability' of society is questioned and in which interests, goods and values seem to be endangered, so that authoritarian or even totalitarian forces present and impose themselves as an alternative" (Zacher, *DEM*, 136).

136. "The assertion of mere liberty produces a tendency toward the total liberation of instinctive desires, thereby breaking down the self-control of man as a person, and because the assertion of mere right produces an inclination to go so far as to demand an unlimited guarantee for one's livelihood, this causes the abandonment of the leading of an autonomous life as a person" (Nojiri, "Values as a Precondition for Democracy," *DAQ*, 100).

137. "Certainly democracy involves the rule of the majority, but equally the other side of the democratic coin entails rights and protection for minorities" (Malik, *DRR*, 391).

138. "The first and most important point is respect for the opinion of the minority. The reason for this lies in the fact that a decision agreed upon by the majority is only an expedient which has been devised in order to decide the will of a whole group" (Nojiri, *DAQ*, 96).

139. "Democracy also presupposes that both individuals and society as a whole have time available. If poverty in a country is so great that daily survival is the prime concern, society cannot [adjust to] the right pace for democratic politics" (Zacher, *DEM*, 132).

McNally: "Poverty creates relationship of an almost feudal dependency. You attach yourself to a clan leader, a tribal leader. There is no point in voting for someone who may be a better man from another group. Anything he achieves will benefit his kinsmen and not you." Ibid., 103; "You cannot build institutions while the people starve. The mind-set established through centuries of poverty does not go away simply because poverty is relieved." Ibid., 106.

140. "Although the incidence of corruption in public life is by no means restricted to Africa, corruption is an undeniable feature of life in many parts of the continent and has a quite discernible impact on the processes of government and economic life" (Thomas A. Mensah, *DAQ*, 359).

141. "The centralization of government has drained decision-making power away from local governments that once served as schools for citizenship" (Glendon, *DRR*, 110).

142. See *DRR*, 110–114.

143. Jacques Maritain, *Integral Humanism*, translated by Joseph W. Evans (South Bend, Ind.: University of Notre Dame Press, 1973). Maritain distinguishes between "practical philosophy" (ix) and "concrete Historical Ideal" (127ff). In this spirit, I have further distinguished "practical-practical" propositions.

144. "I certainly do not draw . . . the conclusion that we are necessarily destined one day to derive the same political consequences as the Americans from the similar social state. . . . It is enough that the creative source of laws and mores is the same in the two countries, for each of us to have a profound interest in knowing what the other is doing" (Lawrence, *Democracy in America*, 18, emphasis added).

Chapter Nine

1. "Muslims are outspoken and emphatic in their disdain for the abuses of the good name of Islam perpetrated by the government in Khartoum. 'Our problem is not religion,' one after another insists, 'but a politicalization of religion, an abuse of religion. They are not true Muslims!'" (quoted by Michael Novak, "Adventure in Asmara: A Report on the Sudanese Resistance," *National Review Online*, September 19, 2002, available at: http://www.nationalreview.com/novak/novak091902.asp).

2. G. K. Chesterton, "Lepanto," in *Modern British Poetry*, edited by Louis Untermeyer (New York: Harcourt, Brace and Howe, 1920).

3. Several writers have analyzed very well the military adaptations that led to Christian victory. *In Carnage and Culture: Landmark Battles in the Rise of Western Power* (New York: Doubleday, 2001), ch. 7, Victor Davis Hanson tallies the military innovations that gave the Venetians the upper hand in battle: replacing the beaks of their galleys with cannons; using superior cannons mounted on swivels and a greater number of harquebuses (guns) with more dependable gunpowder; better firearms; and better training in the use of firearms, yielding greater rates of fire. Jack Beeching is even more vivid: "The West had certain substantial technical advantages. In the Turkish fleet, not even all the janissaries were yet armed with the arquebus. The Turkish leaders consoled themselves with the specious argument that a man trained in the use of a Turkish composite bow could loose off thirty arrows in the time it took an arquebusier to load and fire once. But many of their Christian opponents—and certainly all Don John's officers—would be wearing armor that was virtually arrow–proof, whereas an arquebus slug at 200 yards could put a hole right through a man wearing robes and turban, and perhaps through his neighbor as well. Massed arquebus fire could nowadays sweep decks which in Mark Antony's day could safely have been crammed with infantrymen. The heavy guns carried in the bows of a war galley could be traversed by skillful manipulation of the oars, and aimed with great precision, the whole length of the galley's hull serving as a waterborne gun carriage, so that the entire ship took the recoil as the great guns fired.

"The League galleys were also fitted with boarding nets—then a novelty. And down from their Arsenal to join the fleet the Venetians were towing an unusual weapon which they hoped would disconcert the Turk—galliasses (galleys), six of them. In contriving their version of the galliass, the ingenious Venetians had taken a long stride towards making gunnery prevail in naval warfare" (*The Galleys at Lepanto* [New York: Charles Scribner's Sons, 1982], 197–198; see also Lord Patrick Balfour Kinross, *The Ottoman Centuries: The Rise and Fall of the Turkish Empire* [New York: Morrow Quill, 1977], 269ff).

4. John L. Esposito, ed., *Voices of Resurgent Islam* (New York: Oxford University Press, 1983).

5. Isma'il Raji al-Faruqi, "Islam and Zionism," in ibid., 261–267.

6. Esposito, ibid, 11–14.

7. al-Faruqi, "Islam and Zionism," 224.

8. For these three stages, see ibid., 225.

9. On the high symbolic role of Pakistan, see ibid., 220.

10. "The kind of regime represented by Saddam Hussein has no roots in either the Arab or Islamic past. Rather, it is an ideological importation from Europe—the only one that worked and succeeded (at least in the

sense of being able to survive). In 1940, the French government accepted defeat and signed a separate peace with the Third Reich. The French colonies in Syria and Lebanon remained under Vichy control, and were therefore open to the Nazis to do what they wished. They became major bases for Nazi propaganda and activity in the Middle East. The Nazis extended their operations from Syria and Lebanon, with some success, to Iraq and other places. That was the time when the Baath Party was founded, as a kind of clone of the Nazi and Fascist parties, using very similar methods and adapting a very similar ideology, and operating in the same way—as part of an apparatus of surveillance that exists under a one-party state, where a party is not a party in the Western democratic sense, but part of the apparatus of a government. That was the origin of the Baath Party" (Bernard Lewis, "Saddam's Regime Is a European Import," *National Post*, April 3, 2003).

Sandro Magister writes: "Certainly, with Saddam Hussein fell a Baathist regime that was usually defined as secular. But it was a secularism made of national-socialist tyranny, born of European-style revolutionary atheistic doctrine, aimed at canceling any autonomous political-religious subject, and equipped with an infinite series of coercions and killings concentrated mainly on Islam's Shiite branch, the majority one in Iraq" ("Secularism and Fundamentalism in Iraqi Islam: The Double Misinterpretation," *L'Espresso Online*, April 30, 2003, available at: http://213.92.16.98/ESW_articolo/0,2393,41616,00.html).

11. John O. Voll, "Renewal and Reform in Islamic History: Tajdid and Islah," in Esposito, *Voices of Resurgent Islam*, 44.

12. Ibid.

13. According to Dore Gold, the founder of the modern Saudi nation, Muhammad ibn Saud, and the founder of the resurrected jihad, Muhammad ibn Abdul Wahhab, formed a pact and sealed it with the marriage of their children: "Muhammad ibn Saud [ruled 1744–1765] and Muhammad ibn Abdul Wahhab thus established a mithaq, or covenant, under which ibn Saud established the first Saudi state and ibn Abdul Wahhab determined its official creed. It was, in short, a political bargain: ibn Saud would protect ibn Abdul Wahhab and spread his new creed, while ibn Abdul Wahhab would legitimize Saudi rule over an expanding circle of bedouin tribes, which were subdued through a new jihad. By reviving jihad and condemning enemies as polytheists who have no right to live, Wahhabism set the stage for the swift success and infamous cruelty of its eighteenth- and early nineteenth-century military campaigns" ("The Roots of Terror," in *Hatred's Kingdom: How Saudi Arabia Supports the New Global Terrorism* [Washington, D.C.: Regnery Publishing, 2003], 20–21, 26).

14. Voll, in Esposito, *Voices of Resurgent Islam*, 44.

15. Samuel M. Katz, *Relentless Pursuit: The DSS and the Manhunt for the Al-Qaeda Terrorists* (New York: Forge/Tom Doherty Associates, 2002), ch. 1.

16. Daniel Pipes estimates that "by recognizing the wide backing of bin Laden's evil for what it is, Americans must begin a process of confrontation with 10 to 15 percent of the vast populations of the Muslim world" ("Bin Laden Is a Fundamentalist," *National Review Online*, October 22, 2001, available at: http://www.nationalreview.com/comment/comment-pipes102201.shtml).

17. Fareed Zakaria, *The Future of Freedom: Illiberal Democracy at Home and Abroad* (New York: W. W. Norton & Co., 2003).

18. "Bin Laden's 1998 al Jazeera interview stressed this point: 'There are two parties to the conflict: World Christianity, which is allied with Jews and Zionism, led by the United States, Britain, and Israel. The second party is the Islamic world'" (Paul Marshall, "This War We're In," *National Review Online*, November 26, 2002, available at: http://www.nationalreview.com/comment/comment-marshall112602.asp). With respect to the UN, Marshall quotes bin Laden, justifying his attacks on America in his post–9/11 videotape: "Those who continue to appeal to the United Nations have disavowed what was revealed to Prophet Muhammad. Under no circumstances should any Muslim or sane person resort to the United Nations. The United Nations is nothing but a tool of crime" ("Misunderstanding Terrorism," *Townhall.com*, September 7, 2003, available at: http://www.townhall.com/columnists/GuestColumns/Marshall20030907.shtml.)

19. Coalition Provisional Authority in Iraq, "Law of Administration for the State of Iraq for the Transitional Period," March 8, 2004, "FindLaw: Legal News and Commentary," available at: http://news.findlaw.com.

20. al-Faruqi, *Al Tawhid*, 138–139.

21. Shireena al Nowais, "Teenage Girl to Get 90 Lashes, to Be Deported," *Gulf News Online Edition*, August 17, 2003, available at: http://www.gulf-news.com/Articles/news.asp?ArticleID=95354.

22. Nina Shea, "Shari'a in Kabul? A Theological Iron Curtain Is Descending Across Afghanistan," *National Review*, October 28, 2002, 20–24.

23. Mumtaz Ahmad, "Islam and Religious Liberty: Muslim Perspectives," address to the Second International Conference of the Becket Fund, "Pluralism and Religious Liberty," Jerusalem, December 16–18, 1997.

24. Ibid. Ahmad is quoting one of those secularists, Abdullah Javed, writing on the eve of Ataturk's revolution.

25. Ibid.

26. Khurshid Ahmad, "The Nature of the Islamic Resurgence," in Esposito, *Voices of Resurgent Islam*, 228.

27. *Planned Parenthood of Southeastern Pennsylvania v. Casey*, 505 U.S. 833 (1992), at 851.

28. Quoted in Ahmad, "The Nature of the Islamic Resurgence."

29. Abdulaziz Sachedina, "Why Democracy and Why Now?" address to the Fourth Annual Conference of the Center for the Study of Islam and Democracy, Washington, D.C., May 16, 2003.

30. Ibid.

31. "The founders saw themselves laboring within a long community of inquiry, at home simultaneously in the world of biblical and classical examples and in the practical world of the eighteenth century. For most of them, the Bible and plain reason went hand in hand, moral example for moral example" (Michael Novak, *On Two Wings: Humble Faith and Common Sense at the American Founding* [San Francisco: Encounter Books, 2001], 27).

32. Ahmad, "Islam and Religious Liberty."

33. Ibid.

34. Sachedina, "Why Democracy and Why Now?"

35. al-Faruqi, *Al Tawhid*, 7.

36. Hamid Enayat, *Modern Islamic Political Thought* (Austin: University of Texas Press, 1982), 135; quoted in Bassam Tibi, *The Challenge of Fundamentalism: Political Islam and the New World Disorder*, updated edition (Los Angeles: University of California Press, 2002), 189.

37. Bernard Lewis writes: "Islamic civilization has produced a wealth of theological, philosophical, and juridical literature on virtually every aspect of the state, its powers, and its functions. What is not discussed to any great extent is the difference between religious and temporal powers" ("A Historical Overview," in *Islam and Democracy in the Middle East*, edited by Larry Diamond [Baltimore: Johns Hopkins University Press, 2003], 218).

38. "Khomeini Comes to America," American Enterprise Institute for Public Policy Research, September 26, 2003, available at: http://www.aei.org/events/eventID.630/event_detail.asp.

39. See, for example, the discussion between Hillel Fradkin, Qamar-ul Huda, Zainab Al-Suwaij, and Sohail Hashmi, "Muslim Scholars Discuss Islam and American Democracy," Ethics and Public Policy Center, Washington, D.C., June 25, 2003, available at: http://www.eppc.org/programs/islam/news/programID.36, newsID.1593/news_detail.asp. Other institutions are the Becket Fund for Religious Liberty (www.becketfund.org), the Center for the Study of Islam and Democracy (www.islam-democracy.org), and the National Endowment for Democracy (www.ned.org).

In addition to those scholars referred to in this essay—Abdulaziz Sachedina, Khaled Abou El Fadl, Saad Eddin Ibrahim, Bassam Tibi, Hamid Enayat, Mumtaz Ahmad—one can add, for example, Tarek Heggy, whom Bernard Lewis has called "a courageous and distinctive voice from Egypt"; see his "Tolerant and Intolerant Islam," available at: http://www.heggy.org/recent_articles.htm. See also, for example, Kanan Makiya, "A Model for Post-Saddam Iraq," Journal of Democracy 14, no. 3 (July 2003). For still other voices, see "Liberal Islam Web Sites," collected by Charles Kurzman, available at: http://www.unc.edu/~kurzman/LiberalIslam-Links.htm.

40. Bernard Lewis, "A Historical Overview," 211–212.

41. Cf. David Smock: "Shura is basically a consultative decision-making process that is considered either obligatory or desirable by different scholars. Those who choose to emphasize the Quranic verse 'and consult with them on the matter' (3:159) consider shura as obligatory, but those who emphasize the verse praising 'those who conduct their affairs by counsel' (43:38) consider shura as merely desirable. There is no doubt that shura is the Islamic way of making decisions, but is it obligatory?" ("Islam and Democracy," *Special Report 93* [Washington, D.C.: United States Institute of Peace, 2002], 4).

42. Saad Eddin Ibrahim, "Reviving Middle Eastern Liberalism," *Journal of Democracy* 14, no. 4 (October 2003): 8.

43. Khaled Abou El Fadl, "Islam and the Challenge of Democracy," *Boston Review* (April—May 2003).

44. Karl Zinsmeister and John Zogby, "The First Scientific Poll of Current Iraqi Public Opinion," *American Enterprise*, (December 2003): 26–35.

45. See Alfred Stepan, "An 'Arab' More Than 'Muslim' Electoral Gap," *Journal of Democracy* 14, no. 3 (July 2003). Non-Arab Muslim nations holding at least three consecutive successful elections are Albania, Bangladesh, Djibouti, Gambia, Malaysia, Maldives, Mali, Niger, Nigeria, Pakistan, Senegal, and Turkey.

46. Sachedina, "Why Democracy and Why Now?"

Epilogue

1. Francis Fukuyama, *Trust: The Social Virtues and the Creation of Prosperity* (New York: Free Press, 1996).

2. "Money today is mostly an account, a set of computer numbers always rapidly changing with entries and withdrawals (and occasionally a computer error or a mistaken manual entry by a computer clerk). Money has become more of an intellectual artifact than a physical thing. Moreover, to an extraordinarily high degree, its current value is based on spiritual attitudes such as faith and trust. Burst these like a pin prick in a bubble and the value of money can collapse very quickly. Consult the Asian crisis of early 1998, or the collapse of the Russian ruble.

"These two examples, Asia and Russia, indicate that more is involved in the value of money held on accounts these days than purely economic factors. In Asia, the lack of truly democratic accountability, the lack of transparency, the phenomenon of one-party rule and the rewarding by political authorities of relatives and cronies, and severe problems of transition upon the death of dictators, and other chiefly political factors, undermined confidence in economic transactions. Too many unseen hands manipulate economic factors beneath the table. Imputed valuations collapsed.

"In Russia, the repression of all religious and moral inspirations during seventy long years of Communist Party rule deeply injured the moral ethos of the nation, and the failure of the political system after 1991 to establish the rule of law; to suppress violence, extortion, murder, and gangsterism; and to tie the value of money to real and universally dispersed assets, gravely wounded trust in normal economic life" (Michael Novak, "God and Money," *Catholic Dossier* [May/June 1999], 14–18).

3. Robert W. Fogel, *The Fourth Great Awakening and the Future of Egalitarianism* (Chicago: University of Chicago Press, 2000).

4. Borgna Brunner, ed., *Time Almanac 2002* (Boston: Family Education Co., 2001), 433. See also "Major Religions of the World Ranked by Number of Adherents," updated August 16, 2001, available at: www.adherents.com.

5. Quoted in Charles Calomiris, *A Globalist Manifesto for Public Policy* (London: Institute of Economic Affairs, 2002), 21.

6. Michael Novak, "The International Vocation of American Business," Hansen-Wessner Memorial Lecture (Chicago: ServiceMaster Co., 1998); and *Business as a Calling* (New York: Free Press, 1996).

7. Albert Camus, *The Rebel* (New York: Random House/Vintage Books, 1956), 305.

8. Albert Camus, *The Myth of Sisyphus and Other Essays* (New York: Random House/Vintage Books, 1960), v.

9. Michael Novak, *A New Generation: American and Catholic* (New York: Herder and Herder, 1964), 140–141.

ACKNOWLEDGMENTS

The one to whom I owe most thanks for this and all my work is my wife, Karen, who for forty-one years has maintained a peaceful and productive home around us, with a quiet spirit of self-sacrifice. At the same time, she herself has produced a significant body of sculptures, paintings, and prints, many of them on commission (a few examples can be seen at her website, www.laubnovakartist.com) She has been an unparalleled and much-loved mother of three, wife, friend, and greatly cherished grandmother of Emily and Stephen. I am so lucky to have met her.

Before I saw it myself, my agent Loretta Barrett and editor Liz Maguire saw the unity and book-length promise in some earlier pieces of mine, and nourished this book into being—a far more ambitious and better creation than I had at first. It goes without saying that their vision required of me a lot more work, but the vision and challenge were priceless. I am deeply grateful for their inspiration and friendship.

I was blessed by good solid, patient assistance, especially on the notes, from Grattan Brown, who also did many of the translations from French and Italian sources. The usual top-quality AEI interns of the last three years did yeoman's work surveying the materials we needed, correcting manuscript, identifying ambiguities, suggesting insertions, and other important tasks. Particularly deserving of gratitude are Matt Emerson, Thomas Johnston, Laura Niver, Rick Barry, Tim Foley, and Christopher Levenick. The one who makes our office go—the manager of schedule and manuscript—is Michael Leaser. To him and Grattan Brown, my deepest thanks. Cornelis Heesters and Laurel Cornell also deserve thanks for help at early stages of the writing, back three years ago.

I owe thanks, too, to early readers who corrected many of my mistakes and gave me many helpful suggestions, including fresh sources to consult:

Charles Butterworth, Robert Wilken, Abdulwahab Alkebsi, Sidney Griffith, Imad-ad-Dean Ahmad, Stephen Hayward, and many others. Each of them could have done portions of this book better than I have been able to do, even with their generous help.

I am also grateful to a number of persons and institutions that first invited me to advance arguments about the coming century: To Kevin Hasson of the Becket Fund, James Wilburn of the Pepperdine School of Public Policy, and Dean Kurt Pritzl, O.P., of the Catholic University School of Philosophy for inviting me to lecture on Islam and liberty; the honorable Senator Ferdinando Adornato and Massimo De Angelis for inviting me to present a white paper on environmentalism for the center-right parties of Europe at their annual meeting in Venice in 2002, and on Islam in 2003; Laurence Harrison at Tufts, who invited me to present an earlier and rather different version of chapter 5 for the multi-year "Culture Matters" Project, which he so brilliantly directs; the editors of *The National Interest* for inviting me to review two books with rival approaches to economics, in order to describe a deeper philosophy of economics; Baylor University for inviting me to lecture on religion and economics in the new century; the indefatigable John H. Dunning, for inviting me to contribute an earlier version of the chapter on "Caritapolis" to his superb book, *Making Globalization Good* (Oxford University Press); and the esteemed Dr. Hans Zacher, not only Germany's greatest social scientist but also director of the Pontifical Academy of Social Sciences, for inviting me to review the five volumes on the Catholic Church and Democracy produced by that Academy during recent years. In presenting each of these early papers, I benefitted enormously from the criticism and comments of all who took part.

INDEX